D1572544

HUNTINGTON LIBRARY
PUBLICATIONS

# L. J. ROSE OF SUNNY SLOPE

*1827-1899*

*California Pioneer,*
*Fruit Grower, Wine Maker,*
*Horse Breeder*

BY L. J. ROSE, JR.

THE HUNTINGTON LIBRARY, SAN MARINO, CALIFORNIA

Western
Amer.
F 864
R66
L2
1959a

UNIVERSITY OF THE PACIFIC

© COPYRIGHT 1959
BY
HENRY E. HUNTINGTON LIBRARY AND ART GALLERY
ALL RIGHTS RESERVED
PRINTED IN THE UNITED STATES OF AMERICA
LIBRARY OF CONGRESS CATALOG CARD NO. 93-078983
ISBN 0-87328-144-6
SECOND PRINTING 1993

# PREFACE

In writing his memoirs of early California, my father, L. J. Rose, Jr., was prompted by his great admiration for his father, the builder of Sunny Slope. Grandfather, who was once called one of the "titans of the Southland," was successful in many undertakings. Pioneering in the selection of new varieties of grapes for his thousand-acre vineyard, he discovered those best suited to the soil and developed a fine winery. His wines and brandies bearing the "rose" label became famous on the New York market. Real estate ventures turned his way. His long-cherished dream of breeding fine, fleet horses came true and established for him a national reputation.

Father recorded firsthand knowledge of a remarkable period that saw unprecedented growth in California, the twenty-five to thirty years terminating in 1899 with my grandfather's death. As a child my father was retold many times the experiences of the trip across the plains. As he grew up, he noted with keen interest the happenings of the California about him. He always had an audience when he told his stories and finally wrote them down.

A nostalgia for his childhood days, such as we all feel, impelled Father, with his penchant for writing, to describe the incidents of his young life among the scenes he loved—the natural beauties of the Sunny Slope ranch. An admirer of nature, he found ample time for boyish pranks, and these he took delight in recounting.

In later years Father wrote a series of articles on race horses for the San Diego *Union* and for the *Turf and Sports Digest.* Also, he was selected as judge at race meetings and served as presiding judge at Agua Caliente, Tia Juana, when it was one of the leading race tracks of the world. He judged recurring seasons at Tanforan, San Francisco; Washington Park, Chicago; Reno, Nevada; and Victoria and Vancouver, British Columbia.

Father named the resulting account of one hundred and twenty-five thousand words "Gringo Grandees" and gave the original to the Huntington Library. Several years after the death of my father, I brought the manuscript to the attention of the director, John E. Pomfret, who kindly agreed to have it prepared for publication. To preserve the story and the reader's interest, the manuscript was reduced by deletions of material not pertinent to the whole.

I am indebted to the trustees of the Huntington Library for making possible the publication of this book. Mr. W. W. Robinson of Los Angeles kindly supplied a number of explanatory historical notes. I wish also to thank Mr. Pomfret, Miss Haydée Noya of the Manuscript Department, and Mrs. Eleanor T. Harris and Mrs. Nancy C. English of Huntington Library Publications for preparing the manuscript for press.

HINDA A. ROSE

*San Diego, California*
*May 1959*

# CONTENTS

# *List of Illustrations*

# FOREWORD

FEW MEN have had as eventful careers as my father, Leonard John Rose, around whose life this story is written, and one gifted in letters could make of it a glorious tale.

In the absence of any particular literary ability, I must depend largely upon a recital of the unadorned facts in connection with his spectacular achievements in setting forth his story. Wherein my narrative approaches the historical—aside from a few dates with which I have refreshed my mind—I rely wholly on impressions and recollections in which my memory has been steeped from infancy through many years of personal contact. In support of their authenticity, I offer the fact that of the scores of persons of the long ago, whose names course through my story, there are not ten with whom I was not personally acquainted; that I knew Los Angeles County, the mecca of California's eastern invaders, when there was scarcely more than one home for each town or city which has since risen on her mighty domain, nor more than one individual where there are today five hundred residents; that the Los Angeles which I knew as a pueblo when it had but five thousand inhabitants boasts today of its million and a quarter souls. Nor is this all. It was my great fortune to have been born in California during her golden era and to have lived here almost seventy-five years, the first score of them while her early-day romance was still in flower.

Mine was the time when the small number of us who pioneered and helped to build up the country looked upon ourselves as one big family, and the vast unfenced out-of-doors as all our own; when sympathy, tolerance, and good feeling were dominant; the time when the individual was accepted for his true worth, and ideals were founded on generosity rather than on greed.

It is one thing to read of the early-day life in California, but in no other manner can one gain a correct concept of its romantic grandeur than to have been a part of it. No period in the life of any country was ever so richly endowed with inherent splendor. It is but natural that all this sentimental glamour should have been relegated to the background by the onrush of progress. The Californians of today are of another breed, who know but little of, nor care much about, the pristine glory of the land of their abode. My species—the old-timer—is rapidly becoming extinct, but the few of us who still hover about the side lines surrender our ideals reluctantly, ever harking back to the days that were, seeking comfort in the feeling that

> Though our sun no more may rise,
> Golden are our sunset skies.

LEON J. ROSE

*January 1937*

*L. J. Rose of Sunny Slope*

*1827-1899*

# I

# *Early Aspirations - The Rose Party*

## I

MY FATHER, Leonard John Rose, was born in the small town of Rottenburg, near Munich, Germany, in the year 1827. He was one of three children; the other two were girls. When these youngsters were quite small, their father migrated to the United States and landed in New Orleans, Louisiana, where he opened a small general merchandise store.

His business prospered, and, as he was pleased with the new country, he sent to Germany for his family. In due time his wife, son, and one daughter, Annie, arrived. For some reason which I have never known, the other daughter, Crescent, remained in Europe. At that early date there were no cables across the ocean, and European mail was received only at rare intervals; as a consequence my grandfather knew nothing of the contemplated arrival of the family until they put in an appearance.

They finally arrived and found their way to the store unannounced. To fittingly celebrate the occasion, Grandfather took a yardstick, chased everyone out of the place, locked the door, and they had a grand reunion. This was in 1835, when my father was eight years old.

A young man, a friend of the family, who also had planned to make his home in the United States, was to have traveled with them and been the guide. Being of military age, for some reason which existed or suddenly developed, this young man was drafted and impressed into the army. This change in the plans left the eight-year-old Leonard the only male person in the party, and he took himself quite seriously when informed that it now fell to him to care for them.

The young man who was left behind had a nice guitar, which he gave to his young successor, realizing that he himself would have scant opportunity to enjoy it during his soldier life. One can readily imagine that the family had more than enough other truck to carry, without being thus further encumbered, but the juvenile leader was adamant in his determination and clung to his guitar, learning to play a few airs on it on the journey across the ocean and in later years becoming quite proficient. It was ever a source of great pleasure to him, not alone because of its sweet tones, but also for the tender reveries of the long ago it ever awakened. Happily for him he possessed and prized it up to the time of his passing away.

The family did not remain in New Orleans long as Grandfather sold his business and journeyed up the Mississippi River in quest of a new location. He settled in Waterloo, Illinois, where he again embarked in the general merchandise business.

Grandfather did not Americanize very rapidly; and, as he was of a very irritable and excitable nature, he fell an easy prey to the taunts and jeers of the village youths, who themselves were none too gentle-mannered. They nicknamed him "The Crazy Dutchman," and numbers of them frequently congregated around his store and played no end of practical jokes on him. In desperation he procured a long pole with which from its location in the store he could reach practically every other point in the room, and, when their frolicking reached the "rough house" stage, Grandfather could drop his long pole on their heads. This sudden onslaught would terminate the session for the time being, and the taunters would scamper away, shouting back at him his nickname as they ran.

The children fared better. They were kept in school, soon outgrowing their German appearance, learning English readily, and were very happy and thoroughly at ease in their new surroundings.

Time rolled by and my father finished his education with a year at Shurtleff College, Alton, Illinois, just before he was twenty. He returned to Waterloo and went to work for his father in the store. Having acquired a fair knowledge of the business methods of the country, he naturally could not subscribe to the eccentric ones of his father, and with the ardor of youth he set about to reconstruct the business along progressive lines. His every effort was met with criticism and rebuff, which led to arguments and disagreements so incident to father and son. Realizing the futility of further efforts along these lines, and brimful of the spirit of young America, Leonard decided to leave the paternal roof to shift for himself.

With what few dollars he had saved, the young man bought apples from the Illinois farmers, packed them in barrels, and loaded them on a steamer bound for New Orleans. He carried his own blankets and slept on the deck. Arriving at his destination, he found ready sale for his consignment. Learning that because of an overstocked condition among Louisiana cotton planters horses and mules were very cheap, the aspiring young businessman put all his money into desirable work animals, loaded them on the steamer, and shipped them up the river to Waterloo, where there was an active demand for them.

The animals were at once converted into cash, with which another purchase of apples was made, and the trip to New Orleans repeated. Return shipments of stock were made to various points in Illinois. Each succeeding year grew in volume; and by the end of the season a business of considerable proportions had been done, showing handsome profits from so recent and modest a beginning.

With his comfortable little bank roll, Father spent the succeeding year around Quincy, Illinois, buying and selling anything that struck his fancy and looking for a permanent business location.

In 1848 Father located in Keosauqua, Van Buren County, Iowa, and opened a general merchandise store. Here he met Amanda Markel Jones, whom he married in 1851. The following year a son, William Ferdinand, was born to them. The little fellow's span of life was brief, only two and a half years. Contemporaneous with his taking away was the birth of their second child, a girl, Nina Elizabeth, and about two and a half years later a second daughter, Annie Wilhelmina, was born.

With this growing little family clustered about him, Father prospered in his new business to such an extent that in 1857 he sold it, and by cleaning up the tag ends of his trading and speculations he found himself possessed of $30,000—a fortune in itself at that time and a most pretentious reward for the ten years' efforts of a young man starting with practically no capital in a country where and at a period when the money-making art was still dormant.

Finding himself thus endowed with riches, Father saw the successful realization of his life's dream of a race-horse breeding ranch in California as a possibility, and at once began planning to move his family across the plains to California via the covered-wagon route.

Always inclined to be a plunger, Father decided to invest practically his entire capital in the venture, which at that time, even under the most favorable conditions, must have been regarded as a very hazardous one. Having the courage of his own convictions, he allowed no doubt to enter his calculations and went earnestly about making preparations. To handle an outfit of the magnitude of the one he had decided to assemble would require a number of men sufficient to afford ample protection in case of any untoward occurrence along the long perilous line of march. It was Father's intention from the first to make the trip unaccompanied by others than his immediate family and supported by an outfit absolutely under his own command.

During his residence in Keosauqua Father had become acquainted with Alpha Brown, a man of sterling character and known great courage who had had extensive experience as a plainsman, having been one of those who traveled the covered-wagon route in quest of California gold with the first onrush in 1849. Fortune did not smile upon Brown in his mining venture, and he retraced his steps to his Iowa home and family. When in 1857 Brown heard of the organization of my father's extensive outfit, the spirit of conquest again gripped him, and he was eager to join the Rose party to the Golden West to try his luck once more. Realizing the incalculable value of one of Brown's experience as a leader and helpmate in his arduous undertaking, Father lost no time in securing his services as foreman of the expedition.

At that time the glowing tales of California's gold, her wonderful orchards of oranges, figs, pomegranates, and olives, and her great vineyards and fine climate were a very powerful lure. As soon as this expedition began to crystallize, there were scores of fine young unmarried men who, in their great desire to reach the El Dorado of the West, eagerly sought the opportunity of joining the party as outriders, ox-team drivers, or stock herders, without compensation other than their board. Seventeen of them were selected; finer specimens of young American hardihood were never seen, and they all did valiant service in time of great need.

The physical assembling of such an outfit was in itself a big undertaking and one requiring considerable time and discernment, for, as the animals were for breeding purposes, individual conformation and blood lines had to be taken into careful account. This necessitated considerable research in locating them, then their inspection, and lastly the somewhat tedious transaction of purchasing them.

Father went into Missouri and purchased fourteen mares, all of them of the best trotting blood obtainable at that period in that section. All of these animals were broken to saddle and were to be used on the trip in driving the loose stock. To place at the head of his breeding establishment upon reaching California, Father purchased a very handsome black stallion, Black Morrill. This horse could trot a mile in three minutes, which was considered fast at that time in the rural districts.

Father also had a small gray running mare, Picayune, which had come from New Orleans. She was of unknown breeding but beyond any doubt was well infused with running blood, as she was as fleet as a deer and could hold her own with almost any man's horse at distances up to a quarter of a mile. Father raced her quite frequently, never losing a race with her. However, as all of her races were matches, his astuteness as a horseman, no doubt, contributed considerably to her victories, for, as the old saying goes, "A match well made is half won." A couple of span of good mules and Old Bob—a favorite bobtailed driving horse—completed the equine family. Father also purchased a herd of two hundred purebred red Durham cattle and forty fine work oxen.

In the meantime, the equipment consisting of four large, heavy wagons of the prairie-schooner type, with high sideboards to which were fastened strong wooden bows to support the heavy, painted canvas tops, had been built. These wagons carried two barrels of water on one side with feed boxes on the rear and other side, and those who rode in them entered from the opening in the front end. Each of these wagons was drawn by three yoke (six) of heavy oxen.

My father's immediate family consisted of my mother, my two small sisters, one in arms and the other three years of age, my maternal grandparents, Ezra and Elizabeth Jones, their son Edward, a harum-scarum youth of eighteen, and my father himself. To transport them, with the exception of young Jones, who rode and assisted in driving the loose stock, Father had procured an old ambulance which the clown of the party at once christened the "avalanche." This vehicle, drawn by two mules, was driven by Father.

Twenty-seven thousand five hundred dollars had been expended in assembling this extensive outfit. The equipment was all first class and new, the stock of the very best and manned by as fine a group of young men as was ever mustered together, well mounted and well armed. The outfit made indeed a formidable array and was the talk of the country for miles around.

## II

In the middle of April 1858 all was in readiness, and the Rose party, as this ill-fated one was ever known, went forth with high hopes amid great acclaim from its well-wishers, to make tragic history for itself in the annals of Indian depredations in the early days of the great Southwest.

The line of march was organized with the Rose family's mule-drawn vehicle at the head of the procession. Then followed the four six-ox-team covered wagons, the first of which carried Mrs. Brown and her five young children. The other three were loaded with bedding, provisions, and other supplies necessary for the long journey. The drivers of the ox teams always walked alongside their teams. Then followed the loose stock.

Brown, as director general, rode a good horse and divided his attentions as occasion demanded between the teams and the loose stock. Although this was a one-man outfit, subservient to one head, and as a consequence not likely to be beset with serious dissensions, Brown had with the knowledge born of experience organized the party with military precision. Discipline was paramount—the daily alignment always the same, each person having certain routine duties to perform. "A place for everything and everything in its place."

Even so, the matter of leading one of the early-day wagon trains was at all times sheer heroism requiring the utmost courage and determination, as at times it almost precipitated a riot to preserve discipline. In fact, because of failure to have organized properly and chosen a staunch leader, many expeditions broke up in free fights and were abandoned amid great distress.

After crossing the line from Iowa into Missouri, the train traveled in a generally southwestern direction, with Westport on the Missouri River as its objective. Traveling in easy stages over fairly good roads through a somewhat settled country, with an abundance of feed and water for the stock, the long trek across the broad expanse of Missouri was more of a dress parade for the train than otherwise.

While en route to Westport, a Mr. Bentner and family, consisting of his wife and a young daughter of eighteen summers, another of fifteen years and a lad of twelve, were allowed to join Father's train and became a part of it thereafter. The same wit of the party who had christened the ambulance the "avalanche" bestowed upon this thoroughly anglicized German family the sobriquet of the "Dutch family," as which they were thereafter known.

Upon arriving at Westport where the Missouri River was crossed, a number of wagons joined the train and later on en route several others, until their aggregate number was twelve. They were all of the prairie-schooner type, each drawn by three yoke—six head—of oxen. In addition to their work oxen, this aggregation had about seventy-five head of loose stock. This extensive outfit was the joint property of Joel Hedgpath, Thomas Hedgpath, G. Baily, Wright Baily, Isaac T. Holland, and John Udell, all of whom had families, and besides themselves there were eighteen other men in the party who served as team drivers and herdsmen.

One of the gentlemen amongst these owners, the name of whom I greatly regret to have forgotten, was a clergyman. This lapse of memory, however, is of no moment as the wag of the party soon designated him as the "Missouri preacher," and he was thereafter always referred to as such. Moreover, he glorified himself and his somewhat irreverently applied nickname by his valiance at a crucial moment.

Although this extensive aggregation, which for the sake of convenience shall hereafter be referred to as the Hedgpath party, and Father's pretentious outfit traveled as a unit and under the nominal leadership of Father encamped together at night and fraternized freely, their respective outfits and loose stock were kept apart at all times. Father had exacted this condition from the time of their first affiliation in order that he might be able to preserve the desired regimentation and discipline in his already sizable, individually owned outfit. Moreover, as all of his animals were unbranded, this mode of procedure would avert the possibility of any controversial claim of ownership.

Crossing the Missouri River into Kansas at Westport, the terrain and surroundings at once changed. Kansas was but sparsely settled at this time, practically all of her population residing on her eastern frontier. The Osage

Indians made their home in Kansas, but there was little to fear from them, as they had long been subjugated.

What towns there were in Kansas at that time were infested by the most desperate men in the world. Killings and holdups were of daily occurrence. Organized bands of rustlers (cow and horse thieves) found easy prey in some of the smaller outfits. They frequently "shot them up," took whatever they considered worth while in the way of personal effects, and ran off the loose stock, leaving many poor persons stranded and helpless in a wild country. The Rose party, however, did not fall victim to them.

On numerous occasions, rustlers rode into camp, but after taking an account of stock, of the man power and its accoutrement, they decided to seek for easier game and went on their way.

The caravan had soon left behind all evidences of civilization and was but a part of the broad expanse of wild country in its tedious grind across the apparently limitless plains. The novelty of the affair had worn away, and the stern realities of the rigors of a covered-wagon trip were painfully realized, as the train moved along in snail-like progress, fairly wallowing in the suffocating dust which frequently enveloped them, under a sun that fairly sizzled. With broken wagons to repair, lame and jaded teams to care for, children fretful and quarrelsome under restraint, women forlorn and fatigued, or worst of all under the spell of that awful malady, homesickness, which attacked so many, it is but natural that many tense situations were created.

Heaven knows it tried to the breaking point the courage of strong men, inured to hardships; but contemplate, if you can, the frame of mind of the women, deprived of every comfort, subjected to all sorts of privations. It's a wonder they did not all go mad, and every mother or wife who made the covered-wagon trip was a heroine and worth her weight in gold.

The roads were passably good, except when it rained. Then, in localities where the soil was of black adobe, they would become veritable quagmires, necessitating the halting of the train for a few days. These delays, however, were not without their compensations, allowing the readjustment of living and sleeping conditions and affording greatly needed opportunities for indispensable laundering activities. It also gave the men time to care properly for animals suffering from yoke and saddle galls or those that were sore-footed and lame. The sore places were washed clean and greased and the tender-footed animals shod, and, if their conditions were aggravated, they were replaced from the number of gentle animals running with the loose stock.

A complete blacksmith's outfit had been brought along, and from force of necessity practically every man of the party had learned to do a good job of shoeing and a crude one of iron welding.

Many streams of varying sizes and occasionally a river had to be crossed, a matter always attended with more or less danger, particularly after a rain. If the stream had a rocky bottom, there was naught but its depth and the swiftness of the current to be taken into consideration, but if the bed was sandy, there was always the likelihood that the freshet had stirred up the treacherous quicksand, which meant, if nothing more serious, that the wagons would be stalled. To obviate this, an old-time ruse was resorted to; the loose stock was brought up from the rear and driven into the stream. The great number of hoofs striking the bottom in such rapid succession would tramp the quicksand under, the bottom would become firm, and the wagons could then cross in safety—the loose animals, carrying no extra weight, were able to move freely and extricate themselves when they struck a soft spot. Notwithstanding these precautions there were occasional mishaps. Wagons were sometimes overturned, bedding, provisions, and everything else wet and sometimes swept away by the swift current, and the occupants rescued drenched to the skin.

As all of the party were well equipped and provisioned, there was no imperative haste in their traveling, and when a particularly attractive spot, with an abundance of stock feed, plenty of good running water, shade trees, and firewood, was reached, a halt would be called. A comfortable camp was installed, and a few days passed under something like livable conditions.

During these resting periods, those who were fond of shooting had rare sport. Antelope were very plentiful, and buffalo were in herds of thousands, in easy scouting distance of the camp. Many beautiful specimens of heads and hides were brought into camp, and numbers of the latter were tanned. The fresh meat was always a welcome addition to the larder, and a fat antelope yearling, the loin cuts barbecued on a green willow stick over a bed of hot coals in the campfire, was indeed a feast for the gods. Quantities of these meats were sun-dried the Mexican way—made into *carne seca* (dry meat). To the Mexican people, this is the staff of life, and they are never without it. Their favorite way of preparing it to eat is to grind it in an Indian *metate* (a stone mortar and pestle) and serve it scrambled with eggs or spinach, either of which makes a very palatable dish.

At night the work teams were turned out to graze with the loose stock, unless in territory where it was considered risky because of the possibility of an attack by rustlers, in which event they were kept tied at the feed boxes on the wagons. They were night-guarded by four or five of the men on saddle horses, who would remain on watch until midnight, when the relief crew would be called to stand guard until morning. Of course, this was the procedure every night with the unused stock. The cattle, as usual, were kept apart as they will not settle and rest with horses moving about. The stock gave little trouble at night, as by this time they had learned to know just what was expected of them and, after having satisfied their hunger and thirst, would lie down to rest and remain quiet until the camp began to stir at the first crack of day. The herders and their horses also took advantage of this. A saddle horse broken to this sort of service will do his work almost unguided.

If an animal starts to leave the herd, the saddle horse will immediately prick his ears and start toward the moving animal and head it back into the herd. The riders frequently get off and lie down on the ground and have a good nap, holding the tether ropes of their mounts in their hands, and friend horse, with the man's weight removed from the saddle, will have a good nap standing. If there is any movement among the stock, the horse senses it at once and will take a step or two, giving a little tug on the rope, waking the rider, who immediately gets into action.

At daybreak the camp was alive with activity. Breakfast was being cooked. In the meantime the teams for the day had been caught up, most of them without trouble, the frisky ones quickly lassoed, taken to the wagons, given a little grain, and harnessed. Breakfast was served, everything about camp restored to its proper place and the teams hitched to the wagons, when it was "westward ho" again.

There was a lot of grief but also ample enjoyment when all went well. A number of the people had guitars, fiddles, accordions, jew's-harps, or harmonicas, and impromptu concerts were frequently enjoyed after supper, with an occasional vocal effort thrown in. This was particularly enjoyable to the children, as they danced, or at least pretended to, in the sand. After their idle and close confinement in the wagons during the long day's jaunt, they felt as though liberated from imprisonment and were like bedlam cut loose.

Whenever the expedition happened to be encamped near a settlement, there was always the customary crowd of inquisitors around, who wanted to trade, buy, or sell a horse, bridle, saddle, or anything that struck their fancy. In those days, too, there were men who traveled horseback or in a rickety, light wagon leading another horse or two in quest of a match race. On two or three occasions, my father matched Picayune against them for a fair stake and won each time. Her reputation for speed was soon well known even in that country of magnificent distances, and matches with her were no longer sought. A great trick with those "quarter horse men," as they were called (because about a quarter of a mile was the most popular distance for their races), was to locate someone who had what he considered a fast horse with whom he might make a match race. They would lead their racer as mentioned before, so as to keep it fresh and ready to race at a moment's notice. Arriving at the place where they expected to find their victim, they would take their outfit to a barn, and, if they had not a wagon and harness of their own, they would hire a rickety, old, light wagon and hitch the race horse double with another horse and casually run into the man they were going to try to make a match with. They would discuss every other subject except "hoss racing," adroitly, in their comments, jockeying their intended victim into proclaiming the merits of his horse. No sooner said than done!

The man with his race horse hitched to the wagon derisively says: "If you'll bet me two to one, I'll unhitch Billy and beat your pony to death." The door is now wide open, and after much badinage (for which these people are particularly famous) a race is arranged, not at two to one against Billy, however, who by this time is a prancing Arab, very awake to the occasion, and more than likely his owner is offering the odds. It was a case of "diamond cut diamond" when dealing with these fellows, as what they did not know about the game was not worth while. This trick used to work to perfection with the farmers and the unsophisticated, but these gypsy match-makers were careful first to size up their man from reputation or personal contact to avoid the possibility of being ridiculed by him, if he happened to be of their ilk.

The vast plains of Kansas were finally left behind, and the party moved into Colorado, where the country was practically the same. It was just a short distance across the southeastern corner of that state. They drifted down into New Mexico and soon were in the Raton Mountains. This was a delightful change in scenery, the mountains fairly well timbered, with streams of good, clear water running in the canyons. The mountain air, with the cool, refreshing nights, acted like a tonic, and the entire party was infused with new life. The whole world looked brighter. Any change would have been welcome to their strained eyes and frayed nerves after having viewed nothing for weeks but the apparently endless space of the prairies. This country was rough and rugged, and the roads none too good. Mishaps were of frequent occurrence, and serious accidents narrowly averted. A brake that would not hold, a tire coming off, a wheel caving in, or a tongue breaking were the troublemakers. Rest assured there was always plenty of action in one of these expeditions and few idle moments.

They were soon out of the mountains and came into a very attractive country, which, though sparsely settled, bore evidence of civilization. Water from the canyons was available for irrigating small places, and there were occasional little clearings, some perched up on the mountain side at the lower levels, others down in the edges of the canyon bed, and some of greater dimensions out farther in the valley. These were all homes of Mexicans, with small flat-roofed adobe houses, with the doors and woodwork about them and the windows almost invariably painted blue. They were very homelike in appearance, with a few fruit trees, a few flowers of the hardier varieties, a small patch of corn and garden truck, a small field of grain, a horse or two, a few goats which were the dairy supply, and always a band of cur dogs. These places were small in area, most of them less than five acres. It was not a great distance to Las Vegas, and there were some extensive cattle and sheep ranches in the vicinity.

Small Mexican families, such as were found in this locality, manage to eke out a comfortable existence. From the goat milk a very good cheese is made; enough beans *(frijoles)* are raised to last the season; the corn ripens and is ground into meal, which is used in making *tamales* and *enchiladas*. Green peppers *(chile verde)*, onions, garlic, and peas are dried for winter use, as also the indispensable *carne seca* (dried meat). This meat, which they buy fresh, and flour *(harina)* are about all they purchase in the way of food, money for which they earn either in the town, by day labor on the farms, or by vaquero work on the cow ranges. These families are famous for the beauty of their children. It is not generally known that some of these people are as fair as the Caucasians, many of them auburn-haired and blue-eyed, and the small children and young señoritas are very beautiful, the latter up to the time of young womanhood. It is a noteworthy fact, however, that Mexican girls really do lose their beauty very young.

At this time, 1858, Las Vegas was but a small village, inhabited principally by Mexicans, and all the buildings were of adobe. There was a large general merchandise store, saloons, blacksmith shop, and other small businesses of various kinds. The famous Montezuma Hot Springs were only three miles from Las Vegas. As the detour was such a short one, the party eagerly availed themselves of this, their first opportunity in many weeks, to have a tub bath. At that early date the accommodations were, of course, meager; however, the occasion was none the less glorious.

On leaving Las Vegas, the train continued down the valley a considerable distance and then took up through the low mountains to Santa Fe over practically the same road used by motorists today. At Santa Fe, they encountered a thoroughly up-to-date, wide-awake frontier town. This farthest west of the interior frontier towns of that period was at the height of its glory, saloons and dance halls flourishing on every corner, and gambling of all kinds was wide open. The town was filled to overflowing with desperate characters. Gun fights and killings were of daily occurrence. There were large stores and shops, and the party was enabled to make some very necessary purchases of clothing and other articles. One can readily believe that the women fairly reveled in a shopping expedition, the first in almost three months.

After a few days' sojourn in Santa Fe, the train moved slowly forward to Albuquerque, where a few days' halt was called for a general reconnaissance to determine travel conditions from that point forward.

2

# *Thirty-Fifth Parallel-Indian Massacre-La Fonda*

## I

Prior to this, virtually all emigrant travel to California from the East and Middle West was over the northern route through Wyoming, Utah, and Nevada, then over the Sierra Nevadas by way of Emigrant Gap to Sacramento. All travel from the southern states went over the Butterfield stage road through Texas and what was then New Mexico Territory to Yuma, then across the desert to San Diego and onward to Los Angeles and San Francisco. With southern California as his objective, Father had chosen the intermediate and shorter route over the Santa Fe Trail to Albuquerque. From this point there was a road leading off to the southwest which joined the Butterfield stage road at Yuma. This road, used principally for army movements, passed through the section of country inhabited by the Apache Indians—the most savage and wantonly cruel of all southwestern tribes—and emigrants rarely ventured that way unless assured of safety through the proximity of United States troops.

Lieutenant Edward F. Beale, later surveyor general, undoubtedly the most traveled and best posted of America's pioneer southwestern plainsmen, was at this very time—1858—energetically endeavoring to have the government adopt as the best and standard transcontinental wagon road from the Mississippi River to the Pacific Coast one along the thirty-fifth parallel. The eastern terminus of this espoused route was at Memphis, Tennessee, and on its westward course through New Mexico it passed but a few miles to the north of the town of Albuquerque. From this point westward to California, this route was fully two hundred miles shorter than by way of Yuma, the greater portion of the distance saved being over the worst of deserts after crossing the Colorado River. Whereas by this projected route, shortly after crossing the Colorado, the road struck the well-watered Mojave River country and followed that stream almost until the mountain range back of

San Bernardino was reached. The important fact remained, however, that no emigrants had ever traveled over the road, and there was the ever-present Indian menace to be considered. This latter factor, however, was assumed to be no worse in this section than in other localities. People who should know were of that opinion, and one and all were positive that once reaching the Colorado River there was no further danger from Indians. Father weighed the matter pro and con for a few days, finally deciding to be the pioneer and take the shortcut.

From Albuquerque the projected thirty-fifth parallel route bore due west —I say projected, for such only was its state at the time. Surveys had been made, and there had been a general reconnaissance of it on different occasions by its originator, Lieutenant Edward Beale. No work had been done on its roadbed, which was in reality no more than a devious trail, barely visible at times. In covering the distance to the Colorado River, it wound its way for about five hundred miles up and down and around low rocky hills, mountain ranges, and stretches of desert sand, the most rigorous of which was that section in the Colorado Mountains closely adjacent to the Colorado River.

The road had never been traveled by emigrants, and the Rose party, now consisting of sixteen ox-drawn prairie schooners, Father's family ambulance, Mr. Bentner's small mule-drawn wagon, and three hundred head of loose stock, was the first to care to brave its certain rigors.

The military commander of the district was very reluctant in consenting to allow the train to face the uncertainties of the country. However, the general appearance of hardiness of the train and my father's persuasiveness prevailed. The only proviso was that a United States government guide must escort the party. Accordingly, a Spanish guide by the name of Savedra was employed, and the Rose party drove forth to its doom—the first wagon train that undertook to traverse this portion of the subsequently historical Beale-Whipple Thirty-fifth Parallel Route.

In this rough, weary, toilsome journey but two settlements—if such they could be called—were seen. One, Zuni, an old Mexican village, the other, a deserted sheepherder's camp.

At the end of a week's travel from Albuquerque, they encamped at El Morro, or Inscription Rock, now the nucleus of El Morro National Monument, about twenty miles from Gallup. The texture of this towering sandstone formation is such that its surface can be carved with little difficulty; but when exposed to the atmosphere, the indenture becomes so hardened as to be almost indestructible.

Because of this characteristic, some of the more ambitious passers-by inscribed their names. The earliest of these inscriptions was made in 1605 by Don Juan de Oñate, when he was traveling northward after having—as he erroneously supposed—discovered the Gulf of California, which he christened the Southern Sea. In later years many names and dates, as well as symbols cut by the Indians, were carved here. Father enrolled himself by inscribing on this illustrious roster:

L. J. Rose, Iowa
July 7th, 1858

Today, fourscore years later, the inscription is as clean-cut as if made yesterday.

The terrain, the greater portion of the distance, was very rocky and rough, and much trouble was experienced from tender and broken hoofs in the teams and breakdowns in the wagons. Feed and water in sufficient quantities for so great a number of animals was not at all times available. As a consequence forced marches often extending through the entire night were necessary.

The first number of red men to be encountered were a band of Digger Indians, very small in stature, who subsisted on worms and roots. They were so emaciated and weak, however, that they were more to be pitied than feared, and their appearance had a tendency to disarm the emigrants of fear of Indians. The Hopis, Zunis, Navajos, and Cosninos lived in different localities of this section.[1] The Mojaves, a band of four thousand, lived along the banks of the Colorado River, but none of these tribes were considered warlike.

After six weeks of torturing travel from Albuquerque during which the stock had daily become more jaded and footsore and the party travel-weary, the train reached a point one hundred and twelve miles from the Colorado River, designated as Hemphill Springs by Lieutenant Beale but known to Savedra as Peach Tree Springs. It was here that the emigrants were disillusioned of the impression of the harmlessness of the Indians which they had gained from their contact with the lowly Diggers.

Late in the evening of their arrival they saw a number of Indians moving about stealthily at a distance. This naturally spurred the camp into greater vigilance, but no untoward incident occurred during the night to attract their attention. It was nevertheless discovered the following morning when about to resume their journey that one mare and one mule were missing. And when the train moved onward, three of the herdsmen started out in search of the missing animals. They soon found the trail and started in pursuit. The flight of the Indians had, however, been so precipitate that the

[1] The Cosninos were the Havasupai, an isolated tribe of Yuman stock occupying Cataract Canyon of the Colorado River. *Handbook of American Indians*, ed. Frederick Webb Hodge, I (Washington [D.C.], 1907), 537-538.

herdsmen gained but little if any upon them. During the later hours of their ride the herdsmen were frequently shot at with arrows by the Indians from ambush at a distance. They concluded inasmuch as darkness was approaching and the canyon was growing much narrower that it would not be prudent to assume the enhanced risk of being shot which these conditions provided, and the chase was abandoned.

While en route that day about twenty-five Indians were sighted in hailing distance on a hillside, and Savedra by the use of pantomime and his meager knowledge of their language induced them to come into camp. These were of the Cosnino tribe. Some of them knew a little of both English and Spanish, and in the trilingual "pow-wow" that ensued, when informed by Savedra that it was the opinion that some of their tribe had stolen two animals the night before, the Indians quickly denied their guilt, saying that the Mojave Indians had stolen the animals, at the same time admitting that they, the Cosninos, had taken them from the Mojaves and would return them to the emigrants the next day. The Indians persisted in saying that they were good Indians and the Mojaves were bad Indians, and accentuated their self-righteous proclamations by thumping their breasts vigorously, coincidentally vehemently uttering, "hanna, hanna."

This bit of strategy failed to register true, for Savedra from his extensive knowledge of the tribal habits of the Indians knew that the Mojaves never came so far from their habitat on the Colorado River. The Indians were given all they could eat and finally left, leaving the camp in a state of fervid foment as to things that might occur henceforth, least of which was their belief that the stolen animals would be returned.

The following day while encamped at Indian Springs about ninety miles from the Colorado River, to the utter dismay of the emigrants, about thirty Indians rode in, two of whom were leading the stolen animals, which they delivered to the emigrants amidst an almost endless repetition of their breast stroking and "hanna, hanna" ejaculating. Father gave each of the two Indians who had led the animals in a large butcher knife, a gaudily colored blanket, a shirt, pair of overalls, some beads, trinkets, and tobacco and to each of their remaining number tobacco and beads or trinkets.

Doubtless prompted by fear of reprisal at the hands of the military authorities if this occurrence became known, the wily warriors requested of Father some written evidence that they had voluntarily returned the stolen animals, to be used no doubt to exculpate themselves. Father was equal to the occasion and quickly matched their to him transparent perfidy by writing on a slip of paper that the Indians in question had voluntarily returned the animals stolen from him and that he believed that they had also stolen them in the first place. Whatever had been the motive of this unusually mystifying procedure of returning stolen animals by Indians, it was not confidence-inspiring to the emigrants. The Indians were all given a hearty dinner and supper, and a number remained near camp overnight, doubtless seeking opportunity to commit further thefts. They would have been thwarted, however, in such an attempt by the increased vigilance on the part of the herders.

The following morning while still in camp about fifty Indians came in also seeking a reward, demanding shoes to replace their moccasins which they said had been worn out in pursuing the Mojaves and also asked for a number of cattle. They went through the same rigmarole, breast stroking and "hanna" uttering as had all of their predecessors—all to no avail. While thus engaged, it was reasonable to assume from immediately following discovery that some of their tribesmen were exacting a more liberal reward.

Simultaneously with departure of the Indians, the herders were sent out to bring in the work oxen preparatory to the start onward. It was at once discovered that some of the oxen and six cattle were missing. Some of the herders immediately went to look for the cattle and after a short ride up a canyon found where four had been slain, from two of which all of the meat had been cut, and the other two, though dead, were still warm, the Indians no doubt having been frightened away by flash from some hidden sentry of the approach of the horsemen. From the short time which had elapsed between the departure of the Indians from camp and the discovery of the slain cattle, the inference was justified that some confederate aware of the fact that the herdsmen were at dinner, instead of the Indians who had left the camp, had been the perpetrators of the theft.

Notwithstanding this daylight butchery it was deemed expedient because of the uncertain water and feed conditions ahead at Savedra Springs to leave Brown behind with all of the stock to await a report from Father upon his arrival at that point. It was also deemed prudent to turn the two droves of cattle, which up to this time had been kept separate, into one herd, as by so doing the number of herdsmen would be doubled and better able to cope with any night foray.

From the time the party left Indian Springs the Indians became more annoying. They would appear mysteriously from the bushes and follow along with the train for a while, then disappear. Later on others would come in, repeat the performance, and camp would hardly be reached before they would swarm in. They were more swinelike than human in their snooping about and finally became so bothersome that it was found necessary to rope them out of the camp. Vexatious as was all of this and exasperating as was their thievery, the emigrants found great solace in the belief that the Indians were absolutely harmless.

They were rudely awakened from this comforting delusion the day following the arrival of the train at Savedra Springs. After looking over the ground carefully, Father decided to send my eighteen-year-old uncle, Ed Jones, back to Indian Springs to tell Brown to bring the cattle forward. Jones, an absolutely fearless and headstrong youth, was loath to heed advice from anyone. During the entire trip he had at times helped in driving the loose cattle, using as his mount the fleet-footed, little running mare, Picayune. He would frequently loiter behind at a spring unduly or prospect around about something which struck his fancy.

When what was known as Indian country was reached, although no Indians had been seen, Father not only warned but frequently admonished the young man to cease taking such chances. All of this was to no avail, however; and, when on his way back to camp after delivering his message to Brown, as the weather was very hot, yielding to the enticing shade of a tree, he stretched himself out on the ground for a nap, in the meantime holding the lead rope of his mount in his hand. How long he was there and just exactly what happened, he was never quite able to recount clearly. At all events a number of Indians mounted on ponies having espied him from afar, had, no doubt, stalked him stealthily, until near enough to make a sudden dash in a surprise attack.

At the first sounds of the hoofbeats of their ponies, Uncle was up on his feet and saw them come swooping down upon him full speed. Fortune favored him in that Picayune, who was wild with fright from their yells and onslaught, did not break away and leave him afoot. In one bound he reached the pommel and vaulted into the saddle, and the little mare was away with the swiftness of a bullet, but the Indians were right upon him and unloosed their volley of arrows with telling aim. The fleetness of Uncle's mount soon outdistanced the Indian ponies and carried him out of range. He hung on to the saddle pommel with the grip of death until the party was overtaken about two miles ahead. When the mare stopped, he fell unconscious to the ground, bleeding from seventeen arrow wounds, most of them piercing the skin in his back. Three, however, were still sticking in him, and one of them which had penetrated deeper than the others, down low and in the back part of his side was broken off when he fell from his horse. It was impossible to remove all of the arrow with the means at hand, and the most important matter at that time seemed to be to staunch the flow of blood. All were very excited and feared he would die, but, having done all they could, proceeded to make him as comfortable as possible and hoped for the best. He suffered great pain and ran a very high temperature. After a few days the fever began to abate, and in a short time he was sitting up and in a reasonable period was, though very weak, on his feet again. It was long before he could move quickly, and he was unable to ride a horse again for more than a year. Uncle reached California two years later and lived there with the point of the arrow in his side—or lung, as he always maintained—until he was sixty-five years of age. He enjoyed good health, though he could not lift any weight that he had to stoop to take hold of and never did any manual labor, but could drive a horse, in fact drove some races, and had normal strength in his arms when they were kept above his waistline.

By driving throughout the night, Brown reached Savedra Springs in the afternoon of the following day. He reported that the Indians had repeatedly fired at him during the night and had wounded many of the cattle.

One may ask why this rapid succession of depredations was allowed to go unpunished by so formidable a party. The answer is simple: the emigrants knew that although they might have dispatched a few of the worthless wretches to their doom in their first onslaught, they also knew that if their tribesmen were aroused, a horde of five hundred or a thousand of them would swoop down upon them in a night and exterminate the whole party. Had the men themselves alone to consider, they might have invoked punitive measures and met the Indians in guerrilla warfare. But as the safety of the women and children was the paramount consideration, no other alternative was possible.

From Savedra Springs about seventy miles distant from the Colorado, the train moved forward en masse. For the first two or three days the Cosninos continued their sniping tactics until the imaginary limits of their domain were reached when, true to tradition, they faded entirely out of the picture. There was no improvement in the condition of roads, and the supply of water grew constantly less. Finally the Colorado Mountains were reached and conditions went from bad to worse.

When a point eighteen miles distant from the Colorado River was reached, many of the work oxen of the Hedgpath aggregation had become so weak that they no longer were able to haul their heavy loads. And as there was but enough water at this point for domestic purposes and no feed, resting the oxen here was out of the question. But halt they must. As Father's teams had not, however, suffered to the same extent, he intended to push on forward.

It was therefore decided by Hedgpath to encamp here with ten of his wagons and all of the women and children of his party and send his remaining two wagons and their drivers and four mounted men with the work oxen and loose stock along with Father's outfit to the river, where they could be refreshed and recuperated for three or four days. Whereupon the mounted men were to return the work stock, and the party could then resume its westward march.

It so happened most propitiously that one of these men was a Missouri preacher mentioned in the earlier pages of this narrative. Mr. Bentner, head of the so-called "Dutch family," which we also recall as having joined my father's immediate party before crossing the Missouri River, had also elected to pursue this same course and left his small wagon and family encamped with the others, and came along with Father's outfit with his sole pair of mules.

From the time the Hedgpath party was left, the roads were in many places positively impassable. In one instance, in order to descend from a rocky mesa, it became necessary to unhitch the teams and lower the wagons with block and tackle hitched to a boulder or tree stump. Shallow parallel trenches were dug to accommodate the wheels, and a number of men holding the pole did the steering. This had been a Herculean task and had exacted a heavy toll from the rapidly waning resistance of the men. Hourly the suffering of the ox teams was intensified by the excessive heat and lack of water. Progress was so snail-like that despair was dominant, and the morale of all had reached the ebb-tide stage.

On the afternoon of August 27, 1858, the party reached the crest of the last ridge of the Colorado range. They were dazed with delight at the sight of the Colorado River only four or five miles distant, threading its way through green swards of grass and thicket. Having accepted the oft-repeated information that when once across the Colorado River there would be no more rocky roads to travel, no further Indian menace to contend with, the party had, notwithstanding the fact that there were yet one hundred and fifty miles to encompass before the genial clime of southern California was reached, come to regard the Colorado River as the very threshold of their journey's end. Hip Hip Hurray! The mecca of their pilgrimage was at hand! Little did they realize that instead it was to be their Waterloo. Hope was renewed and faith was in the ascendant.

A halt was called atop the ridge to prepare a meal, the first they had partaken of throughout the day, having traveled two days and a night without cessation. While thus engaged, a number of Indians, the first of the Mojaves, put in their appearance. In friendly attitude they brought with them a little green corn and a melon which were eagerly purchased.

When supper was over and the party started forward, the Indians who had meantime remained in camp marched along with them and pointed out the road. Even so, instead of negotiating the short distance which Father had expected to accomplish shortly before midnight, it was midforenoon before the woody district adjacent to the mountains, still a mile distant from the river, was reached. By this time the work animals had about reached the limit of their endurance, and as an act of humanity they were unhitched and driven along with the loose stock to the river.

At this point a boisterous, impertinent lot of Indians put in their appearance and were anxious to know if the party intended to settle on the Colorado. They were informed to the contrary and that there were more people coming, and then they would all proceed to California. From their furtive glances and their continual mutterings it was evident that this information was somewhat suspiciously regarded. In the course of an hour and a half the animals were returned and rehitched.

When the start was made to the river, as a means of lessening the burden of the mules drawing the ambulance, Father and Mother decided to walk. While thus engaged, a swarthy, impudent Indian stepped between them and placed his hands upon Mother's shoulder and breast. Mother screamed and fled to the nearest wagon and climbed on the tongue and remained standing there between the oxen until the river was reached. The instant the Indian's hands touched Mother, Father pushed him aside with a display of as little temper as his mounting rage would permit, bemoaning the fact, however, that only the safety of his wife and children precluded him from treating the insolent wretch as his conduct merited.

A little farther along, the wagon occupied by Mrs. Brown and family was reached, it having been left a short distance from where the other wagons had halted, about a furlong from the river. Mrs. Brown was in tears and great anguish because of the delay in Mr. Brown's return with water. A number of Indians were encircling her, and in her frenzy she had asked them to bring some water for her suffering children. They expressed their willingness if she would take off her dress and give it to them. She countered this impertinent demand by offering them a number of articles far more valuable, but nothing but her dress would suffice. They also took hold of her three-year-old boy and threatened to take him away. Father at once had the wagon drawn near to the others, and they bothered her no longer.

This section of the Colorado River country which at that time, 1858, was in the confines of New Mexico became a part of Arizona when it was admitted as a territory five years later, and the location can be more definitely designated as being two hundred miles north of the present city of Yuma, Arizona. Yuma, an army post at that time, was known as Fort Yuma, and, because of the torrid heat which prevailed there, there was an early-day legend that a soldier who had died there and had gone to hell sent back for his overcoat. Measured by the brand of weather which prevailed when the emigrants reached the Colorado River, the same tradition could be applied locally without slander.

The instant the teams were unhitched, all of the drivers and all of the herders except two who had been left with the cattle fell in their tracks from exhaustion when shade was reached and soon were dead to the world. Some of them in semidelirium, still driving the oxen, gnashed their teeth and shouted aloud. Others who had drunk inordinately of water were prone, helpless, racked with violent nausea.

The Indians, still hovering around like so many vultures, became so bothersome that they were roped out of camp. Had they made an attack at this particular time, they could have exterminated the party in short order as there were but five men in camp awake. Manifestly this helplessness of the emigrants had not, however, gone unnoticed by the wily red devils, as within two hours thereafter they had inaugurated their reign of rapine without even the formality of theft and were having a glorious time in plain view of the camp, cooking and eating the meat of the beef which they had openly driven from the herd and slaughtered.

As there was nothing that the emigrants could do but start a battle, to prevent such a procedure they were forced to endure it passively. Night came and though fitfully spent the party awakened refreshed and somewhat rested. A day for further recuperation and readjustment was nevertheless decreed.

As Mr. Bentner's mules were shod, their only suffering had been from thirst and lack of food, and true to their species the full night and upward of half a day of rest with an abundance of feed and water found them restored to working condition. And as soon as Mr. Bentner had eaten his breakfast, mounted on one of the mules and leading the other, he left for the Hedgpath camp to bring his family and light wagon to the river, expecting by driving all night to be back at this camp early the following morning.

Shortly after breakfast on this, the 29th day of August, it was decided to move camp to the river's edge, in order to have water more accessible for laundry and ablutionary purposes.

Soon after the noon hour, an Indian chief with twenty-five or thirty bucks came to camp, and he also was anxious to know whether the party was going to settle there. He also was given the same reply, that many more were coming, and, as soon as they could get across the river, they would all proceed to California. Father brought forth many blankets and butcher knives, shirts, overalls, liberal quantities of tobacco, and numerous trinkets, consisting of bells, beads, and looking glasses, which he gave to the chief, and he in turn divided them amongst his followers. Apparently well satisfied, the chief told Father that the party could remain until they were able to cross the river and that they would not be molested, and thereupon left.

About an hour later another chief, a huge, bombastic individual, arrayed in war paint and a gorgeous headdress of feathers and many bells and gewgaws dangling from his belt, also accompanied by about twenty-five bucks, put in his appearance. He made the same inquiry as his predecessor, was given the same answer, and after being presented with a like number of blankets, knives, and so forth, repeated the promise of his predecessor that the emigrants could remain unmolested while preparing to cross the river. That the worthy warriors did not consider the butchery of the emigrant's cattle a molestation was manifest as it continued apace thereafter with the Indian appetite for fresh beef.

The observance that on each occasion of their visits the Indians had invariably come from the California side of the river was very disconcerting to the emigrants as it entirely invalidated the oft-repeated advance information that when once across the Colorado River there would be no further Indian menace to contend with. Another shattered hope! What next?

## II

The morning of the thirtieth found all hands refreshed and restored to their normal physical condition. The practically forty-eight hours of personal contact with the Mojaves, despite the assurances of the chiefs who visited them the day before, had in no wise minimized the emigrants' realization of their precarious helplessness. For, as a matter of fact, they were thoroughly convinced that they were sitting atop a powder magazine, and their only speculation was as to if, how, and when the lid would be blown off.

There was nothing which they could do, however; flight was impossible even if they were across the river, as the Indians afoot could travel twice as fast as the emigrants could with their plodding ox teams. There was no alternative but to watch and wait. There was no need to fret or worry—that would avail them nothing. In the final analysis, however, if they were to escape without a fight, it would be by crossing the river. They therefore decided to expedite this undertaking with all haste. Their courage was one hundred per cent plus. There was nothing to do but assume their natural aplomb and await eventualities. And if fight they must, fight they would to the bitter end.

The river at this point was about five hundred yards in width, composed of alternate broad expanses of shallow water and swift-running, deep currents in the more confined areas. The bottom throughout, shifting in nature, was composed of atomic particles of silt and sand, which caused the formation of more or less quicksand in the shallow places. Although it would be possible to cope successfully with these conditions with the loose stock and mounted horsemen, to undertake to haul the heavy wagons across would be but to court certain disaster.

It therefore became necessary to construct a log raft and rig a ferry crossing with which to transport the women and children and the wagons. This would entail a delay of three or four days. Mr. Brown having located a point about one-half a mile down the river where there was an advantageous crossing with an ample supply of trees from which to get the logs for the raft, it was decided, both as a matter of expediency and safety of the women in case of a surprise attack by the Indians, to move the camp down within hailing distance of the men at work on the raft.

Accordingly, immediately after breakfast, the eventful 30th day of August 1858, the camp was moved down the river in close proximity to the proposed crossing. Although the terrain was otherwise considerably overgrown with desert brush, a bare spot was encountered at the proper location, about one hundred feet in width and several hundred feet in length, one end of which closely abutted the riverbank. The large wagons were placed in two parallel rows of three each about fifty feet apart. The strategic importance of this location and arrangement is manifest. The opening toward the river fenced off an enemy in that direction, and the other, which was used as a means of ingress and egress, with its long range of vision prevented a frontal attack from that direction.

The women, Grandmother Jones, Mrs. Brown, and Mother, were in passive accord and went about arranging their fireside camps with a partial degree of permanence. Hope, the good Lord's eternal comforter, gave them courage. How long was it to abet them?

While these activities were in progress at the camp, an unusually great number of Indians were seen crossing the river in the vicinity of the first camp, and upwards of two hundred and fifty of them were counted. In the course of a short time most of them had vanished as though swallowed up by the earth. Along in the middle of the forenoon two Indians came near camp and looked about in a superficial manner, saying nothing, and after a while left. About an hour later, a lone Indian repeated the same procedure. Savedra's suspicions were aroused to the extent that he said, "I don't like the way them 'Injuns' is acting. We are going to have trouble with them, and I bet before night."

Somewhat aroused by this statement, suddenly recalling that Mr. Bentner, who had expected to be back early that morning, was now considerably overdue, Father resolved to send in quest of him. As dinner was about ready, however, he decided to wait until it had been eaten and thereupon sent a young man by the name of Young and Billy Stidger, a nineteen-year-old youth, on their horses to see if they could encounter Mr. Bentner and family. Mr. Brown, Lee Griffin, and Ed Akey, after partaking of their dinner, went back to where they were working on the raft.

From immediately subsequent events it transpired that the large number of Indians which had been observed that morning had craftily divided into two parties, one of which deployed at a distance unseen and approached the camp on the side near which Brown was working, evidently expecting thereby to prevent Brown, Griffin, and Akey from reaching camp when hostilities began. The remaining half of the Indians, with equal cunning, had maneuvered themselves stealthily around the cattle and by darting from bush to bush had approached camp on the opposite side and likewise secreted themselves behind brush and bushes. By this move they had cut off the four herdsmen who were tending the cattle from reaching camp. Having by this stratagem reduced the twenty-five fighting men in camp by seven, when the number was further reduced by the departure of Young and Stidger, the wily devils evidently thought the time was opportune for an attack.

Young and Stidger had barely passed from view, when Sally Fox (the twelve-year-old stepdaughter of Mr. Brown), who was playfully climbing on one of the large wheels of a wagon, espied some Indians surreptitiously darting from bush to bush approaching camp. She at once jumped down, simultaneously shrieking, "The Indians are coming and they will kill us all!" Coincidentally the Indians rent the air with their demoniacal war whoops, and pandemonium broke loose. Each bush within arrow shot of the camp secreted an Indian or two, and a veritable flock of arrows coming from all directions greeted the appearance of anyone in camp.

Strangely enough the first one to be wounded was little Sally Fox. The instant the battle started, bedding, blankets, and boxes of all sorts were placed alongside of the wheels of the wagons to serve as a barricade to screen the women and children from arrows that might be shot underneath the wagons. While Sally Fox was hovering together with her four little sisters and brother in one of these improvised breastworks, an arrow impaled her tiny abdomen from side to side, miraculously escaping her vital organs.

When the first report of a gunshot reached the men working on the raft, Griffin exclaimed, "What's that mean?" "Great God, it is the Indians," Brown replied, and hurriedly mounting his horse raced at top speed for camp. He was showered with arrows from either side, one of which entered from the back in close proximity to his heart. Yet onward he fled and, riding hastily to where Mrs. Brown sat, exclaimed, "Where's my gun, Mother?" and toppled from his horse dead.

In the meantime Akey and Griffin, who were not mounted, were running at breakneck speed, revolvers in hand, toward the camp when Akey, observing an Indian not more than twenty feet away, his arrow leveled at him, promptly shot him dead, and his arrow sped harmlessly over Akey's head. A few steps farther along Akey killed another Indian under the identical conditions.

Shortly he came upon Griffin, apparently dazed, standing perfectly still, dangerously exposed. Akey said, "What in the world are you doing here?" In reply to which Griffin indicated a copious flow of blood from two wounds on his right arm and side. Akey gave him a terrific shove toward the camp and said, "Run for your life!" And while thus engaged, Akey received a serious, though not dangerous, wound, extending from under his left armpit out through the flesh in the upper part of his breast.

The herders, likewise alarmed at the gunshots, raced their horses at full speed around the battle area and reached camp without serious injury through the long frontal approach and took their places in the firing line. Young and Stidger, similarly aroused, rushed madly into camp, bearing the sickening tidings that they had found Mr. Bentner's wagon near the place where the party had encamped the first night—Miss Bentner, the eighteen-year-old daughter, lying on the ground beside the wagon stripped of every stitch of her clothing, her head beaten to a pulp and her face frightfully mutilated. No trace, however, was found of Mr. and Mrs. Bentner, their fifteen-year-old daughter and twelve-year-old son and their team of mules. And the only further indication of their fate, a gruesome one, was furnished by an Indian observed across the river during the battle, triumphantly waving a pole from the end of which dangled a number of scalps.

Some of the Indians with animal-like dumbness exposed themselves to pistol fire at a distance of not upwards of fifteen feet. Whether this was because some of them at that early date had positively no knowledge of the dangers from gun fire, or that they had expected to find the same passive nonresistance from the emigrants in battle as they had shown when the Indians were wantonly butchering their cattle, is problematical. Bravery it surely was not, as the Indian has not yet lived who would give the white man an even break, to say nothing of a decidedly advantageous one.

Be all this as it may, the Indians were not long in discovering their error. The first half a dozen or more of these imprudent ones were dropped in their tracks by revolver fire. This had a steadying effect upon the rest of them, and henceforth their movements were gradually backward. In the meantime they kept up a constant barrage of arrow fire.

Some of the wily red devils, in the hope that none would escape their murderous attack, shot their arrows high into the air at an angle so that they would fall within the camp area, hopeful of killing or maiming some helpless woman or child. In this they all but scored, as one of their random missiles struck Grandmother Jones, who was sitting on a sugar box behind one of their improvised breastworks, holding in her arms my year-old sister, Annie. The arrow which struck Grandmother in the wrist missed the child's head by inches.

The effectiveness of the Indians' arrow fire was diminished in ratio to their backward movement. This, however, did not reduce their personal peril as those who exposed themselves at the greater distances were picked off by rifle fire.

While the battle was at its height, the Indians gave a sickening exhibition of their savage brutality in connection with the stallion Black Morrill, who we recall was to have headed Father's trotting breeding farm in California. Before starting on his journey, Father had, as a safeguard against escape or theft, fastened a strong chain so securely around the horse's throat that it could not be removed without the use of a heavy pair of blacksmith's pincers. The chain was then passed through the ring of the halter, and the other end was always fastened with a lock and key when and wherever the horse was tied. Throughout the journey the stallion had been secured to a feed box at the rear end of one of the wagons. The man whose duty it was to take care of the horse was custodian of the key.

On this particular occasion, to escape the torrid heat of the sun, the horse was tied in the usual manner in the shade of a mesquite tree at a considerable distance from camp. Far be it from the Indians to allow such a handsome prize to escape them. A number of them made a dash for the horse, and finding their efforts were vain to unloose him, they cut his throat and left his carcass hanging in the halter.

When at a little upwards of two hours after the battle had begun and practically all of the Indians had withdrawn from the battle area, their chief, in gaudy war paint and a gorgeous array of furs and feathers, stood forth in plain view about two hundred yards distant from the camp, defiantly stroking his breast inasmuch as to say, "Here I am! You can't get me!"

Here the Missouri preacher re-enters our story and in a most glorious manner. He was known to be a crack shot, and one of the other young men whose sight was so impaired by the flow of blood from an arrow wound over his right eye that he could not shoot, observing the Indian, said to the parson, "Why don't you shoot that fellow?" The preacher replied, "My gun won't carry that far." The wounded man then said, "Take mine. It will hold up true that distance." The proffered rifle was accepted, and the parson took aim at the vainglorious chieftain, but from excitement or fatigue his aim was unsteady. The gun was lowered, and finding a place to rest it, the Missouri preacher again took aim. This time there was no wavering. The trusty rifle barked and the chief fell dead in his tracks. A number of husky warriors picked him up and bore him away as had they all others of their dead who had fallen at a sufficient distance from the camp to permit of their doing so without unduly exposing themselves. This according to the Indian ritual of war was a signal for the cessation of hostilities, and the Indians left en masse, taking with them upwards of four hundred head of stock.

In the hectic rush of the battle, there was so much of more importance to be done than keeping count of the Indians killed that the exact number was never known. It was generally accepted, however, that seventeen were killed in plain sight of the camp, and that number was no doubt considerably augmented later by those who had been fatally wounded. The casualties amongst the emigrants were the absolute extinction of the Bentner family, comprised of five souls, the killing of Mr. Brown, and the wounding of eleven, of whom Lee Griffin was very dangerously hurt and three or four others, including Grandmother Jones, seriously so, and the remainder, including my father, only superficially.

The smoke and smell of powder had barely cleared away before the all-absorbing topic of what next to do presented itself. Escape in any direction seemed impossible, as if the Indians were so disposed they could soon overtake them. There was no time for hesitation or indecision, however. They decided that the best course to pursue would be to retrace their steps whence they had come, gravely doubtful, however, of the efficacy of the undertaking. But each and every one of the men resolved to sell his life as dearly as possible.

Terrifying as was their plight, it would have been infinitely worse had it not been for the fact that the oxen and mules which had been used that morning in moving camp had remained close at hand with a few other animals which had become separated from the main herd. It thus transpired that there were enough oxen—three yoke (six head)—to haul one of the large wagons and two mules to draw the ambulance, and Old Bob, a favorite bobtail riding and driving horse, and ten or fifteen other nondescript animals.

As many provisions as it was possible to carry and only the most absolutely essential articles were loaded in the large wagon and ambulance. Grandmother Jones and my sisters, Nina and Annie, four and one year old respectively, Mr. Brown's five children and my wounded uncle, Ed Jones, accommodated themselves as best they could in the ox-drawn wagon. Mrs. Brown was mounted on Mr. Brown's horse, which had borne him into camp after he was shot. Mother was mounted on Old Bob. Grandfather Jones was so very lame he was assigned the task of driving the mules and ambulance in which Lee Griffin was prone on an improvised stretcher. The men, about twenty-five in number, including Father, walked.

It was about five o'clock before their flight began, and the moment was indeed a tragic one to leave behind five wagons loaded with practically all of their worldly possessions. Their progress was so slow that they had proceeded only about three miles into the mountains until, because of their inability to see the road, they were halted by darkness. They were fearful of making a light, and, there huddled together in the deathlike stillness of the desert, they constantly strained their ears for any sound of approaching danger.

Along about ten o'clock the solitude of the occasion was rudely shattered by a tumultuous chorus of war whoops, punctuated here and there by loud beating of tin cans and kettles by the Indians, who had returned to the scene of the battle. Their revelry increased in volume from time to time, resulting no doubt from additional numbers who were arriving, until at the zenith of their orgy there were in all probability more than one thousand of them who had come fully determined to exterminate the party with war clubs as they slept. When the revelry was at its height, one of the young men not altogether bereft of his sense of humor remarked, "I guess they have broken into the medicine chest and got hold of Rose's $8.00 brandy!"

Why the Indians did not pursue the fleeing emigrants can be ascribed only to their great satisfaction over the extensive amount of loot they had taken.

The moon rose shortly after midnight, and the party resumed its tedious grind. The daytime weather was extremely hot, animal water and feed were scarce, and in their desire to escape they had hazed the poor teams to their limit every moment.

As the day wore on, Grandfather Jones, who was bringing up the rear with the mule team and ambulance, fell farther and farther back. The mules would frequently stop, and each succeeding time it took more and more whip and tongue lashing to get them started again. Finally when dark was fast approaching, they came to a determined stop and could not be budged by an endless amount of prodding and profanity. The vanguard of the party was fully a mile ahead, and Grandfather no doubt under the stress of excitement reasoned that the mules could not or would not go any farther without water, which he himself was unable to provide, that the best thing to do with them was to turn them loose and let them forage for themselves, giving no heed, however, as to what would ultimately become of them. Thereupon he unhitched them and turned them loose, and, insofar as the Rose party was concerned, the mules were never seen again.

A tragedy unto itself and the act of a madman for the time being at least. There could have been but the one result—the loss of the mules. Whereas had he remained patiently where the mules had come to a halt, it is a moral certainty that the moment the vanguard of the party realized the tardiness of his arrival someone would have come back to succor him. We must admit in all fairness that the old man was under teriffic mental and physical stress, but one cannot help but wonder why self-preservation did not assert itself to the extent of safeguarding this valuable means of transportation. It would have been but little less needless and senseless to have deliberately thrown away his firearms in a country still full of dangers.

Conjecture as to the mental processes which dictated this inane rashness is needless, for that part of his anatomy was certainly not functioning at that time. And my guess founded on the impressions which I gained from my close contact with him during the first seventeen years of my young childhood and adolescence would be that it was temperamentality of the 90% temper and 10% mentality brand. This does not mean to say that the old gentleman was in any wise mentally deficient, for far from that he was a wise old owl, well informed and competent. He was however a self-willed, headstrong individual with a volatile temper, a person hard to get along with.

Leaving poor wounded Griffin prone in the ambulance, Grandfather limped his way laboriously onward for about a mile until he overtook the rest of the party, which very fortunately had reached the encampment of Hedgpath's ten wagons, which as we recall had remained there on the way out while their work teams were sent to the river to recuperate. The instant Grandfather Jones reached camp, Ed Akey, himself severely wounded, without waiting for his supper, started back in the darkness to succor his pal Lee Griffin. He finally located the ambulance, and then by partially carrying Lee Griffin and stopping frequently he returned with him two or three hours later.[2]

Throughout the day the physically racked and mentally distraught fleeing party had striven midst hope and apprehension to reach this encampment, fearful as they were that the Indians might have killed the whole party. And their joy in finding that their fears were not justified was unbounded. Needless to say these weary guests were greatly revived by a well-cooked, frugal supper, and the realization that their man power was now double was the source of unlimited comfort.

The following morning the party that had been in camp at this place played their role in the tragedy of the occasion. They were without teams with which to move their wagons. Contemplate if you can the mental reaction that these poor people must have had from the realization that they must abandon their ten wagons and all of their worldly goods and start, God alone knew where, on foot via Albuquerque five hundred miles distance—and then?

When the party pulled out, it numbered about forty-five men and an equal number of women and children. The only vehicle in the outfit was Father's ox-drawn wagon. The loss of the mules and ambulance had necessitated the readjustment of the human cargo. Mother surrendered her mount to one more decrepit and walked along with the rest of the party.

The hardships which they endured beggar description. The road was flinty and mountainous, and before the first day had passed the shoes of the women and children were worn to shreds. And thereafter they hobbled and staggered along on blistered and bleeding feet. The heat of the sun was torrid, fully 130 degrees. The water supply was scanty. Their food was fragmentary and their rest fitfully spent on the bare ground, and their minds overwrought with apprehension and sorrow. Still they trod on and on.

After three days of this torturing grind, during which not upwards of

[2] John Udell's account of the tragic adventure with the Mojave Indians is contained in the *John Udell Journal*, introd. Lyle H. Wright (Los Angeles, 1946).

twenty miles had been covered, this tatterdemalion brigade had the good fortune to meet a large outfit, California bound over the same route which they were abandoning. Needless to say it did not require any oral persuasion to induce the westward-bound travelers to call a halt. Verily the good Lord had his protecting arms around the fleeing aggregation at this juncture, for had they not encountered this outfit, tragedy would surely have stalked in their wake before another twenty-four hours had passed. As it was, many of them were in a state of utter collapse, and another day's session with the torrid heat would have beyond all doubt seen numbers of them dropping in their tracks, dead or hopelessly prostrated.

Strangely enough the owners of this California-bound outfit, Messrs. Caves, Perkins, Jordan, and Davis, were friends of my father's, hailing from the same county back in Iowa whence he had come. All of these gentlemen had their families with them, and besides the owners there were thirty other men in the party. The men and women alike did everything humanly possible to comfort and succor them. They opened their bountiful larders and even went so far as to kill their own cattle to supply them with fresh meat. The women ministered to the bodily ills and aching hearts of those of their sex with motherly care, going so far as to share their raiment and shoes wherein it was practical. And as for my mother, I know that someone made her a pair of sandals of cowhide, which she wore Indian fashion, secured with thongs between her toes and around her ankles.

These benefactors reported that they had been continually harassed by the Cosnino Indians, and many of their cattle had been stolen. After about two days allowed for the recuperation of the foot brigade, the entire party, now numbering fully one hundred and fifty souls, started its march back to Albuquerque.

When they reached a point five or six days distant from Indian Springs, fifteen of the young men were sent ahead with the loose stock to take advantage of the good feed and water conditions existing there. When the main party had approached to within a few miles of Indian Springs, another young man decided to walk ahead and join his comrades there encamped. Within a couple of hours the young man in question rushed breathlessly back to the party with the terrifying information that the Indians had killed all of the young men of the advance party and, wearing their clothes and carrying their guns, were surrounding the Springs, evidently intent upon keeping the emigrants away from the water.

This calamitous situation was by far the most dangerous that they had encountered. Indians with bows and arrows—yes, ad infinitum—the massacre had revealed could be worsted by the emigrants. But armed with fifteen good revolvers and rifles, they would exact a sanguinary toll before they had been wiped out by the preponderance of numbers of the emigrants.

There was no way of dodging the issue. The party was in frantic need of water, and have it they must at any cost.

There was therefore nothing to do but face the situation fighting. Accordingly, all of the fighting men took an extra hitch in their belts and unlimbered their shooting irons, and when the proper position was reached went forth to do battle. Upon arriving at a point where an unrestricted view could be had of the men and their encampment, a situation of incalculable gravity was instantly transformed into one of ecstatic joy, when they observed that the reportedly dead young men were much alive and were waving their hands in salutation. The constant Indian menace had evidently produced a severe case of "jitters" for the self-appointed young advance agent.

The young men had nevertheless been in a fight with the Indians, and two of their number were severely wounded, one of them by an arrow and the other by a ball from an old-fashioned muzzle-loading rifle, in all probability the only firearm at that early date in the possession of any of the southwestern tribes of Indians other than the Apaches.

At this point, Indian Springs, another westward-bound party belonging to the brothers Smith was encountered. With the traditional pioneer kindness, they also opened their hearts and their larders to these distressingly bedraggled wayfarers. The Messrs. Smith rightabout-faced. And, when the beef cattle of the main party had been exhausted, they too gave of their own freely. It was about this time that Mrs. Brown suffered the loss of her highly prized horse which had borne Mr. Brown into camp upon the occasion of his death, and she was then reduced to the foot brigade.

When Peach Tree Springs was reached, as it was then considered the eastern limits of the domain of hostile Indians, another crew of twenty young men, feeling that it would lessen the tension somewhat, decided to again strike out for themselves. They were given an ox that one might say was so poor that you would have to stand him up to knock him down. They slaughtered him and dried his beef, rather a perfunctory proceeding as it had been almost dried on the hoof. To further accelerate the process, they salted the meat freely. They left camp about noon one day, expecting by nightfall to reach a point where there had been water on the way out. Upon arriving there, they found that the water had dried up. The heat was intense, and, having nibbled a little of their salt beef, they were in great need of water. They therefore decided to push right on through during the night, expecting to find water the following morning. Again they were disappointed, and their thirst had become so acute that they realized that they must go on.

They proceeded throughout the day and night semidelirious, staggering and falling like drunken men, and the second morning out they encountered water, if such it could be called. The water was so putrid that they could detect the odor of it from a distance. It was literally alive with white worms, and in order to drink it the men had to strain it through their bandanas. Even so, it was a veritable godsend and certainly saved their lives, and they remained encamped there a couple of days.

Henceforth the retreat was one calamity after another. Provisions and the supply of beef were gradually exhausted, most of the work stock gave out and died, and wagons had to be abandoned by the wayside. Their progress was so slow that at one period it took eighteen days to cover ninety miles. Fate was merciless in its toll from Mrs. Brown. Her youngest child and only son, the sole issue of her marriage with Mr. Brown, was taken sick and died and was laid away in a lonely spot along the desert roadside.

When the party was nearing Albuquerque, the United States Army, hearing of their plight, sent out a wagonload of supplies and later on sent two more loads. Father with Mother and the rest of the family together with a few others of the party and Old Bob, Father's one surviving animal, in the vanguard of the scattered remnants of the once-spectacular Rose party, reached Albuquerque October 28, 1858—fifty-nine days having been consumed in their flight following the massacre at the Colorado River.

Perforce with death playing such a tragic part in them, there was no gauge by which to measure Mrs. Brown's losses. Although measured by dollars and cents Father's losses of $27,500 amounted to practically as much as those of the Hedgpath party combined, from the standpoint of human misery, notwithstanding the fact they had all but ruined him financially, they were by no means so personally distressing as those of some of the individual members. Some of them already in the sunset of old age had put all of their worldly possessions into this venture in the anticipation of joining a son or daughter who had preceded them to California, reasoning that when they themselves reached that Midas land of opportunity they could cash their stock and outfits advantageously, and with a little nest egg acquired thereby they could so arrange as to pass their remaining days in ease and tranquillity in that sunny clime.

With this dream shattered, themselves reduced to penury and marooned in a strange land, their plight was indeed desperate. Whereas with Father, though the blow was staggering, he was yet young (thirty) and virile. He had amassed this, for that period, very considerable fortune within the past decade. He still had a small bank roll. Hope beckoned him onward.

Fortunately for Mrs. Brown, her husband, who was a Mason, had fraternized with that order on his way westward. When Mrs. Brown reached Albuquerque, hearing of her plight, the Masons took her in charge and did all that was humanly possible to comfort and succor her. Shortly thereafter, a Mr. Smith who was going to San Francisco took Mrs. Brown and her four little girls with him at his expense. Mrs. Brown had a brother and sister living in San Francisco, and they at once reimbursed Mr. Smith.

There is a famous landmark along the highway near Vacaville, California, not far from Sacramento. It is an immense black walnut tree grown from a nut carried across the plains in a covered wagon by Sally Fox, heroine of the Indian raid on the Rose party on the banks of the Colorado River in August 1858. On the renewal of the westward trip of Mrs. Brown and her family the following spring, her twelve-year-old daughter, Sally Fox, playing under a tree on the bank of the Gila River, then in New Mexico Territory, picked up four queer-looking nuts. These she carried in the pocket of her apron to the ranch of her uncle, Josiah Allison, in California. And from one of these nuts planted in 1859 grew this magnificent tree.

When our little heroine, Sally Fox, attained her majority, she taught school in San Francisco. In 1870, on her first visit back to Iowa, she carried with her as a souvenir the same little white apron, with the two telltale arrow holes in it, which she had worn on that fateful occasion.

## III

On reaching Albuquerque, the party scattered. The young men who were of Father's immediate party, all stalwart specimens, found employment with the government as surveyors' helpers and road builders. My father and his family took a small house in Albuquerque. Undaunted by his straitened circumstances, Father at once cast about for some inexpensive business to be acquired by making a small cash payment. Unable to find one, he sought vainly for such employment as befitted his capabilities. The only thing offered him was waiting on table in a restaurant. To conserve his remaining small bank roll, he took the job and started anew the climb to success from the lowest rung of the ladder.

Quite naturally, Father was not at all contented in his menial occupation in Albuquerque and continued in it only until the family had partially recuperated from their harrowing experiences. He had been greatly impressed with the business activity of Santa Fe, when passing through on his way west. At the front, so to speak, of western emigrant travel, Santa Fe was the trading center for all prospecting and mining outfits and extensive cattle and sheep operations from the outlying country for hundreds of miles around.

Concluding to cast his lot there, Father loaded the family and their few belongings in two two-horse wagons. One of the animals of one team was the faithful Old Bob, which had carried Mother away from the battlefield.

It took but a few days to make the short journey. Upon arrival, camp was pitched in the outskirts of the town, and Father started immediately to look the ground over in quest of some business in which he might be able to embark. After spending a week or more in careful observation and inquiry, he entered into negotiations for the purchase of the business of La Fonda (The

Inn), an old hotel later known as the Exchange. It was a dilapidated, old, flat-roofed, one-story adobe, located on one corner of the old Pueblo Plaza, built after the manner of most of the old Mexican structures, with the sleeping rooms opening on a patio. Each room, of course, had a door, but all of those along the interior walls were without windows, and the only source of ventilation was the iron-barred openings in the upper part of the doors. The few windows of which La Fonda boasted were in the outside walls opening flush with the sidewalk, protected from intrusion by heavy upright iron bars.

It was not, however, the hotel part of La Fonda that appealed to Father, but the bar business and gambling games. He had never had any experience in either of these lines of business, rarely took a drink, and had an absolute abhorrence of a drunken man. He was, however, very fond of card playing and was rated as a first-class poker and seven-up player. This, though, was to be his first experience on the "inside," as the gamekeeper's end of it is termed. Although lacking in actual experience, Father had a good general knowledge of the varying angles of gambling and relied upon this to enable him to protect himself from the ever-present menace of the shrewdest of card sharps and collusive dealers. He was short of money and wrote to his brother-in-law, H. K. S. O'Melveny, who was practicing law in Cairo, Illinois, asking him for a loan.

O'Melveny scraped up all the cash he could and sent it to him. Father bought the place and took charge. He did not do any of the actual work as barkeeper or dealer of any of the games, but hired the most dependable men he could get in these branches as well as in the alleged hotel. He was around all the time and made it his business to see that everyone got a square deal. It was a very tough spot and not one that women and children should abide in, and my mother and her parents and the little girls lived in other quarters.

Human life was the cheapest thing there was in Santa Fe, and killings were frequent at La Fonda. The town was a seething hotbed of gamblers, killers, and lewd women. There were many men in those days who killed others simply to get the reputation. They were rarely arrested or tried and usually were killed later by someone quicker on the trigger. If they ever got it in their heads one was afraid of them, they would make it so uncomfortable for him that he would have to leave town. But let it be known that a fellow would not back away, they gave him a wide berth.

My father was a very even-tempered man with a very clear, penetrating eye. Every lineament of his countenance indicated determination. Though he had to do with all sorts of bad men in very trying situations, he never had to use a gun, but having it on him and having inspired the belief that he would use it no doubt saved him a lot of trouble. He soon became well known and very popular, and his business flourished. There were some very rich cow and sheep men and miners who drifted into Santa Fe occasionally, and some poker games for big stakes were played at the Fonda. Father took a hand with them once in a while usually making it highly profitable.

After the family had been here little over a year, my mother gave birth to my older brother, Harry Ezra, January 6, 1860. In the summer of the succeeding year, Father sold his business, paid off all debts, and had a new bank roll of $14,000.

# 3

## *Butterfield Stage Road - Early Gringos - The Mission*

### I

WITH the determination to reach California still uppermost in his mind, Father availed himself of the first opportunity presenting itself that seemed reasonably safe. A few months later, with a number of other families he joined a government expedition under command of Lieutenant Edward F. Beale. On this occasion with Uncle Sam's soldiers in attendance, there was no fear of Indian attacks.

With water facilities perfected and roadbeds improved, some of the rigors of the trip were removed, not, however, to the extent of making the journey a pleasure jaunt. The torrid heat, stifling dust, and irksome daily routine still prevailed. As the expedition carried a liberal assortment of supplies for almost every need, and with the army physician at their command, the prospect was particularly alluring to the women who had little ones.

This expedition took the southern road from Albuquerque, crossed the Colorado at Yuma, and took the Butterfield stage road across the desert to the mountains in San Diego County. The desert part of this route, which descended to almost three hundred feet below sea level in what is now the heart of Imperial Valley, was certainly the Great Creator's most worthy effort in desert-making. In one section the road passed through large dunes of sand of extreme fineness. With the heavy winds sometimes prevailing, these dunes were shifted bodily from one place to another completely covering the road, and the air was so charged with the very fine dust that it all but suffocated one and rendered visibility impossible. Emigrants were frequently stalled and compelled to dig a new roadbed for short distances.

The only habitations seen in this—at that time—barren waste were the stage stations located about ten miles apart. These were forlorn makeshift affairs, usually presided over by a lone hostler, who bached by himself in a shack made partly of lumber and partly of brush. A rough manger was built in the center for two teams of six horses each, which was the necessary complement for a daily two-way single stage line. At stations where meals

*Amanda and L. J. Rose on their wedding day, 1851.*
*Courtesy of Miss Hinda Rose, San Diego.*

*Section from* Map of the County of Los Angeles, California, *comp. by* J. H. Wildy (*1877*), *showing* L. J. Rose *ranch (Sunny Slope) to the left of the Chapman property near center of map.* Huntington Library Collections.

were served, the personnel was augmented by a cook, usually a male person. The teams were generally used for but a single trip daily, as when on the road they were pushed to their limit, time being the essence of the journey. As stated before, ten miles was the daily stint over these sandy roads; however, in localities where feed and water were plentiful and the roadbeds firm, the distance between stations was frequently fifteen miles.

Stations of the latter character, built where materials were of easy access, were well and conveniently constructed, the usual assemblage being a horse barn of sufficient size for the necessities of the line; a commodious hay mow and corral and a small rough cottage for a man and his wife, who, if it was an eating station, prepared the meals. If the station was a one-stage-a-day outfit, the man was the hostler. If more than one stage came daily, he had an assistant; a blacksmith shop, granary, chicken coop, outhouses, a well, and water trough completed the layout. These stations, standing out in bold relief on the broad expanse of plains, were a cheering beacon to the weary road-sore emigrant in the country of magnificent distances.

Leaving the trying sands of the desert behind, the road went out through the rough, heavily rock-ribbed Borrego (sheep) Canyon. From the moment the canyon was entered, as the road slowly wended its way onward and upward over the Cuyamaca Mountains at an elevation of twenty-five hundred feet, the landscape grew constantly more beautiful. The stream in the main canyon, fed into volume by the trickling flow of its many tributaries, gurgled merrily along through its rock-strewn course. The rough, jagged, rocky mountain sides were soon replaced by others solidly covered with fresh green growth of chaparral.

Then, after a few miles travel over a practically level, sparsely wooded country, the broad flat valley on Warner's Ranch was reached, where a glorious climax was added to nature's already lavish adornment. Here were found large streams of clear running water, with thousands of acres of level ground, with a luxuriant growth of California's native grasses blanketing the entire terrain six inches deep. Here were acres upon acres of magnificent oaks with lusty dark green foliage, some of them shading a space almost one hundred feet in diameter; thousands of cattle grazed listlessly, contented. The entire valley itself, of an elevation of about twenty-five hundred feet, was surrounded by mountains of fully that much greater altitude with the higher peaks white-capped, with a recent flurry of snow sparkling in the cordial sunshine. The scene was one of serene tranquillity to the road-sore travelers, who concluded they had finally reached the El Dorado of their hopes.

## II

Warner's Ranch, a magnificent property of 45,000 acres, was owned at that time by Jonathan Trumbull Warner, to whom it was granted by the Mexican government in 1843.[3] Warner, who came to California in 1831 from Connecticut by way of Missouri and Salt Lake, partly for his health and also to buy mules, was among the first flight of the "Gringo Grandees" of southern California. As a matter of fact, I have in mind but three who antedated him. John Temple came to Los Angeles in 1828, Don Abel Stearns, the most aggressive of them all, came in 1829, and William Wolfskill in 1830.[4] A census taken in the pueblo of Los Angeles at the latter date shows that there were but thirty white persons, men, women, and children, living there at that time.[5] In 1837 Warner married Miss Anita Gale, adopted daughter of Don Pío Pico. Warner was a man of large physique, standing considerably over six feet in height, because of which he was called "Juan Largo" (long John). He also had the nickname of "Juan José" (John Joseph). I cannot, however, get the connection between Juan José and Jonathan Trumbull.

Warner's Ranch was on the main line of horseback travel—renegade and otherwise—from Sonora, Mexico, to Los Angeles, and was the scene of many thrilling incidents. Warner was a warrior every inch of his great size, who always stood up for his rights, regardless of consequences. He once came to grief during the Mexican War, when Ensign Espinoza attacked his home. While forcibly remonstrating over the wanton and reckless ransacking of his personal effects, Warner's arm was broken. Far more thrilling, however, was his experience when the notorious bandit Antonio Garra and his band of outlaws made their attack and were repulsed by "Juan Largo" (Warner), who escaped on horseback leaving in his wake four or five dead Indians.[6]

[3] Warner's Ranch (Rancho Agua Caliente or Valle de San José) was granted by Governor Alvarado to José Antonio Pico in 1840 and by Governor Micheltorena to Juan J. Warner in 1844. It contained, as patented, 26,629.88 acres.

[4] John Temple came to Los Angeles in 1827; Stearns came to California in 1829 and settled in Los Angeles in 1833; Wolfskill came to California in 1831 and settled in Los Angeles in 1836.

[5] The census report made by Alcalde Vicente Sánchez for the year ending Dec. 31, 1830, showed 764 whites within the town. The first census of the Los Angeles District (not merely the pueblo) made in 1836 showed 1,675 whites.

[6] Antonio Garra was bandit or patriot, depending on the point of view. He was a Warner's Ranch Indian, who had been educated at Mission San Luis Rey. To resist the imposition of a tax, he tried to organize the tribesmen of southern California from the Colorado River to the San Joaquin River. The so-called Garra Revolt ended at San Diego when Garra was shot by a firing squad.

Warner's Springs, located on Warner's Ranch, was originally the property of the Mission tribe of Indians, who lived there for many years and built a very attractive village.[7] Their houses were all of adobe, with roofs thatched with *tule* (tu-ly), a large native bulrush. There was also a small tile-roofed church, where visiting padres held services occasionally. In later years, through the vagaries of the law, the Indians were dispossessed and moved to the Pala reservation near by, and title to the springs given to the grant owners.

This tribe of Indians was famous for the baskets they made of grasses, bulrush, or willow twigs, in varying shapes and designs, with small colored breaks or figures in the general outline, which carried a legend or told a story in Indian lore. They also made *ollas* (o-yahs), large earthen jugs for holding drinking water, which, when in use, are usually suspended by a rope in the shade, where the breeze strikes them and keeps the water very cool.

Before California came into the possession of the United States this Warner Ranch property was known as Agua Caliente (hot water). And it was here in 1846, during the conquest of California by the United States, that Colonel Kearny was encamped with his detachment of Dragoons, which he brought across the desert after taking Santa Fe from the Mexicans. In marching his forces from here to San Diego, for the purpose of co-operating with Commodore Stockton, Colonel Kearny, when reaching the site of the present town of Ramona, took the wrong road. Instead of taking the direct road over Mussey's grade into San Diego, along which his progress would have been unopposed, Kearny took the one off to the right which led down to Poway Valley and San Bernardo. In so doing, Kearny ran into a detachment of the Mexican army under General Andrés Pico, brother of Don Pío Pico, then governor of California, in fact the last under Mexican rule. In his engagement with Pico, Kearny's forces were severely worsted and driven up onto the top of a mountain peak, where, beleaguered for four days, they all but perished before being relieved by Stockton and his marines.

From Warner's Ranch, the Butterfield stage road ran down through Santa Ysabel, Ramona, and Foster into San Diego. The party Father was traveling with took the road which left Warner's Ranch through a draw in the mountains that led down through the San Jacinto range out onto the broad plains of San Bernardino County. This section of country on which the beautiful city of Riverside and scores of others of lesser note have risen to their glory, surrounded by splendid orange groves, was practically unsettled.[8] Truly enough, most of it was held under Mexican grants, the extent

[7] The so-called Mission Indians of southern California were of Shoshonean and Yuman stock. They had been under the jurisdiction of Franciscan missionaries; other Indians in other California areas were under similar jurisdiction but died out.

[8] At this time San Diego County extended to the borders of San Bernardino County.

of which was so great, however, that one might travel a day over them and not see the homesite. Scarcely a habitation was seen after coming out of the mountains into the valley until the fair-sized, then, Mormon settlement of San Bernardino was reached.

San Bernardino at that time, the terminus of competing stage lines carrying passengers from the seaport at San Pedro, via Los Angeles, was a thriving village, wearing considerable of a frontier air. The stage road to Los Angeles, sixty miles distant, passed through the settlements of Cucamonga, Spadra, and El Monte, which, about fifteen miles apart, were used as stage stations. The convenience in distance of their location along the route and the fact that provisions and other necessities could be purchased caused the party to use these settlements as camping grounds at the end of a day's travel.

A settlement, as then spoken of, consisted of a small tavern, where meals were served and sleeping accommodations could be had for three or four persons; always one, and sometimes two saloons, with the indispensable card and billiard tables. There would be a small general store, with a motley collection in the way of stock; a barn and corral, where horses could be stabled or run loose overnight; a blacksmith's shop; a public watering trough; and the homes of the local merchants. A few others lived on small acreage tracts on the outskirts, with the greater portion of population tributary to the settlement living on larger holdings in the outlying districts.

If the settlement had the distinction of being the stage station, the number of buildings was correspondingly augmented. Post offices were seldom an adjunct. The stage driver carried a few letters for friends he was sure of seeing. The country folk depended on the Los Angeles post office for their mail, making weekly pilgrimages for it from places thirty or forty miles distant. The long round trip was generally made the same day, Mexicans invariably going on horseback.

Cucamonga, the first settlement on the stage line out of San Bernardino, was located on a Mexican grant of the same name, consisting of 13,000 acres, owned—at the time, 1860—by Colonel Julian Isaac Williams, who arrived in California from Pennsylvania in 1833.[9] After residing in the pueblo of Los Angeles until 1842, he moved to Rancho del Chino (the Chinaman's ranch) and succeeded to the ownership of it. The Rancho del Chino grant of 22,000 acres was patented to Don Antonio María Lugo in

---

Only a northern strip of the later Riverside County was created out of San Bernardino County.

[9] Williams did not own Rancho Cucamonga; it had been acquired by Tiburcio Tapia in 1839 and passed to other owners. Instead, Williams acquired two ranchos lying to the south of the Cucamonga: the 22,000-acre Rancho Santa Ana del Chino in 1841 and the 13,000-acre addition to Santa Ana del Chino in 1843. The combined ranchos of Williams totaled over 35,000 acres.

1841. The combined acreage of the Rancho del Chino and Cucamonga gave Colonel Williams a domain of 35,000 acres in one piece. Shortly after taking up his abode in the rural district, Colonel Williams, an ardent worshiper at the shrine of Eros and the fair señoritas, capitulated to the charms of Señorita Francisca Lugo and took her as his wife.

Don Antonio María Lugo, the father of this fair señorita, was a member of one of the oldest and largest of California's early families and himself a Croesus among the natives. Early history tells us of his being possessed of seventy-two thousand dollars in personal property, half of which was in gold kept in his home. This amount was exclusive of his landed estate, which was spoken of as so many leagues of land. Colonel Williams built a magnificent adobe home on Rancho del Chino, the furniture and furnishings of which were only exceeded in lavishness by their elegance. Scores of native servants were kept busy caring for it.

Very generous and hospitable and of magnetic personality, Colonel Williams at once became a central figure in social life and La Hacienda de Williams (the Williams estate) was famed from San Diego to San Francisco for its *fiestas* (feasts) and *bailes* (pronounced "by-lays"—dances). Aside from his high social attainments, Colonel Williams gained laurels for his valor during the turbulent period of Mexican insurrections and the reign of banditry. His generosity was proverbial. On many occasions he sent messengers forty-five miles to Los Angeles for clothing and supplies for emigrants who had reached his hacienda stranded, and also advanced money to many young men to start them in business.

The settlement of Spadra, the half-way point between Los Angeles and San Bernardino, was the home of "Uncle Billy" Rubottom, a very popular and picturesque character in early California life. The 22,000-acre Rancho San José grant belonging to Ignacio Palomares and Ricardo Vejar was adjacent to Spadra on the east. Off to the southwest was La Puente (the bridge), the regal domain of 49,000 acres granted to William Workman and John Rowland in 1845. Rowland and Workman came with a party by way of Santa Fe in 1841. The year following their arrival, they joined Pico's Mexican army against Micheltorena and the illustrious and ill-fated Sutter of Helvetia, leaders of another faction, Workman serving as captain and Rowland as lieutenant of a company of volunteers.

El Monte (the woods), the largest settlement on the stage road from San Bernardino, was the last station before reaching Los Angeles—its inhabitants lived in two sections, one bearing the high-sounding name of "Lickskillet," the other "Shirttail bend." The country about El Monte had been settled en masse by a large party of families, and as they were somewhat of the fire-eating class, peace did not always reign serene with them. They had, however, the virtue of making short work of outlaws.

Leaving the stage road at El Monte, taking another bearing a little to the northwest, after traveling four miles, the then almost century-old Mexican settlement built around San Gabriel Mission was reached.

This was in late December 1860. Early rains had fallen and nature was rapidly donning her festal robes. The entire country as far as the eye could reach was an apparently limitless sward of green. Although yet too early for the plains to have fully adorned themselves with their Joseph's coat of wildflower bloom, there were scattered splotches of brilliance from early-blooming varieties. Cattle and horses already shed of their winter coats, sleek and fat, moving aimlessly about, were grazing in native grass up to their knees; large flocks of sheep were feeding on the hillsides as their newly born lambs gamboled to and fro. A few orange trees near the old church were heavily laden with fruit just taking on a golden hue. Roses in full bloom were climbing over the arbor in the padre's garden. Streams of clear running water, fresh from their subterranean home beneath the not far-distant Sierra Madres rippled merrily along on every side.[10] The entire landscape was enveloped in an atmosphere of prosperity and serene contentment. Such was the ecstatic first-day midwinter panorama that decided my father to cease his weary wanderings and make his abode in San Gabriel Valley.

Father rented the comfortable adobe home of J. D. Woodworth on his forty-acre tract about two miles distant toward the mountains from the settlement of San Gabriel, where the family was soon comfortably settled. So confused was Father's mind by the labyrinth of alluring locations surrounding him on every hand, plus the fabled tales of greater virtues and potentialities of other sections of southern California reaching his ears daily, that he deferred purchasing temporarily. Ready to believe almost anything, regardless of how extravagantly spoken, of this wondrous country, he decided to cruise about and see for himself. Many attractive places were investigated in other sections of Los Angeles County. Journeying over into Santa Barbara County, he was particularly impressed by the great fertility of the southern portion of it, which later became Ventura County.

Happening to encounter one of the disagreeable east-wind storms quite prevalent there, his good opinion was somewhat tempered. Then he traveled on through the northern portion of Santa Barbara County into San Luis Obispo and Kings counties. In Kings County, he found the country more barren and arid-appearing than any before visited. In fact, it occurred to him that the farther he got from San Gabriel Valley the less attractive were conditions, and he returned to the land of his first love.

The San Gabriel Valley, as it was then known, can be described as that section of country about ten miles in length nestling against the Sierra

[10] "Sierra Madre" or "the Sierra Madres" refers to the range now called San Gabriel Mountains.

Madre range of mountains, its western boundary taking in the site on which Pasadena was later built, and its eastern one including Baldwin's Santa Anita Ranch. With an average width of six or seven miles, it reached the Repetto Hills back of Montebello on the western part, and the moist lowlands of El Monte on the eastern portion of its southern boundary.

The particularly attractive feature and, as a matter of fact, the deciding one in Father's conclusion to locate in San Gabriel Valley, was the splendid water conditions prevailing. Extending its full length east and west, about midway between the floor of the valley and the mountains, there was an undulating section, which rose into gentle rolling hills in its western limits, from which in its eastern extent it descended into a flatter formation, with a more pronounced incline upwards toward the mountains. Immediately adjacent to this formation in its full course, there was a strip of water-bearing land, varying in width from seven or eight hundred to a thousand feet, from which constantly flowed streams of pure, crystal-clear spring water, which percolated through the many strata of gravel from the Sierra Madres, five miles distant. All that was necessary to develop a fine stream was to open a trench and give it an outlet, and a flowing well could be had by sinking fifty or sixty feet.

The soil was soft and porous, of decomposed granite and fine alluvial silt, the erosion of ages from the mountain slopes. It had a good subsoil for drainage and stood irrigation splendidly. Even after a heavy rain, it never became muddy. The roads themselves, of a very firm formation of granite texture, bore the appearance of a washed-off pavement after a heavy storm. There was a gradual rise of about thirty feet to the mile from the valley to the base of the mountains. During the winter, "Old Baldy" (San Antonio Peak), the towering sentinel of the Sierra Madres, ten thousand feet in height, stands out in bold relief with its snow-capped crest. At times in winter there is a little flurry of snow to be seen on the rest of the range, giving a slight tang to the air with an impression of winter, while down on the floor of the valley wild flowers of every color and hue, of exquisite fragrance, grow in profusion. The orange, fig, olive, pomegranate, and vine, and about every fruit which grows in a tropical or temperate zone are laden with fruit or are resplendent in fragrant bloom, or the budding foliage of springtime. It would really seem that the beautiful mountains had been a special dispensation of Providence to shelter and protect this fairyland from storms and rough winds.

The entire country has been so radically changed by the great influx of people that the newcomer has positively no conception of the natural beauties of the flowered and wooded landscape prior to its usurpation for subdivision purposes. There were tens of thousands of acres in absolutely the same condition as they were left in the beginning of time. There were no large herds of cattle or flocks of sheep feeding in this immediate locality, and the entire terrain was just as nature had created it.

There were very few native trees growing in the lower areas of San Gabriel Valley, an occasional isolated oak, or a cluster of sycamores or cottonwoods flanking the bank of a creek. On the elevated and undulating section immediately contiguous to the stretch of water-bearing land, in the direction of the mountains, there was a beautiful, heavily wooded strip, varying in width from one and a half to two and a half miles. This was a particularly sightly section, commanding an unobstructed view of the entire valley. There were acres upon acres of massive oaks, shady nooks, wild flowers, and babbling brooks, small game in great abundance, and an occasional deer astray from its mountain home. The land was of the most fertile, with just sufficient slope to irrigate nicely.

Thus endowed and adorned with nature's gifts, it is not to be wondered that, when the Americans first settled San Gabriel Valley, this section should have been sought by the more ambitious as their homesites. As a consequence, this section soon became the nucleus of all major developments in the way of tree and vine planting, which ultimately made San Gabriel Valley famous for the superiority of her oranges and the excellence of her wines.

Practically all of this favored section was on the 14,000-acre San Pasqual grant of Don Manuel Garfias, extending from Rancho Santa Anita to Arroyo Seco.[11] The señor's hacienda stood on that western portion of the grant just a few rods south of the hill the Raymond Hotel was later built upon.

At this time there were a few Americans living in the flat areas of San Gabriel Valley raising stock and grain but giving little attention to orange and vine culture.

William Stockton started a nursery and vineyard near the mission in 1855, and there was a small vineyard and orange orchard on Santa Anita, but the first real apostle of both the orange and the vine was Mr. Benjamin Davis Wilson, who came to California from Tennessee by way of Santa Fe

[11] In the early 1850's Benjamin D. Wilson began buying land in what is now the Pasadena and San Marino areas, as well as elsewhere. In 1854 he obtained a deed from Victoria Reid for the 128-acre Huerta de Cuati (the Lake Vineyard property), where he built his home near the lake (sometimes called Wilson's Lake), now the site of Lacy Park in San Marino. In 1858 he bought a 700-acre rancho adjoining the Lake Vineyard property, this rancho being the Cañada de San Pascual or San Pascualito. As a climax, in 1859 he expanded his holdings by buying Rancho San Pasqual, site of Pasadena, which as surveyed and patented contained a little more than 13,500 acres. It had been granted by the Mexican government to Manuel Garfias, who sold it to Wilson. The following year he sold Dr. John S. Griffin a half interest in this rancho. In 1873 Wilson and Griffin partitioned the unsold part, Griffin's share being 4,000 acres, Wilson's 1,600 acres. The Griffin land included the site of Pasadena.

in 1841 in a party with John Rowland, William Workman, and others.

Mr. Wilson purchased about 2,000 acres out of the center of the San Pasqual grant—a piece so abundantly supplied with water that a lake of a number of acres had formed upon it. This was known as Wilson's Lake, and in naming his place Mr. Wilson had chosen for it Lake Vineyard.

"Don Benito" (Mr. Benny), as Mr. Wilson was affectionately called by all the natives, was a very jovial, generous, and hospitable person, typically southern in manner and appearance, with the broad expanse of white linen collar, ruffled shirt front, and flowing black tie of the Jeffersonian period.

In 1844 Mr. Wilson, having basked freely in the sunshine of the smiles of the señoritas, fell a victim to their irresistible charm and married Señorita Ramona Yorba, daughter of Don Bernardo Yorba, the head of a very prominent and wealthy family. Misfortune overtook Don Benito, and his charming señora went to her final rest in 1849, leaving behind a son, John, and a daughter, Sue (María de Jesus). In 1853 Mr. Wilson married Mrs. Margaret S. Hereford, a southern widow, who bore him two daughters, Misses Nannie and Ruth.

Mr. Wilson had many thrilling experiences during the Mexican insurrection prior to California entering the Union. In 1846 he joined the riflemen that took up arms against General Castro's Mexican troops. In 1848, while in charge of twenty men with which he had been sent to San Bernardino to protect that border from Mexican recruits coming in from Sonora by way of Warner's Ranch, Wilson answered a call for help from his friend Colonel Williams at Rancho del Chino, who was besieged by the Mexican army under General Castro.[12] In the engagement which followed, Wilson's ammunition gave out, and he and his men were taken prisoners.

By the time Father arrived in San Gabriel, Mr. Wilson was well advanced as a grower of oranges and grapes. He had quite a number of acres of orange trees in full bearing, and many young ones in different stages of advancement toward production. The vineyard was of even greater proportions, and Mr. Wilson had been making fine wine in commercial quantities for some time prior to this.

Mr. Wilson was very progressive and amassed quite a fortune. It was he who built the first trail up the Sierra Madres to the high peak which bears the name "Wilson's Peak" in his honor. This peak is now surmounted by the country's most powerful telescope and is reached by the famous Lowe incline. Mrs. Cooper, a widowed southern lady, a sister of the second Mrs.

[12] The minor skirmish sometimes called the Battle of Chino took place during the Mexican War, not in 1848 but in Sept. 1846. A few pro-Americans, including Wilson, were besieged by a larger group of *Californios*. Each side had friends, neighbors, and in-laws on the other side. When the roof was fired, the "foreigners" surrendered and were held prisoners until the capitulation at Cahuenga in Jan. 1847.

Wilson, lived with her charming daughter, Miss Mamie, and grown sons, Isaac and Thomas, on a portion of Don Benito's place, as did also Edward Hereford, a son of Mrs. Wilson's by her first marriage.

Another very early settler, Captain Michael White, who came to California in 1828, also located on the San Pasqual grant, acquiring a 200-acre piece adjoining the Woodworth place on the west.[13] Captain White, an old English seafarer, was married to a Mexican woman, with whom he had reared a large family. One of his daughters was married to José Heslop, a Chilean, another was the wife of Francisco Alvarado, a Spaniard, and still another was the wife of a ne'er-do-well Englishman by the name of Courtney. Both Heslop and Alvarado, good citizens, had nice small places on the White Tract and raised fine families. The captain, not overly thrifty, had a small mixed orchard of oranges and deciduous fruits and a few acres in vineyard, and made some wine of indifferent quality.

Colonel E. J. C. Kewen came to Los Angeles in 1858, and in 1861 purchased the 450-acre tract in the San Pasqual west of the Wilson place, locally known as El Molino (the mill). The padres had many years previously built on this tract a small stone flour mill, which had gone into disuse with the collapse of the mission. The old stone mill was remodeled and transformed into a most attractive residence. The colonel was a veteran of the Mexican War and thereafter practiced law in St. Louis, Missouri. He moved from that city to San Francisco in 1852, and he served as California's first attorney general. The colonel was known for his great oratorical ability, and his speech before the Society of Pioneers in San Francisco in 1854 has gone down in history as a classic. Colonel Kewen's forte as a lawyer was criminal practice. Somewhat undersize, but every ounce of his anatomy filled with southern fire, he on one occasion took recourse to the duello as a means of satisfying a grievance.

Colonel Kewen married Miss White, a southern lady, whose people lived in a very attractive colonial residence in Los Angeles, approached by an avenue of large English walnut trees, and surrounded by a number of acres of vineyard. The Cudahy packing plant now occupies the site.

The colonel himself, very gallant and hospitable, and his wife, possessed of all the grace of her southern ancestry, were wonderful hosts, and social functions at El Molino were considered the *pièce de résistance* of the season by the neighborhood.

S. Richardson, a New Englander, with his fine family lived on a small

[13] Michael White's grant was not a part of Rancho San Pasqual but was a 77.23-acre ranch in the San Marino area. It was one of a group of small Mexican grants—the Courtney grant being another one—that are often confused with the larger San Pasqual and Santa Anita.

tract adjoining El Molino on the south. Two daughters of his family, Mary and Alice, attended the old adobe schoolhouse with us.

In 1858 Don Manuel Garfias, grantee of Rancho San Pasqual, in need of money with which to enlarge his hacienda, which I have stated stood just below Raymond Hill, borrowed $3,000 from Doctor John S. Griffin, of Los Angeles, a brother of Mrs. General Albert Sydney Johnston. Garfias gave as security a mortgage on the western 6,000 acres of the grant, agreeing to pay 4% interest per month, compounded monthly, for the use of the money. With his poor management, he did not pay even the first month's interest. Unable to secure any other settlement, Dr. Griffin took over the property in 1859, paying Garfias $2,000 additional, acquiring all the stock, horses, and ranch tools and leaving poor old Garfias well advanced toward the end of his journey to financial ruin.

In 1860 Dr. Griffin sold 600 acres of the property to Don Benito Wilson and his wife for $500.[14] The Wilsons, in turn, a short time thereafter, sold 260 acres of their purchase to Mrs. Albert Sydney Johnston for $1,000. In a short time, Mrs. Johnston built a fine home on the property and called the place Fair Oaks, the name of the plantation in Virginia on which she was born. From this, Fair Oaks Avenue in Pasadena later took its name.

When the Civil War broke out, General Albert Sydney Johnston resigned his commission in the United States army, and with a hundred companions started overland for the South by way of Warner's Ranch. The party was detained temporarily at Yuma by orders of Captain W. S. Hancock. Upon reaching the South, Johnston was made brigadier general in the Confederate army and lost his life at the Battle of Shiloh.

Kindly ponder with me just an instant. The Wilsons, Coopers, and young Hereford, the Kewens and Richardsons, Captain White, J. D. Woodworth, and Mrs. Albert Sydney Johnston, largely on the Rancho San Pasqual, and Henry Dalton, on Rancho Santa Anita, were the only Americans residing in 1861 in that glorious section on which today stands Pasadena, Oak Knoll, Huntington Library, and millions upon millions of dollars worth of palatial suburban homes along the entire route of Huntington Drive to Arcadia.[15]

After the death of General Johnston, the splendid country estate Fair Oaks became the property of Benjamin S. Eaton, an attorney, who arrived in Los Angeles shortly after 1850. Judge Eaton, as he was generally called,

[14] See n. 11 on Rancho San Pasqual, acquired by Wilson and divided between him and Griffin.

[15] Henry Dalton had sold Rancho Santa Anita to Joseph A. Rowe in 1854. He later acquired Rancho Azusa, where he made his home.

was highly respected and prominent in the community during his long life. He was the father of Frederick Eaton, onetime mayor of Los Angeles, and very prominent in the story of the construction of the 250-mile Los Angeles Aqueduct from Inyo County.

A short time after the war Colonel W. H. Winston, a dyed-in-the-wool southerner, who, I believe, was still fighting the war at his death, arrived from Alabama and settled in the San Pasqual area. Colonel Winston wore a white beard of the same style as that of General Robert E. Lee, to whom he bore a very striking resemblance. The colonel always went about his estate horseback, followed by a pack of fine foxhounds, a bugle made from a cow's horn swung over his shoulder and his army saddlebags hung on the pommel of his saddle. Very taciturn, but quick of speech when speaking, the colonel created a decidedly military impression. Bobcats and coyotes were plentiful, and when one was jumped up, the colonel's typically rebel yell could be heard a mile away. Colonel Winston lost his first wife before leaving the South and brought with him to California the second Mrs. Winston with their family of small children. Langston and Miss Lucy, grown offspring of the first marriage, came with them.

Langston Winston at the height of his young manhood came to a tragic end—he was a great deer hunter, and although he had at times trod every canyon and scaled every peak in the adjacent Sierra Madres, he perished there from unknown causes while hunting. The children of the younger generation were of the small roster of Americans that attended the little adobe school.

In 1858 Judge Volney E. Howard, who had reached San Francisco in the early fifties, came to Los Angeles and settled with his wife and grown family on a ranch within a stone's throw of the old San Gabriel Mission church. Judge Howard practiced law in San Francisco during the turbulent reign of the vigilantes, under the leadership of the valorous William T. Coleman. Judge Howard succeeded W. T.—afterwards General—Sherman in the leadership of the law-and-order contingent. Because of his activities in support of that organization, Judge Howard was asked to leave San Francisco. That was not a time to tarry, and Howard took the first river boat to Sacramento, thence proceeded by stage to Los Angeles, where he resumed the practice of law, and stood at the head of that profession for many years. He served two terms as superior judge of Los Angeles County, and one on the supreme bench of California.

In 1863 J. De Barth Shorb of Baltimore, Maryland, came to California in the interest of Tom Scott of the Pennsylvania Railroad to exploit California for oil. Shorb was for a while assistant manager of the Philadelphia and California Oil Company. He also did some mining at Temescal. In 1868 Shorb had occasion to call on Don Benito Wilson at his very hospitable Lake Vineyard home in connection with a business affair. With his customary cordiality, Don Benito prevailed upon young Shorb to take luncheon with the family. Miss Sue, the charming daughter of Don Benito's first wife—nee Yorba—was one of the luncheon party. Shorb told the story on himself that the moment he laid eyes on the bewitching young woman, he made up his mind not to take his hat from the rack until he took the young lady with him. Hence the romance had its birth, and the young people were shortly married and built a princely home on land presented to the bride by Don Benito.

The location was a very sightly one on a hill and commanded a view of the whole valley. The Shorbs gave their place the name of San Marino. Mr. Shorb was a man of very striking appearance, of very gracious manner, and the polish that befits a southern gentleman. He had good clothes and wore them well, was a fine conversationalist, and one always realized his presence. He was a high liver and entertained lavishly. He planted an extensive vineyard and built a large winery at Ramona, now a suburb of Alhambra, and in later years was a producer of high-grade wine and brandy. The Shorbs raised a large and very interesting family, and it is upon the site of their elegant home that the Huntington Library stands today.

The place east of the property Father later bought was acquired by Mr. William Chapman, who came from one of the southern states about 1870. He had a wife and two young children, Paul and Lucy. While they were building their house, the Chapmans camped out under some immense oaks, and I shall always remember the first time my brother Harry and I came across their camp accidentally, while they were at lunch, on one of our Saturday weekly exploration trips on foot. They were typically southern and lavish with everything. The table was adorned with cut glass and elegant silverware and fairly loaded down with quantities of food of endless variety. I am prepared to admit that I had never seen nor had I ever dreamed there was anything so sumptuous on earth. We were mighty poor at the Rose house, plain food enough, but no surfeit—meat, potatoes, beans, and bread all right, but fancy dishes, glassware, and even fine silver, and in a camp! This was beyond our conception, and it took a long time for us to tell of it when we reached home.

We were ragged as usual. As soon as we were spied, though he did not know who we were, Mr. Chapman left the table, hurried to us and extended a welcome fit for some dignitaries, and would not take no for an answer to his invitation to join them at lunch. We were, naturally, very abashed. Here it was that I tasted my first chicken gumbo. My age and the occasion had much to do with it, but I have never since been able to satisfy myself that I have tasted any so delicious. My brother was but ten years of age and I not yet eight; we were as green as two young gourds, but, as we were fairly well housebroken, managed not to disgrace ourselves at the table.

There were a few other families living scattered about San Gabriel Valley at the same period, with whom our family were well and favorably acquainted. As I grew up I knew them and also the new arrivals from time to time, and loving memory of them still endures. I forego the pleasure of mentioning them all, confining myself to those who were an active part of my daily young life. Their homes were the first landmarks, and they themselves were the first persons I knew from my infancy, and to omit them would be tantamount to leaving out a member of the family.

## III

The only settlement in San Gabriel Valley was that surrounding the mission, originally called by the padres San Gabriel el Arcángel (Gabriel the Archangel). This mission was founded by the Franciscans in 1771. The original location was on the banks of the San Gabriel River, about five miles south of the ultimate location. The first structure was of adobe and the locality where it was built, known as Misión Vieja, still bears that name. Worshiping was carried on there for about three years while the new edifice was being constructed; the parish then was moved to San Gabriel.

The padres, known for their astuteness in selecting positively the most desirably located sections for their orchards and flocks, must have overlooked the vast superiority of the country around San Gabriel to that of Misión Vieja, when making their first selection. The church edifice, considerably smaller and much less ornate than the majority at other missions, stands on a corner of the road passing through the settlement. The burial ground is immediately adjacent, surrounded by a high adobe wall. The building has always been kept in a fine state of repair, and services have been held in it unfailingly every day since it was dedicated a century and a half ago. In the heyday of its glory this mission, the wealthiest of the entire chain of them in California, boasted of 80,000 cattle, 30,000 sheep and 3,000 horses, 160,000 grape vines (160 acres), and 4,000 fruit trees (40 acres). All of them had vanished long ere the American came. The only evidence left—a mute one—was portions still in good condition of an enclosure to one of their fields, made of the prickly-pear variety of cactus, known to the Spanish as *tuna*.

In starting the fence, the large leaves of the tuna were planted in rows four feet apart, with a like distance separating them in the rows. They were planted with the butt end embedded in the ground three or four inches. With the least bit of moisture, small roots were immediately thrown out, and, growing rapidly, the plant attained a height of three or four feet in the first year. In four or five years it attained a height of about ten feet and the parent trunk six inches in thickness, forming an absolutely impregnable barrier to animals.

The settlement was built around a scissorslike intersection of four roads, the buildings, principally small adobe huts, built flush with the dirt sidewalk, some having a small porch attached to the front. The water supply was from an open *zanja* (ditch) which ran along one side of the main street. The population of about one hundred and twenty-five were practically all Mexican peons and half-breeds or domesticated Indians.

Amongst the few Caucasians residing in San Gabriel, N. Tuch, a grotesque little Hebrew, married to a Mexican woman, kept the only store. Cæsar Twitchell, an early-coming New Englander, kept a saloon, as also did William Soulé. An eccentric old Scotchman, Doctor Money, owned an odd structure of three connected round rooms with pointed roofs, which he called the "Moneyan Institute." In this he kept a few stuffed birds and small animals, pelts and bones of others, a few Indian metates and relics, odd-shaped stones, pieces of metal and whatever he could pick up. Admission to this wonderful exposition was twenty-five cents.

David Hall, known to the natives as Don Davi (Mr. David), kept a tavern in which he and his wife and their young son, Charles, lived. Mr. Hall was also postmaster, and kept the post office in the same building. It is in the yard of this same tavern that the historic old grapevine of San Gabriel stands today.

Some later-day California historian, imported from I care not where, after about all the California of Californians has fled, has had the effrontery to placard this vine as having been planted by Father Junípero Serra in the year 1771. Along about the year 1870 I played under this very vine and ate grapes from its luscious clusters. The trunk then was not over five inches in diameter, and in 1879, I courted in the moonlight under its sheltering foliage a perfectly respectable and very charming young lady of Los Angeles, who was visiting with the Hall family. The trunk of the vine then was no more than seven inches in thickness. As a matter of fact, David Hall procured the cutting from which this vine grew from Sunny Slope. My father planted the parent vine sometime between the years of 1863 and 1865.

# 4

## *Sunny Slope - The First Vintage*

### I

FATHER bought 1,300 acres lying near the eastern boundaries of the San Pasqual grant for a little more than a dollar per acre. This section of the tract was locally known as La Presa (the dam) from the fact that the mission padres in early days had built thereon a dam of cobblestones and mortar, by which they took an open stream of water a number of miles down the valley to irrigate some of their lands. In later years, having procured other water more conveniently located, this project was abandoned.

La Presa had ever been a favorite place for clothes washing with the Indians and Mexicans who lived in the Rancheria (a group of huts) near by —others, living within a radius of two miles, also came there to avail themselves of the unlimited supply of water, firewood, and the smooth surface of the broad dam on which to arrange their tubs and kettles.

The Woodworth property, where our family had been living since their arrival, was also a part of the San Pasqual grant and abutted on the west against the piece Father purchased. As a matter of expediency, in the way of saving the time necessary for building a house and of further conserving his capital, Father decided, because of the proximity of the Woodworth house to the scene of his immediate operations, to continue living in it indefinitely. It thus occurred that I was born in that house June 11, 1862. During the Mexican rule squatters frequently settled on lands embraced within the grants of others, invariably seeking quite naturally a spot conveniently located with reference to water. This had occurred on this particular part of the San Pasqual purchased by Father. A man by the name of Courtney, married to the half-Spanish daughter of Captain White, had constructed a four-room adobe house with a shed made of lumber attached. A stream of water from the dam had been brought down close to the house; a little garden truck was raised and a small orchard grown.

Father finally dispossessed Courtney by paying him a small sum; however, although the transaction was justly and legally consummated, it was

*The Rose wine label, promoted from coast to coast, made Rose's Sunny Slope Brandy a staple item with wholesale druggists. Huntington Library Collections.*

*First vintage at Sunny Slope, 1864, L. J. Rose seated on platform. Courtesy of Miss Hinda Rose, San Diego.*

*During the 80's the Sunny Slope house played host to such notables as Rutherford B. Hayes and Helen Hunt Jackson and was on the itinerary of eastern excursion companies. Courtesy of Mrs. John P. Gallagher, Paso Robles, and J. V. Wachtel, Santa Barbara.*

*Stern & Rose Distillery boasted an annual output of 500,000 gallons of wine and 250,000 of brandy. Huntington Library Collections.*

almost interminable. Just so soon as things took on an air of prosperity about the place, Courtney assumed a menacing attitude. Attorneys were finally employed, and the case dragged along to its slow death for fully ten years. The adobe part of the Courtney house was used as storerooms. The shed part was increased in size to accommodate six work animals, and a small blacksmith shop and tool room erected close by. A conveniently located space of about an acre in extent was selected as a site for the house, to be built later. Three pepper trees, three eucalypti, and a weeping willow were planted in appropriate places around the outline of the grounds. One of the eucalypti grew to tremendous size, and, if still standing, is seventy years old. When last I saw it, in 1919, it was the largest of the species I have ever seen, fully one hundred feet in height and seven or eight feet in diameter.

From the center of the house plot an avenue was laid out, extending a half mile to the southward. Two rows of orange trees, twenty-five feet apart, with the same distances separating them in the rows, were planted on either side.

Father followed right along in the footsteps of others and planted the Mission grape. This variety, a hardy growing and prolific yielder, bearing medium-sized, round, purple grapes of high sugar content, was introduced into California by the Franciscan missionaries. There were at this time, 1860, possibly seventy-five, mostly small, vineyards in Los Angeles County, practically all of them located in the town of Los Angeles or its environs, many of them where skyscrapers stand today. These, however, were all irrigated, and everyone shook his head askance at Father's temerity in undertaking to grow a vineyard with no irrigation and, moreover, on the high lands.

In no wise daunted by their skepticism, he planted about 60 acres the first year. The vines flourished as the green bay tree. Each of the succeeding two years he planted 100 acres, and at the end of the third he had 260 acres growing in fine condition. Thus again had Father pioneered and demonstrated to the astonished natives that vine irrigation was not necessary.

The advantage of this was manifest as the grapes were of deeper color and much sweeter than those on irrigated lands, both qualities very essential to the best results in wine making. True enough, the yield was increased by irrigation, but at the expense of coloring and saccharine matter.

Somewhat studious by nature and a great reader, Father soon realized that the adaptability of certain varieties of grapes to climatic and soil conditions would in the final analysis be the measure of success. Cuttings of different varieties were obtained from other localities, and later rooted slips were imported from France and Germany.

As soon as the vines grown from these were two or three years old, cuttings were saved from them at the fall pruning and planted the following spring. When the yield of grapes was of sufficient amount, a small quantity of wine was made. If the sample betokened quality and the prospective yielding capacity of the variety was commensurate, further propagation and acreage planting resulted. If the test did not come up to standard, the variety was discarded as a wine grape.

We had at one time thirty-five distinct varieties of grapes on Sunny Slope, and not more than half a dozen of them had the particularly characteristic quality for wine making. A fact not generally known of the grape is that it is not only not true to seed but goes still further in its caprice. A score of vines might be started from grapes of the same stem, and all of them would be different and more than likely none like the original, varying in size, color, and taste.

All vineyards in California are planted from cuttings. Vineyards are pruned in the fall, and the prunings are cut into lengths of thirty inches and tied in bundles of one hundred each. The butt ends of these bundles are laid in a shallow trench, and about six inches of their length well covered with dirt. In this manner the sap is retained, and, as it is the period of dormancy, no growth takes place. Early in the spring, planting is done by sinking a hole with a small bar eight inches in depth to moist dirt, into which the cutting is placed and the earth solidly tamped around it with the foot to exclude all air.

California vineyards were planted with the cuttings six feet apart in either direction; after deducting the space next the boundaries and of the crossroads necessary in hauling the crop at vintage time, 1,000 vines per acre were planted. Though the soil was very fertile and deep, the surface appearance was that of a desert. The land was thickly covered with a growth of chaparral, cactus, elders, sagebrush, and large weeds. All of this had to be grubbed out by the roots, then burned, the ground plowed, evened up, and cultivated ready for planting. This and all other labor on the ranch, except the extra amount required for grape picking at vintage time, was done for the first few years by a dozen or fifteen Mexicans and domesticated Indians, who with their families lived at the Rancheria, near La Presa.

In speaking of Mexicans and Indians the distinction is with practically no difference in appearance or temperament. The Indians had much coarser hair, which was never wavy. Their complexions were invariably dark and cheekbones more prominent than those of the Mexicans, whereas some of the Mexicans were fair, occasionally having blue eyes and curly, auburn hair. Their modes of living were the same. They fraternized readily and frequently intermarried. The Indians had long since lost their racial instincts and were very peaceful. Both were bibulously inclined but rarely indulged in drink other than Saturday nights.

Their marriages were of the common-law order, but they were very true to their mates, and their only quarrels were over their women, when in their cups. Unafraid to shed blood, they were quick to take recourse to their *puñal* (dagger) to settle their differences. In the many years which we employed them, in changing and increased numbers, there was but one serious affray among them. A stranger on horseback from the mission started a quarrel in front of the hut of one of the men, Juan de Diego. When the intruder turned and fled, Diego hastily mounted his saddled horse, which stood at the door, and overtook him in full sight of the winery. Both horses on the dead run, the pursuer, riding on the left side, drew his *puñal* and with a backward thrust sank it into the other's heart, toppling him from his horse, dead.

The Rancheria, as we called the place where the workmen lived, was a plot of ground about five acres in extent. Their small huts were made of tule (bulrush), which grew in the swamp near by. The tule was stood upright six inches in thickness for the sides of the house, held in place by thin willow rods within and without, fastened together by pieces of raw cowhide. The roofs were of the same material and construction. Mother earth was the floor. Their picturesque little abodes were proof against rain and were warm and comfortable. For a kitchen, a lean-to made of brush, open on one side was built—stoves were rarely used, but in their stead a number of flat stones conveniently placed about the fire to support the cooking utensils.

Great coffee drinkers, meat and bean eaters, these were their thrice-a-day fare. Their sun-dried meat was roasted over the embers, their beans, the small rose-colored variety, fried with their own juice, after boiling, with a small quantity of lard added. Few had chickens or took the trouble to have a garden; as a consequence eggs and vegetables were rarely indulged in. Bread was not used; as a substitute they had *tortillas,* made from a dough of ground corn and water and a little salt, of a proper consistency to handle easily, as they took a ball of it the size of an orange and patted it out between their hands into pancake shape about an eighth of an inch in thickness and ten or twelve in diameter. This was toasted on a large piece of sheet iron, placed on the rocks over the coals. The *tortilla* took the place alike of bread and plates. A piece of meat, some stew or *frijoles* (beans) was wrapped in it and eaten as a sandwich or piece of pie.

These people were scrupulously careful in the preparation of their food. Delmonico in his palmiest days never concocted anything more palatable than their primitive fare was to me then, and still is, with my plainsman's tendencies and love for the great outdoors.

These simple-minded, goodhearted souls had no thought beyond the moment. They were very fond of brother and me as the sons of Father, whom they idolized, and any hour of the day or night that we might come to one of their huts, they would get up and prepare one of their rustic meals for us. In the twilight hours, they played their guitars and accordions and sang their soft ballads in the open air. The gorgeous rising moon peeping from behind the crest of the slumbering Sierras charged every note with thrilling romance.

Many of the happiest hours of my young life were those I spent playing with the children of these people. We were very fond of their *tortillas* and *frijoles* and spent many evenings after supper at the Rancheria. From these children I learned to speak Spanish as a native, in fact the first word I ever uttered was *agua,* Spanish for water. These little Mexicans were my only playmates up to the time I was five years of age and started to school. The three older children, Nina, Annie, and Harry, were attending school, and I offered the argument to Mother that it would be best for me to attend also, lest the other children would be lonesome without me. I was allowed to join them, and walked two miles and back daily. Later on we drove with a donkey and cart. The school, a single-room adobe about twenty feet square, was located out in the open country in a forest of large oaks. There were only about twenty scholars, two-thirds of them Spanish speaking. As a memory test, I will offer the information that my first teacher's name was Mrs. Sarah Jabesine Loomis Loop, who with her husband, a clergyman, and their two sons had come from Syracuse, New York, in 1865 or 1866 and established a home on a fifty-acre tract about a mile north of the mission. They lived here a number of years, then sold their place, and moved twenty-five miles east, where they bought a good-sized tract from the Palomares family, part owners of Rancho San José, and founded the town of Pomona—today a thriving city of thirty or forty thousand—in the center of one of the most productive citrus districts in southern California.[16]

Father christened his new possession "Sunny Slope." On it there were about 300 acres of stately oaks and sycamores, bush oaks and sumacs, manzanitas with their dark-red, highly polished, crooked trunks, and elders with their profusion of saffron bloom or purple berries; thickets of luscious wild blackberries and gooseberries; acres of wild roses; many trailing vines of wild clematis and chilicothe in their clinging, graceful growth, climbing high among the branches of the trees. In the sunshine of springtime or, for that matter, at any season, for here is almost perpetual sunshine, the air is so clear in its purity that "Old Baldy" in stately repose fifty miles away seems but a few miles distant. The entire range varies in shades of blue, brown, or gray with the changing lights. Mockingbirds were caroling to the sun; California canaries singing their dainty lullabies; the meadowlark rising to the rhythm of its own melody; highly colored orioles, bee martins, and the

[16] Charles F. Loop was a Pomona pioneer rather than founder. Loop and Alvin P. Meserve bought 2,000 acres and planted the "Loop and Meserve Tract" to oranges, lemons, and olives.

native "witticoche" darting back and forth; wrens and linnets twittering in one's very ears; doves cooing for their mates; and large coveys of quail releasing themselves from cover with the speed and whir of a cannon ball.

There were tree squirrels and ground squirrels, cottontail and hare scampering hither and yon, small ground owls and large tree owls, the chicken hawk warily watching in its gentle flight for unsuspecting prey, and also the American eagle soaring serene and undisputed in skies as blue as the sapphire.

There were wild flowers, acres of them, of every imaginable color and hue—the air redolent with their perfume—growing in such denseness as to fairly enmesh one's feet. One could walk for hours continually discovering new varieties. When I say acres of them, I speak advisedly. There was a field of possibly 100 acres of California poppies on a ranch belonging to Jesus Rubio, a native-born Mexican, in the identical spot where Altadena later rose to her glory. The field was situated on an exposed, slanting piece of land quite near the base of the mountain. The natural golden color of the flowers, with the bright rays of the sun beaming upon them, looked like a sea of gold and could be seen from any part of the valley as far as the eye could reach. This was one of the natural beauties of the country over which every late winter tourist marveled. All of this was of daily occurrence in springtime. Was not this enchanting spot very appropriately called "Sunny Slope"?

In the late fall of 1862 the house having been completed at Sunny Slope, the family was moved from the Woodworth place to the new home. Everything was of the most primitive. We made our own candles, smoked our hams and bacon with corncobs, rendered lard, provided casings for sausage, leached ashes for lye with which to make hominy, and put up all our jams and jellies and canned fruits. We roasted and ground our coffee and made our corn meal. We pickled olives, and also made oil by crushing ripe olives, which were then placed in a barrel and covered with water, fermentation started, the oil rose to the surface and was skimmed off. The butcher came from Los Angeles but once a week. The household water supply was from a ceaseless stream of water running through the yard within ten feet of the front door. Father's little bank roll had melted and he was hard pressed to keep the family pot boiling. Hay in quantities in excess of the demands of the ranch work animals was raised for sale; oak wood cut and sold for $2.50 per cord on the ground, or delivered, plus cost of the hauling. Native California horses were very cheap. Mares, small in size but likely looking and of good conformation, could be purchased for $5.00 per head. With his strong penchant for horses, Father soon found himself possessed of a *manada* (band) of forty or fifty mares and a fair stallion. These ran loose, living on the native grass in the pasture at no particular expense.

Occasional sales and trades were made. Good work mules were bought and sold. Father never rode horseback. Old Bob was still doing yeoman service and was used in driving back and forth for mail at San Gabriel, or on business trips to Los Angeles. When going afield among the horses or overseeing the laborers, Father always walked and carried a double-barreled shotgun. As game was very plentiful in all directions, he always brought home enough quail and cottontail rabbits to supply the family table with meat for a meal.

One day in his meanderings he passed through the field where the wood was corded and was dumbfounded to see a man loading some of it on a two-horse wagon. Upon being asked why he was taking the wood, the man replied that it belonged to him. An argument quickly ensued, and the thief, with a large six-shooter strapped around his waist, assumed a bellicose attitude. This, Father quickly quelled by getting his shotgun in a position to fire. The fellow then proposed to pay for the wood or unload it, neither of which propositions was acceptable. Having the drop, Father ordered the remnant of the cord loaded on the wagon and taken to the ranch house and thrown on the woodpile, following behind the way, himself on foot.

After the wood was unloaded, Father forced the man to reload it on the wagon. Then with a severe reprimand, he ordered him to leave the ranch and take the wood along.

Father, though practical and reserved—he was one person who rarely said anything that would have been better unsaid—was visionary and a great dreamer, but with his great determination was one who made his dreams come true. He was of artistic temperament, had high ideals, knew good things when he saw them, strove for them and usually attained them. He was always out of money, though he did not waste or lose it. He had set his goal and kept expanding toward that end regardless of intermediate circumstances. This caused him to see some very hard times, and the family often went without sugar and the children barefoot, and delicacies of all kinds were unknown. The family kept increasing, and I wonder how my dear good mother lived through it.

By the time I was eight, there were three children older than I and two younger. There had been three younger ones, Hinda Alice, Guy Orlando, and Cora Daisy, but Hinda Alice passed on before she was three years old.

Mother made all our clothing, even the suits for my older brother and me. My two older sisters were naturally very helpful. With all this on her dear hands, at vintage time Mother did all the cooking for from fifteen to thirty Mexicans and Indians, who came from afar to pick the grapes, cooking out of doors in immense cauldrons and serving on long rustic tables with benches in the open air.

## II

The first wine was produced at Sunny Slope in 1864. It was made in the primitive way still in vogue in some parts of Europe, tramped out by men with their bare feet. Over a large vat of two-thousand-gallon capacity was placed a box four by eight feet, with a bottom made of hardwood slats three inches wide laid with spaces between them of about three-eighths of an inch in width. The grapes were dumped in from boxes and baskets containing about fifty pounds, in which they were picked and hauled from the field. When all the juice was tramped out, the residue, or "pumice" as it is called, was scooped up and thrown in with the juice. When this vat was full, the box and crew were moved to another one. Three men usually worked in a box of this size. Fermentation started in a couple of days or so, depending upon the weather. Saccharimeters were not in vogue in this faraway country at that time, and the palate was depended upon to determine the proper state of fermentation requisite for the class of wine desired. The juice was then drawn off and placed in large, one-hundred-and-fifty-gallon puncheons with the bungs tightened. Here it settled for a while, was again racked off into other containers, with care not to disturb the lees or sediment in the bottom. This process was continued from time to time and the settling process was sometimes expedited by the use of whites of eggs or gelatine until the wine was perfectly clear.

In making a sweet wine, grape spirit (brandy) is added after the first fermentation, which checks it, preserving the sweetness. Sweet wines were fortified to show a twenty per cent alcoholic content. In making dry or tart wines, fermentation is allowed to go to a point beyond that necessary in making sweet wines and then held in abeyance by placing the wine in a well-filled, tightly bunged container, thereby eliminating the air. Improvement is greatly hastened by repeated drawing off, until all the sediment or yeast-producing matter is eliminated. The coloring matter of a grape is all in the skin, and from a purple grape four distinct wines can be made, viz.: to make port, a colored sweet wine, the juice and pumice are allowed to ferment together and the wine, when drawn off, is fortified with grape spirit. To make claret, a red tart wine, when a certain stage of fermentation is reached, the wine is placed in a container, as above stated. To make a sweet white wine, one has but to eliminate the pumice from the fermentation and fortify the wine, and to make hock, a tart white wine, eliminate the pumice, and use the same after-methods as with claret. The grape stems were eliminated at all times.

This practice, however, is not productive of the best results, for the very quality of high sugar content—which gives the desired heady strength to sweet wines—is the detrimental factor in the process of making dry (tart) table wines. All early California used the native Mission grape almost exclusively until experience taught them their error.

The adaptability of varieties to localities had long been the secret of success with the wine producers of France and Germany. Experience had taught them that a certain variety would give excellent results in a circumscribed district, whereas slightly removed from that locality the undertaking would be an absolute failure. This condition is most forcefully illustrated by the restricted district in which champagne is made in France.

In 1867 some small shipments of wine were made to New York. With a growing demand locally, also in Arizona and Utah, the increase in revenue was considerable—however, with Father's constantly expanding ideas, the income would not take care of the outgo. All ranch supplies and provisions were bought in wagonloads of H. Newmark and Company, and settled for once a year, January first. Though cash demands then were about the ratio of one dollar to ten of the present time, they were no less urgent, and Father became nothing short of an inveterate money borrower. So persistent was he in his demands for money that it became a standing joke with his bankers and some of his closest friends. As soon as he was seen on the streets of Los Angeles on his business trips, the comment would be passed—"Rose is in town, I guess he is out of money." He kept himself in financial close quarters at all times and took many scoldings from his banker. He would in some way extricate himself in a measure, and then, like the story of the frog that jumped one foot out of the well each day and fell back two, he would get deeper in debt than previously. Withal, he battled along courageously, supported by the knowledge that although his debts were increasing constantly, the value and beauty of Sunny Slope, which soon became the show place of all southern California, were increasing in much more rapid ratio.

All of the ranch work and hauling was done with mules. In trading around, Father had acquired an extra number of mule teams and wagons. Tucson, Arizona, was at that time headquarters for the United States Army of that territory. Learning there was a good demand there for large freighting outfits for hauling to outlying districts, Father decided to send out one of his teams for sale. In order to kill two birds with one stone, he decided to load the wagons with wine, brandy, and cigars, also to be sold. We had in our employ as teamster Charles Durfee, a young man not yet twenty years of age, of exemplary habits. His family, well-to-do, lived on their ranch in El Monte, where they had located with a large number of emigrant families in the early fifties. Young Durfee had some cash and bought a half interest in the team and wagons from Father.

Durfee selected a team of eight mules that graduated in size from eleven-hundred-pound leaders back to wheelers which weighed about twelve hundred and fifty. Their manes were carefully roached and tails properly tasseled, the wagons carefully gone over, tires set, brake blocks relined, all bolts tightened. The barrels for carrying water on the sides of the wagon were soaked up, feed boxes repaired, harness washed and oiled, and all was in readiness for the long six-hundred-mile trek across the thirsty desert, which would take about thirty days. Durfee was a past master as a teamster and took great pride in his team, adorning the leaders each with a coyote's tail tied to the outside of the bridle. A light steel arched frame with bells attached, that jingled merrily as the team traveled along, was fastened to the hames of the leaders.

Off to a spectacular start, nothing was heard from Durfee till he reached Tucson. The understanding with Durfee was that, upon reaching Tucson, he was to dispose of the cargo for Father's account; that the team could be sold for $1,500 for their joint benefit, and any sum realized in excess of that amount would be Durfee's personal gain. Good fortune was with Durfee, and he sold the team for $3,500 the day he arrived. Tucson was booming, and, experiencing a little difficulty in disposing of the liquor and cigars, or in finding suitable storage for them, Durfee conceived the idea of going into the saloon business for the joint account of Father and himself, and opened up a place forthwith. He started out flourishingly and was clearing $50 a day.

In great glee he wrote Father of his doings. Durfee was not yet of age, and Father, very fond of him, was greatly distressed over his actions. Father wrote him quite a sermon on the ethics of the occasion, telling him that he was too fine a young fellow to be in the saloon business and commanding him to sell out and return to Sunny Slope at once.

The business was still going famously, and Durfee, loath to part with it, wrote Father to that effect, stating he would continue the business for his own account and pay for the liquor and cigars when he returned to California. In a short time, the army headquarters were moved from Tucson, and business flattened out completely. Instead of showing a daily profit of $50, Durfee's saloon showed a considerable deficit. He stuck by the sinking ship, however, until all the liquor was gone and along with it all his cash except $500. He then took the stage home and arrived at Sunny Slope somewhat contrite but with his head held high. The episode was discussed in a friendly, dispassionate manner, with the adjustment of it left to young Durfee. His proposition was to pay Father the $500 in cash he had salvaged out of the wreck and turn over to him 100 head of cattle. The proposition was at once accepted. Durfee mounted his saddle horse, galloped away five miles to his father's place at El Monte, informed his father what he had done, and the next day with the assistance of another man delivered the 100 cattle at Sunny Slope.

This is an ordinary instance of the way business was done between the old-timers in California's early life. Today a like transaction would entail an arrest and volumes of legal lore.

Durfee was very kind to me, and I was very fond of him. He slept in a room in the old Courtney adobe, near the ranch house. Evenings after supper he frequently played his violin for me—often I went to ride with him, perched high on the seat of an old prairie schooner at least seven feet from the ground. One evening while he was putting the mules in the barn, he left me on the high seat, playing teamster. The wagon had been stopped on a sloping piece of ground. In some way I managed to kick the big brake loose, and away the wagon coasted down the hill, leaving the road after going two or three hundred feet, and parked itself deep in the swamp. The swamp was so muddy that animals could not be used, and it took about half the men on the ranch to get the wagon out.

After this episode I was not so popular with Durfee for a few days, but shortly thereafter was restored to the fold by his rescue of me from a runaway horse and the certainty of a very bad fall, which could have been quite serious. This incident in my childish mind caused me to regard Durfee as my savior.

One evening just before sundown my Uncle Edward Jones and the young "schoolmarm" who was living with the family had just returned from a horseback ride and were dismounting in front of the house. Childlike, I was bothering for a ride. Impatient because of my importunities or mayhap with the young lady with whom he was engaged in earnest conversation, Uncle rudely raised me into the saddle and struck the horse with his hand. Away went the horse on a gallop, which he immediately increased to a run in his hurry to the barn a half-mile distant. I was but a little over four years old and had never ridden alone except on a donkey, had not taken the reins in my hand in my hurried departure, and at all events had scant chance in any case of staying put on the broad smooth Mexican saddle. I did have gumption enough to grasp the pommel and hang on for dear life. The first lap of the journey was about five hundred feet straight away, then a sharp right-angle turn to the right for about half the same distance, then a sharp turn to the left, and a long run to the barn. Just before reaching the second turn, the road passed within forty feet of the adobe house where my friend Durfee slept. He happened to be sitting out in front, heard the clatter of hoofs, and, though there was an orchard between his place and the road, he could see beneath the trees that the horse was running away. In an instant he had taken down his riata (cowhide lassoing rope) and hurried to the edge of the road, uncoiling the riata ready for action as he ran. Just as the horse was about to pass, he tossed the loop over its head, and the horse, accustomed to being roped, stopped within a few strides, and I slid to the ground none the worse for wear save that I was very frightened. It was a neat catch, with a loop just big enough to make sure of the horse's head and not so large that it might take me in also and injure me when the pull was made to tighten it. No doubt I would have taken a hard fall making the next turn. In my youthful way I was very grateful, though for a long time I was undecided as to who was the greater hero, Durfee or I.

Durfee continued in our employ happily for some time, during which he was courting Señorita de la Osa (of the bear), who resided in San Gabriel Mission. The young lovers married and moved to Los Angeles, where Durfee went in the livery stable business with Dan Reichard on Aliso Street. Father took particular pride in going around with Durfee, introducing him to all the tradespeople, recommending him highly, and volunteering to stand good for any of his purchases.

In the summer of 1868 a large consignment of wine was made to a firm in New York. The shipment was made through Rodmond M. Gibbons, a broker doing business in San Francisco and residing in Oakland. It was hauled by our big teams from the ranch to Los Angeles, there transferred to a team-freighting company, which hauled it to San Pedro and delivered it to a coast steamship company, which took it to San Francisco, delivering it to a company operating a line of sailing vessels by way of Cape Horn to New York. It took upwards of six months for the trip. Along in the spring, my father received notice from the New York people that the wine was of poor quality and in bad condition, asking advice as to its disposition. Very perturbed, Father at once went to San Francisco to consult with Mr. Gibbons, who was also greatly exercised, knowing what the loss would mean to my father. Some of the same wine was still in the cellar at Sunny Slope and was of excellent quality. My father reported this to Gibbons, who with good business sense, insisted that Father go on to New York and see for himself.

My father could not see how he could absent himself from the ranch for the necessary length of time to make the trip, and, as usual, he was out of money. Mr. Gibbons was insistent and suddenly remembered that, when the shipment was taken from the steamer to be transferred to the sailing vessel, a cask was leaking and its contents changed to another, which happened to be a little smaller, and there were a few gallons over, which were put in a five-gallon demijohn and sent to Mr. Gibbons' home. It was arranged that Father dine with him that evening, and they would sample the wine. The demijohn was found in the attic, where it had been forgotten. The cork had been left out and a piece of burlap tied over the opening—a severe test, but very beneficial if survived, the atmosphere having an aging influence on wine that has sufficient alcoholic content to preserve it from souring. Just such a test was most convincing as the wine was found mellow and delicious, fortifying the belief that all was not straight in New York.

Mr. Gibbons was more insistent and Father acquiescent. Money was now the stumbling block. By morning, their belief about the New York end of the transaction had become a conviction, and without further ado Gibbons told Father to go take out an insurance policy on his life for the amount required, payable to him (Gibbons), and he would advance the money, to be returned out of the proceeds from the sale of the wine. He was confident the only chance he was taking was that he (my father) might die. Father insured his life for thirty-five hundred, sending what money was necessary home.

This was in 1869, the year the Central Pacific Railroad was completed, forming, in connection with the Union Pacific Railroad, the first transcontinental carrier. Father headed direct for New York. Upon arriving, he first made arrangements for a place to which to transfer the wine. He called on the consignees, and it took him but an instant to verify his conclusions. He saw the wine all moved to another firm, sold it to them for $10,000, paid up all freight charges, sent Mr. Gibbons his thirty-five hundred, bought a lot of nice presents for all at home and was happy as a clam at high tide.

# 5

## *Thoroughbred Trotters - Agricultural Park - California Wines*

### I

At this moment a new era began for Father. Still dreaming his dream of his blooded-horse ranch, he had always had in anticipation the returns from this lot of wine for its fulfillment. He had been in correspondence with Mr. George C. Stevens of Milwaukee, Wis., about the purchase of some standard-bred colts and fillies, and now the time had arrived when he could look at them. He went direct to Milwaukee. There he purchased six head, one a two-year-old black stallion, Beau Clay (later changed to The Moor); Overland, a yearling bay stallion; Pilot, a yearling gelding; and Barbara, Maggie Mitchell, and Minnehaha, yearling fillies.

After closing the deal with Mr. Stevens, he went to Cairo, Illinois, to visit his brother-in-law and sister, Mr. and Mrs. H. K. S. O'Melveny. This was his first trip east and he had not meantime had personal contact with O'Melveny—who had so greatly befriended him in Santa Fe—since his departure for California eleven years earlier. He had great stories to relate about the covered-wagon trip, the Indian massacre, and the many wonders of the new land of milk and honey. When he got to telling of picking oranges, figs, olives, and pomegranates from the trees, he started a miniature riot among the children. Mr. O'Melveny suffered greatly from malaria. Father advised him to wind up his law business, move to California, and resume law practice there. Consulting his wife, Mr. O'Melveny asked when she could go and received the reply "tomorrow." She and her two daughters got ready and came on with my father, and visited at Sunny Slope until Judge O'Melveny and the two boys, Edward and Henry, arrived. A house was rented on Fort Street (now Broadway) between First and Second streets, and the O'Melvenys moved into it and remained there until their imposing home, corner Fort and Second, was completed.

Father had formed a partnership for Judge O'Melveny in advance of his arrival with Judge Anson Brunson, a talented gentleman and brilliant attorney. He was somewhat addicted to the use of liquor, and during his indulgences was not altogether dependable. Judge O'Melveny was the direct opposite of Brunson in disposition—temperate, mild-mannered, and the soul of honor. Their partnership did not endure long; Judge O'Melveny withdrew and formed a partnership with Henry T. Hazard. Later Judge O'Melveny was elected to the superior bench of Los Angeles County, and Mr. Hazard elected to the mayoralty of the city of Los Angeles.

While in Cairo, Father employed a young man, James Hurd, whom Mr. O'Melveny knew and recommended highly as a horseman, to go to Milwaukee to ship the colts to San Gabriel. They were shipped by rail to San Francisco, then transferred to a coast steamer for San Pedro. The landing facilities were meager, and each horse had to be hoisted from the steamer's hold to the wharf in a box. The horses were then led overland to San Gabriel, a distance of about forty-five miles, taking two days for the trip. I shall always remember their arrival. It was a big event in our lives. They did not arrive until an hour or so after dark. We awaited them with lanterns at an improvised barn adjoining the old adobe house. The Moor (Beau Clay) was very beautiful. Being a stallion and two years old, he showed to better advantage than the others, who were but yearlings and suffered more from the wear and tear of the long trip. The Moor was jet black with a shield-shaped white spot about the size of small apple in the center of his forehead.

The young horses were allowed to rest for a couple of weeks, were well groomed daily, and given plenty of green feed along with their rations of hay and grain. The Moor had been broken to drive, and after a time Hurd hitched him daily to a light road cart and jogged him a few miles. The yearlings were turned out one at a time in a corral, with bitting harness on them for a few days, then driven around the yard with no vehicle hitched to them, taught to guide and to stand. When they were tractable, they were hitched double with a gentle mule to a light spring wagon and driven a mile or two. The mule was perfectly gentle and true and just simply marched the colts along beside her. They soon became very gentle, were then hitched single, given short drives, and in the course of two or three months were turned loose in the pasture with the other stock to run until spring. Then they were taken up again, and, after the rough edge was taken off them, they were hitched to a track sulky and given spirited brushes on a quarter-mile ring, which had been graded around the barnyard. Hurd was a good man with colts, and they all developed speed rapidly. With the advent of this precious cargo, a fine large barn was built with box stalls and all other accessories in a field about half a mile from the ranch house, with a cottage near by for

Hurd, whose wife joined him. Hurd was a Kentuckian, had good game chickens, and, it finally developed, liked whiskey very much.

Old Bob, after his eleven years of heroic service, had died the year previous and was buried beneath the sheltering branches of a large oak. Father constantly nibbled around in the horse business, always managing to have a speedy road horse. The first I remember was Jack—a very handsome large white pacer, with eyes, nostrils, hoofs, and exposed parts of his skin as black as ebony. He had a fine flowing mane, a beautiful tail set just at the right angle and properly carried—really a show animal. He could outbrush every horse we met on the road, and I fancied he was the fastest horse in the world as Father let him step on the way home from Los Angeles, where he had taken my brother Harry and me to see our first circus.

Although I was but seven or eight years old, I remember the occasion as though it was yesterday. Away back in that long ago, Father had a buggy made by the noted Brewster and Company, of Broome Street, New York. It was stationed about two stories high on half-elliptic springs and was a monstrosity in comparison to Brewster and Company's later-day works of art—the dainty sidebar piano-box buggy, famous the world over as the gentleman's pleasure vehicle, before the advent of the automobile. Father had also acquired a fine-looking bright bay mare of unknown breeding but unquestionably running bred, as was indicated by her every appearance. This mare was bred two years in succession to Fireman, a thoroughbred stallion of fine breeding and individuality brought from Kentucky by E. C. (Keno) Parish, a horseman of the old school, who settled near El Monte in 1854. The first foal of this mating was a black colt, which we named Billy Buffum; the second, a bay filly, Katy Did. Billy Buffum showed considerable speed, and Father let Silas Mulkey, who was at that time sheriff of Inyo County, take the colt there.

Mulkey, a keen horseman, had located a victim for a match race, and it was primarily for that purpose that he wanted the young stallion and incidentally to use him in the stud. Mulkey won his match and a number of other races, ultimately purchasing Billy Buffum. We raced the filly Katy Did with indifferent success, then sent her as a matron to The Moor's harem.

Father's trip to New York in 1869 to salvage the consignment of wine had given him an insight into the possibilities of introducing California wines more generally on that market. On the eastern seaboard, where ocean transportation made California wines available, they were coming into use. In the sparsely settled Middle West they were comparatively unknown; in fact, many people there had never heard of California wines. With production mounting annually, better marketing facilities became imperative, and Father decided to take upon himself the missionary work of their introduction. Accordingly, in the early spring of 1870 he started on an eastern trip, which consumed three months. Disembarking at Omaha, he visited the large cities along the Missouri River and worked his way eastward. He found it an uphill road to climb but was indefatigable in his efforts, calling on wholesale druggists, wholesale dealers in liquors, wholesale grocers, and saloons and even sold a case of a dozen bottles or a five-gallon keg to private consumers.

From Chicago onward in the larger cities along the Great Lakes, sales were much better, and by the time Baltimore, Philadelphia, and New York City had been canvassed, Father's fondest hopes had been surpassed. Buoyed by this success, he could not resist the urge to further augment the breeding ranks of his horse business. From New York he went direct to Kentucky and bought ten mares and fillies, eight of trotting and two running bred. Part of them were purchased of Mr. Robert Aitcheson Alexander, master of Woodburn Stock Farm in Kentucky, at that time the leading breeding establishment of both runners and trotters, not only of America, but the entire world. The others, including the two running fillies, were purchased from General Jackson, of Belle View Meade Stock Farm in Tennessee. One of the running fillies had been named Lulu Jackson for a daughter of the general, the other, Irene Harding for the daughter of his neighbor General Harding.

The animals were at once shipped by rail to San Francisco, then by steamer to San Pedro, then overland, and arrived at Sunny Slope in good condition after a long tedious trip. They were a choicely bred lot and all fine individuals. Four of them—Gretchen, Sea Foam, Kate Tabor, and Belle View Maid—were of matronly age. The remaining six, including the two running fillies, were two years old. Sea Foam and Gretchen had been to the court of Woodford Mambrino, and Kate Tabor to that of Mambrino Patchen, both of these stallions being held in high favor.

The arrival of ten animals from famed Kentucky—a great event—was heralded all over the state. Some fine stallions and mares had found their way to California much earlier, and some stallions from far-off Australia. In 1860 F. P. F. Temple, who came to California in 1841 and later married Señorita Workman, the daughter of William Workman of La Puente, imported the stallions Black Warrior and Billy Blossom from Kentucky, paying $7,000 for the former and $10,000 for the latter. Many southerners found their way overland to California. It required men of great valor and hardihood to endure the pain and distress of the rigorous journey across the plains. It likewise required a horse of unusual courage and stamina to stand up under the strain of the arduous trip. It was, therefore, quite natural that the men from the South who were to be outriders to the long covered-wagon caravans, with the love of their horses inborn in them, should select as their mounts, when leaving on the long tiresome western trip, the best mare or stallion they possessed.

In this way it occurred that individuals of the most prized thoroughbred strains of the South, found their way to California and were a most potent factor in the uplift of the horse family in future generations. There naturally was some breeding done in a sporadic way, but Father's was the first instance of an exclusive blooded-horse stock farm.

Early in the spring of 1871 L. H. Titus, with his married daughter, Mary, and her husband, Captain J. C. Newton, a veteran of the Civil War, arrived from Buffalo, New York, and at once purchased the J. D. Woodworth place. A few months later Mrs. Titus and Clara, an unmarried daughter, came from the East, and the family at once became a prominent factor in the community. Miss Clara, a beautiful auburn-haired young woman of convivial temperament, greatly to the surprise of all, quietly forsook the social sphere and entered a convent.

Mr. Titus, who had owned trotting horses in the East, brought with him Echo, a four-year-old stallion, a son of Rysdyk's Hambletonian. The latter had established beyond all controversy his supremacy as a progenitor of trotting speed. So fashionable was the Hambletonian blood that its partisans considered it paramount and fairly decried all other strains.

The Moor, the young stallion which Father had placed at the head of his breeding venture, was of the not generally well-regarded Clay Pilot family, famed for its speed, but condemned for lack of endurance. As in all his other undertakings, Father, guided by his own convictions, had sought the path of the pioneer; when embarking in the horse business, he espoused the cause of the discredited Clay family, having in mind that their faintheartedness could be overcome by the infusion of the blood of strains of known stamina in subsequent generations.

There was a serious controversy over the breeding of The Moor's dam, Belle of Wabash, at the time Father purchased him. The *Trotting Register*, the accepted authority, gave Belle of Wabash's breeding as standard (trotting), whereas her breeder gave it as of thoroughbred (running) blood. Father saw the mare himself, and because of her appearance, which so perfectly supported the thoroughbred contention, relied upon his own judgment and accepted and always maintained the thoroughbred version. In fact, it was this stout-blooded reinforcement, close up in the Clay pedigree of The Moor that decided Father in purchasing him. That the conclusion was a correct one was abundantly demonstrated beyond peradventure, not alone by the courage of The Moor himself, but also through the wonderful stamina he imparted to his tribe.

It was indeed strikingly coincident that Mr. Titus should move all the way across the continent from the state of New York to California and locate in almost the same barnyard—our barns were not over five hundred feet apart—a breeding farm, headed by his fine stallion Echo, whose blood lines were so diametrically opposed to those of The Moor. It seemed a certainty that one must fail, with the burden of proof lying on the side of Father. Time was to tell. It told a glorious tale for both, admittedly more generously for the clan of The Moor; Echo, however, had worthy compensations for his merit in future generations.

With Father's importations from Kentucky and the advent of Mr. Titus, horse racing gained quite an impetus in Los Angeles County. There was a track in the outskirts of Los Angeles, where races were occasionally held, but there had been no regular organization or racing. In March 1871 a meeting was held in Los Angeles for the purpose of organizing an agricultural society, with horse racing as an adjunct, for the counties of Los Angeles, Santa Barbara, San Diego, San Bernardino, and Kern. Many of the foremost citizens attended, among whom were Judge H. K. S. O'Melveny, Doctor J. S. Griffin, Judge A. J. King, Colonel J. J. Warner, ex-Governor John G. Downey, F. M. Slaughter, Harris Newmark, L. H. Titus, and Father, who were delegated to form the Southern District Agricultural Society.

Father was the leading spirit and was elected its first president. A suitable piece of ground was purchased in the southwestern part of the town, a grandstand, a suitable number of box stalls, and pens for show stock erected, and a good mile track laid out.

The place was known as Agricultural Park, and the initial fair and race meeting was held in October 1871. The association at first was a private corporation; then the land was deeded to the state, becoming known as the Sixth District Agricultural Association, and received annual state appropriations. Later, the property was involved in some litigation, but finally, under a fifty-year lease, it became the present home of Exposition Park, Los Angeles.

Our trainer, Hurd, had been busy giving the younger trotters their early education and also had The Moor well advanced in his training in anticipation of racing him at the fair.

Father employed J. W. (Billy) Donathan, considered the best in the country at that time, to train the running fillies Irene Harding and Lulu Jackson. When Donathan came to Sunny Slope to take them in charge, he brought with him two horses of his own—Snipe, a bay, and Maneater, a bay with white face and four white legs. With these two horses, riding one and leading the other, Donathan traveled through the country, running match races—the long distances with Snipe, and the sprints with Maneater.

Training methods were positively farcical at that time. Donathan, two or three times weekly, would gallop these horses three miles and occasionally work them a mile at speed, heavily blanketed and hooded with openings for their eyes and nostrils only. When the horses were pulled up after being worked, the sweat would almost puddle as it ran from them—enough to kill an ordinary animal, but it was the proper way then, copied from the Virginians of the era of the mighty Boston.

Even with these aboriginal methods, trainers took themselves quite seriously, and we looked upon Donathan as almost psychic. He lived to be an old man, had plenty of success and ample opportunity to laugh at himself about his early-day experiences as compared to his later and much saner ones, when coverings of any kind were used only in the rarest of instances merely to sweat a horse about the throat.

Racing saddles were grotesque in structure, weighing four or five pounds, a sort of miniature McClellan tree with far more bow in proportion over the withers, no leather covering, with stirrup leathers and girth straps riveted to the tree.

A week before the date of the fair, the Rose contingent hied itself to the scene of battle—the horses were all walked the fourteen miles, the trotters to harness and the runners under saddle, with the two horse wagonloads of trappings following in the rear.

The fair was the event of the season, and everyone from San Luis Obispo to San Diego who could get there was on hand. There were many ranchers who could be termed race-horse men, who knew and liked good horses and sought to own the best there were about. The fact of the matter is that there was little of the best to be had, and their contributions to the speed contests at the first fair were necessarily very mediocre, but with each succeeding year they became more assertive and in the end were prominent factors in the race-horse game in all parts of California.

Captain George A. Johnson of San Diego, a retired sea captain, owned some first-class horses and was a regular patron of the race meetings both in San Francisco and Sacramento. He brought three runners to the fair, Pelee and Eva Coombs, both very fine mares that had earned laurels in San Francisco in competition with first-class animals from the East, and Mission Bell, a beautiful little gray miss, bred in San Diego.

Charley Thomas, a cowman originally from Maine who lived at Strawberry Valley in the San Jacinto mountains, was always a prominent factor at the races, not in consideration of the horses he raced, but because of the broad scope of his acquaintance and his ardent love of the sport. The soul of honor, voluble, loud-spoken with a Yankee twang, and very reminiscent, he was always a central figure in conversational groups. Lame, wizened, and weather-beaten, though not aged, he looked as old as the hills he lived in. Thomas was married to a Spanish woman, nee Badilla, the sister of the notorious early-day chicken fighter "Six Toed Pete," who actually had six perfectly formed toes on each foot. Mrs. Thomas was also lame, and both she and Thomas carried canes.

Thomas was somewhat bibulously inclined—far be it from me to say the señora also was—however, when Thomas looked upon the wine when it was red, under cloak of sentinel, *no mas a ver que el Viejito no tome muy demasiado* (only to see that the old man does not drink altogether too much), the señora went into the saloons with Don Carlos, and each time he had his *traguito* (small swallow) the señora also had hers. When both had reached the proper state of mellowness, and the wee small hours of morning were well advanced, the Thomas duo wobbled to their hotel, arm in arm, each with a cane in the disengaged hand, one well propped to the starboard the other to the larboard.

Another of the hardy pioneers was Fin (F. M.) Slaughter of Rincon, who had raced his good mare Belle Mason against Dashaway a few years before Agricultural Park was established. Slaughter had blazed his way to the distinction of being classed as a hardy pioneer. While engaged in mining in the San Gabriel Canyon, he had the satisfaction of making three "Good Indians" of an equal number of bad ones who attacked his camp.

The San Bernardino district contributed Doctor Dickey, who later owned the good one-eyed horse Pescador; Alexander Brazelton and Edward Kenneston, who later owned Inca; and from San Jacinto, near by, came the Aguirres, Picos, and Estudillos; John Reed of La Puente came through El Monte with his beautiful Monte Belle and Careless and was joined by "Keno" Parish and "Monte" Smith. The Forster brothers—Marcus and Chico—of San Juan Capistrano, whose father owned upwards of 200,000 acres in San Diego County, made a *fiesta* of the entire week. Their trainer, Tom Case, was never out of their sight. Steve Stroud of Norwalk was also there with Bow Hocks, as were all of the Machado family of La Ballona, with their favorite, home-bred little horse Bandera (flag), on whom all the natives wagered regardless of his competitors.

From away off in San Luis Obispo came "Shot Gun" Taylor, an old stage man, and from across the mountains near Los Alamos, "Cap" Harris and the old Spanish don, M. Rochin, and his neighbor, Stanislaus Cordero. From Santa Barbara drove Nick Covarrubias accompanied by his friend Manuel Den, covering the long hundred and ten miles behind a pair of native-bred horses in twelve hours; Ramón Malo, also of Santa Barbara, the social arbiter among the Mexicans, came by steamer. Mr. Jacques, English, debonair, and very gentlemanly, wearing, hung over his shoulder, beyond question the only pair of racing glasses in the community, brought along his gallant little mare Mariposa (butterfly). Jack Hill and Jake Gries, big farmers, made the trip from Ventura County with their speed flash, Dottie Dimple, and swapped yarns with Hill's brother Ben, of San Diego County, who later raised many good horses, running wild in the hills surrounding El Cajon Valley, a number of them later finding their way to New York City, where they met the best and won their share of races.

Jim Adams, who owned California, Ten Broeck, and had the distinction of breeding peerless Geraldine, who held the half-mile record for many years, was in mighty evidence with his new stallion Ben Wade.

Hancock M. Johnston, son of General Albert Sydney Johnston, and Los Angeles County's personal pride, Billy Rowland of La Puente, were liberal patrons of the pool box. The pillars of the speed contests—Oscar Macy, E. B. Gifford, George Butler, William Babcock, T. D. Mott, L. H. Titus, and Father—were all keen for the fray. "Whispering Johnny" Donahue, Ed Dupuy, John Reynolds, and Ed Beecraft were the resident trainers.

As a special attraction, a race was arranged for nonprofessional owners to drive their own horses. Mr. Mott drove Lugo; Mr. Macy drove Billy Blossom; Mr. Babcock, Brown Dick; and Father drove The Moor. This contest was the social event of the meeting, creating a vast amount of interest, and rivalry was keen, not alone as to victory, but also regarding the appearance of the horses, and each got a hearty cheer when coming on the track. The Moor outclassed the others considerably in speed and won the race handily, Mr. Mott with Lugo taking second money. The little running mare, Irene Harding, won both her starts, beating Mission Bell and Mariposa, and Donathan's distance runner, Snipe, won a two-mile race for him.

The town of Los Angeles and the county as well turned out en masse; from banker to baker few were missing. Leading merchants, who did not know one horse from another, entered right into the spirit of the occasion, taking partisan sides with some owner-friend and fairly threw their coin into the pool box, winning or losing with the utmost good cheer.

Having no pavilion at the track in which to house the exhibits, they were displayed in a one-story building on Market Street, just across from the old courthouse, which was used as the first roller-skating rink in Los Angeles.

The fair at once became a festal event and was looked forward to from one year to the next in joyful expectancy. It stimulated competition in all lines; the farmer showed his prize bull, friend wife her jams and jellies, sonny his "big" pumpkin, and the little girl her fancy needlework. Not only did it accomplish all this, but it became a means of reunion of friends, who lived so far apart in the vast domain of meager intercourse that it required just such an event to induce them to take the long journey.

Father being the president of the association, members of his family were naturally franked to both, at the races and the pavilion. I laugh when I think how often we are fooling ourselves when we think we are deceiving others. At that time, 1871, Los Angeles did not have more than five thousand inhabitants, about half of them Mexicans, and the man at the door of the pavilion taking tickets knew every white man, woman, and child in the town, and more than likely by name. The occasion was my brother's and my first introduction into town life, and, enshrouded in our rural verdancy, we did not take this fact into consideration. We kept up a procession, going back and forth bringing in boys from the street, shouting "The President's sons" to the ticket taker as we entered, and he undoubtedly enjoyed as much as we our fancied deception, just as effective as the ostrich hiding itself by concealing its head in the sand. The experiences of the week were epochal to Brother and me and marked the first milestone in our young lives.

The life of my brother and myself in the country had been just one long happy holiday, toying around with nature and enjoying her bounties—all sorts of fruit to choose from—apples, pears, peaches, plums, nectarines, apricots, cherries, figs, pomegranates, and oranges; loquats, guavas, persimmons; gooseberries, blackberries, raspberries, and strawberries; walnuts, almonds, and pecans; such a great variety of grapes that we found sport in searching for new varieties—unlike Sparticus and his shepherd boy friend, we did not have to scale lofty peaks, but we did bear the grapes home in childish triumph and ate them.

The daily routine was varied Saturdays only, when we cruised farther from home on foot, drifting about with no particular thought. Sunny Slope's broad expanse of thirteen hundred acres, with an occasional sortie across the *arroyo*—the summer dry wash—of the freshet waters from Eaton's Canyon, gave us ample scope for exploration, and each occasion uncovered to us places of beauty before unseen. Our excursions to a distance were confined to an annual trip to the circus at Los Angeles and occasional Sunday visits with friends near El Monte, five miles distant, or, if to spend the day, a five-mile-farther jaunt to see the Rowlands at La Puente.

If the family chose to make a daybreak start, we went twenty-five miles to the crossroad settlement of Anaheim, where the Doffelmeyers lived. In sections of the country in the late spring, the narrow road would be skirted for miles to its very edge by a growth of wild mustard, so dense that it stood wall-like, a mass of lusty green leaves surmounted at a height of seven or eight feet by a solid blanket of bright yellow bloom, so intensely fragrant that it all but sickened one.

With the advent of the fair, our aspirations grew; we were soon allowed to have our own saddle horses and the occasional use of a team—with these the latitude of our Saturday pleasures expanded into visits to the near-by neighbors. A particular one of them still stands forth in happiest remembrance—that was to Mrs. Cooper's place, near Don Benito Wilson's. Mrs. Cooper with loving southern mother instinct gorged us with small hot biscuits and jam, which were delicious, but the alluring feature was a small species of pear, brought to the country by the missionaries, which grew on age-old trees in Mrs. Cooper's orchard. They were locally known as "San Juan" pears, from the fact that they were ripe by the 24th day of June, a Mexican feast day known as "San Juan's."

My brother and I had good saddle horses, rode well, and occasionally we would carry a lunch and join some of our schoolboy friends, and go three or four miles to Eaton's Canyon, or a few miles farther over through the Baldwin Ranch to Santa Anita Canyon, where there was fair trout fishing.

In the very heart of the mountains, easy of access, this canyon was a favorite spot for picnics. Frequently an old-fashioned Concord coach with four horses would leave Los Angeles early in the morning with six or eight couples, come by Sunny Slope and pick up my two older sisters, and drive on to the canyon in time for a basket lunch—joined perhaps by some of the Cooper, Howard, or Wilson families—return by way of our home, partake of refreshments or supper, and on back to Los Angeles by moonlight. The canyon was quite wide, its bed very rugged, strewn with boulders of all sizes, some of them very massive, dislodged from the ledges by the erosion of ages. The mountains sometimes rose in sheer bluffs or at others from flats into gentle slopes upwards, the lower confines fairly covered with flowers—matilija poppies, red Indian paintbrush, Mariposas, lupine, blue and white, red and blue larkspur, buttercups and bluebells. Higher up the slope was studded with manzanita, sumac, chaparral, with swards of mountain lilac in full bloom, dotted here and there with the Spanish bayonet, with its towering, cream-colored pinnacle of clustered flowers. Large sycamores and alders grew at the edge of the stream, which danced merrily onward from ripple to pool.

With our rapidly advancing ideas, we commenced to hanker for a shotgun. There was an old muzzle-loader hidden away in a corner, which Father, who was very fond of hunting, used before his various enterprises overtook him. He had a narrow escape from great injury with it one day. In hurriedly reloading after firing it, when pouring in the charge of powder, there must have been a live spark which exploded the charge, blowing the powder flask violently from his hand a great distance, luckily with little injury to that member, burning him, however, quite seriously about the forehead. With this in mind, we were forbidden to use this gun; as a matter of fact, we were too young anyway. When the O'Melveny boys spent the week end with us, Ed, the older one, was allowed to use it. Going along with him when hunting, he occasionally allowed us, by resting the gun on a board of the fence, to have a shot at a tin can. Little by little, we encroached and finally got to using the forbidden blunderbuss ourselves; to solve this dilemma, Father bought each of us a double-barreled, breach-loading Remington.

Starting on our hunting trips after a six o'clock supper, going out through the walnut field, passing a small piece of vineyard of an imported variety, we were certain to have killed a quail or rabbit by the time we reached the mill dam, not over a quarter of a mile on our way. Passing along, we were soon at the Rancheria. Fortifying ourselves there with a fresh, warm *tortilla* at any of the huts, we rigged this into a cornucopia-like affair, filled with hot *frijoles* (beans), and sauntered along down across the arroyo to the Chapman ranch, walking around the edge of that place about half a mile then through part of our pasture. We were back home before dark with from six to a dozen quail and two or three rabbits each—and we did this any time we chose. Hunting so often, we soon became expert and confined ourselves to wing-shooting and looked derisively upon our city boy friends who shot at birds before flushing them.

## II

The second fair of the Southern District Agricultural Society was held in October 1872. There were several recruits to the racing ranks; notable among whom was our neighbor L. H. Titus. Mr. Titus had constructed a half-mile track, on which he had been training his stallion Echo for the approaching contest with Father's stallion The Moor. Both of these horses had their partisans, and their meeting in a race was looked forward to with unusual interest.

The day of the race arrived, and, although the two equine warriors met, neither bore home the laurel wreath. With the paucity of fast horses in California at that time, shrewd horsemen in the East shipped horses of considerable speed to the races in San Francisco and usually swept the deck. On this occasion Henry Welsh of Chicago brought to the fair via San Francisco Vaughn, a rather inferior-looking, sway-backed animal, which he started in the race with Echo and The Moor. Vaughn so outclassed both of them in speed that as far as he was concerned the race was simply a procession with Echo and The Moor battling valiantly for second honors which, after a hard tussle, fell to The Moor.

A few days later at the same meeting The Moor, driven by our trainer Hurd, started in a two-mile heat race against Longfellow, owned by George Butler and driven by Ed Dupuy. The Moor won the first heat after quite a spirited contest. At the end of the second mile of the second heat, not a hundred yards from the finishing line, both horses racing courageously, Longfellow suddenly swerved to the outside fence and fell through it, dead. A few days prior to this sorrowful occurrence Longfellow had been driven, in a race with owners driving, by George Butler against Milk Boy, driven by E. B. Gifford, Brown Dick by Mr. Babcock, and Gretchen, driven by Father. Father again carried off the amateur honors, and this marked his final appearance as a reinsman.

Irene Harding, the running mare, was the only other animal taken from Sunny Slope. In fact she was not taken from the ranch but joined the other horses in Los Angeles on her return from Sacramento, where Donathan had raced her against keen competition, winning two races and losing one. Her only competitor at Los Angeles was Captain Jack, a very flashy good-looking *palomino* (cream colored), carrying some native California blood, as his color would indicate. Captain Jack was no match for Irene, and she beat him, both at mile and two-mile heats.

At this same meeting, at the behest of a number of young English society gentlemen who held forth at the Union Club, the leading organization of its kind in Los Angeles, a hurdle race for gentlemen riders was given. Seven of the beaux gallants, gayly attired, paraded to the post and were at once dispatched on their pirouetting journey. There were four hurdles, and the number of riders was decreased one or more at each obstacle, until there were but two of their number remaining. Mr. Seymour, riding a slowgoing sorrel nag, won the race, and Mr. Arthur Herdman, riding Shark, a light roan with white points, finished second. The event created quite a bit of merriment at the expense of the unseated knights of the pigskin. As a means of recovering their equestrian aplomb, another hurdle race was arranged to take place a few weeks later.

The natives, none of whom had ever seen a hurdle race, were very much struck with it. Manuel Den of Santa Barbara, whose mother was of one of the famous old Spanish families of that county, was so impressed with the idea he declared his intention of taking part in the renewal of the event. Den, as good a horseman as I have ever known, always riding a saddle with pommel, had never ridden—on what he chose to call a *tortilla*—the English saddle. Equipping himself with one, he returned to Santa Barbara, put up some hurdles, schooled a horse of his own breeding, brought it to Los Angeles, and won the race with great ease. About the same number of English gentlemen as of the former contest tarried by the wayside.

The following year, 1873, The Moor was liberally used in the stud and was not raced. Gretchen was returned to the fold of matrons, leaving nothing but Irene to race. Donathan again took her to the State Fair at Sacramento, where she met the best horses of the state, giving a fair account of herself by winning one race in three starts. Irene, a very beautiful small mare, was a great local favorite, and her unbroken chain of victories in Los Angeles had caused her to be considered well-nigh invincible. People bet heavily on the races in California at that time, pools selling for four and five hundred dollars for first choice. With this in mind, some smart horsemen were lured into bringing a horse to the Los Angeles races they believed could beat Irene.

On this occasion a man by the name of Hall came from San Francisco with Target, a really fine, very dark chestnut—almost black—horse, counting on a great betting coup. These two animals met in midweek of the fair in a mile and repeat race. Irene was ridden by George Howson, California's leading jockey at the time, still vigorous and under thirty; he looked much older with his long chin beard and moustache. The first race was a worthwhile affair, with Target contesting doggedly every foot of the way, but, unable to wrest the lead at any time, he was beaten by Irene in straight heats. The following Saturday, the last day of the fair, the same animals met in another singlehanded race of two miles and repeat.

Howson was again up on Irene and won the first heat with greater ease than she had beaten Target in the shorter distance of their first meeting. The second heat was taken by Target with such ease that it did not look wholesome, particularly to our old friend Charley Thomas, to whom we had traded Irene the morning of the race for sixty Durham cows and calves and in whose interest she was racing. Exercising his prerogative, Thomas substituted Charley Smith, a waif of a boy who exercised Irene in the mornings, as jockey in place of Howson. Smith had never ridden a race and was so small he had to carry fully twenty pounds of lead to make the required weight. When Donathan mounted the lad on Irene, he instructed him to "hurry her away from the start, take a steadying hold on her and let her run." Irene at once took the track, was never threatened, winning by a number of lengths on her own courage in a number of seconds' faster time than that in which Target had beaten her. The scene was one of great excitement when Smith brought Irene back to the judges' stand to dismount. Smith, trembling and almost exhausted from his efforts of the "steadying hold" he had been instructed to take on Irene, complained that his hands hurt him, whereupon Thomas, with a number of us following, took the lad across the track to the bar and got a beer glass full of whiskey for him in which to bathe his aching fingers.

At this same meeting Jim Eoff, a first-class trainer from San Francisco with a none-too-savory reputation, showed up with a good-looking dark chestnut horse called Temecula. Eoff conspired with Chico Forster, a popular, wealthy, and profligate scion of one of the most affluent native families, to enter the horse in his (Forster's) name. The twain went so far as to claim the horse was reared on Forster's father's 200,000-acre domain in San Diego County, and it was to give this contention a further metallic ring of verity that the name Temecula, which was that of an Indian village on the Forster property, was taken. The horse was entered in one of the slower classes and won the race with such consummate ease and so mannerly a fashion that not even Forster's supposed probity could screen the performance from suspicion. Hasty telegraphic inquiries disclosed the horse to be Professor, an eastern animal of some class, with a record twenty seconds in advance of the class in which he had started. The horse was not allowed to race again, but the gratuitously serving, politically prominent, distinguished citizen judges took no punitive action.

## III

In order to keep consumption on a par with the yearly increase in production of wine, Father found it expedient to continue his eastern missionary work of 1869 and 1870 and made a trip annually, leaving Sunny Slope in the latter part of March and spending three months in visiting all the larger cities. His experimentation along the lines of better adaptability of certain varieties of grapes to local climatic and soil conditions had determined him to adopt the zinfandel and black malvoisie for red table wine production, and Blaue Elben and Burger for white wine—the zinfandel and malvoisie perforce, because of their usage in making dark wine, were purple grapes, carrying about equal saccharine strength. The Blaue Elben was also a purple sweet grape, having, however, a latent suggestion of acidity. The Burger was of white variety, with just a bit of golden glow in its skin, a very prolific yielder, the grapes growing so closely clustered that they were pressed out of shape, were very thin skinned and fragile, with an unusual amount of juice, not sweet, nor yet sour, somewhat of a watered sweetness.

Cuttings from these varieties had been sold, and the zinfandel generally adopted in lieu of the Mission for red table wine making. Earlier in this story, the statement was made that the pioneer wine makers used the Mission grape alone for making all sweet and dry wines, which was generally true, due to the fact that the Mission was the only variety easily available, and furthermore those who entered the field lacked experience in wine making.

Europeans were among the early pioneers, and it is quite possible that some of the number who were somewhat versed in the technique of wine making may have sent home for vines of some favorite variety, which ultimately found its way into wine casks in limited quantities. The only well-known early case where the introduction of foreign varieties was turned to commercial account was that of Louis Vignes, who came to Los Angeles from France in the early thirties, where he had had some experience in wine making. So impressed was he with the great viticultural potentialities of the fertile soil and sunny clime that he sent back to France for vines of favorably regarded varieties.

Before the end of the decade, he had produced wines that were pronounced excellent, and history of 1858 tells us of some of Louis Vignes's fine twenty-year-old white wine—whether sweet or dry is not stated. Mr. Vignes's vineyard of one hundred and five acres was located on Aliso Street, now in the heart of Los Angeles. Along about 1860 he sold his vineyard and stock of wines to his nephew, Jean Louis Sainsevain, for $40,000. Mr. Sainsevain continued the business, but, as grapes from his vineyard alone were used, the output would not be in excess of twenty-five thousand gallons—a sizable quantity at that time, but infinitesimal as compared to later-day productions, when California wines were in general use.

Mr. Sainsevain was the pioneer California wine merchant of New York City, locating there in 1861. I am not conversant with the measure of his success, nor of that of Mr. Vignes with their table wines, but I know from personal experience that there was no halfway-good California claret sold in quantities to the eastern trade until the zinfandel grape supplanted the Mission. In later years the zinfandel was relegated to the background by other varieties which produced claret equal to that of European countries.

To get back to the adaptability, our own later experience at Sunny Slope forcefully illustrated that hypothesis with this same zinfandel grape. We were at once gleeful over the superiority of the first claret made from the zinfandel to that made from the Mission. Our glory was short-lived, however, for we soon learned from competitive sales in the East that the zinfandel claret made in the northern counties of Sonoma and Napa was far superior to that made at Sunny Slope—so vastly so that we curtailed our production of it to our local needs for the bottle trade and bought from our northern competitors for our quantitative wants in the East, and went more actively about developing a new variety to replace it.

The malvoisie was early thrown into the discard; not so, however, with the Blaue Elben and Burger, from which white table wines were made. Both of these varieties were pronounced successes from the beginning, and with a few years' age the wines made from them would gratify the taste of the most fastidious. Our port was of the best. Angelica, a sweet white wine made from the Mission grape by eliminating the skins, was a nice palatable drink, with no particular virtue.

Sherry was the weak link in our chain; in fact little wine of that class produced in California was worthy of the name. All of it lacked the nut-brown characteristic of the Spanish sherries. At Sunny Slope we tried to supply this flavor by leaching unripe English walnuts with high-proof grape spirits (brandy) and adding a small amount of this extract to each cask. This process changed the character somewhat but after all was but a makeshift. A wine in great favor with the ladies was muscatel, made from the grape of that name, a small, round, white grape of the same flavor, only of higher degree, as that of the raisin grape, muscat of Alexandria. The wine—very sweet, with the pronounced aroma and flavor of the muscatel—was very like a cordial.

Our brandy was our trump card. The process in distilling it was the same as in producing whiskey, except with the substitution of wine for grain mash, which was boiled in copper stills, the vapor evolved, condensed by passing through a copper coil immersed in a large vat of continually cooled water. The product is crystal white and about one hundred and eighty proof, which is reduced to one hundred by the addition of pure water. Whiskey and brandy absorb their color from the charcoal on the inner side of the barrel staves which are charred during construction. As a means of hastening the coloring process of our brandy, we added a very small amount of syrup made by burning white sugar; this also added a slight characteristic flavor. "Rose's Sunny Slope Brandy" was a staple article with wholesale druggists all over the country. None was just like it. This little dash of syrup—the story of which never before has been publicly known—no doubt had something to do with it.

Our demands for steady laborers had mounted beyond the number of regulars living at the Rancheria. It was particularly urgent for labor in the winery, to the detail of which Mexicans did not respond very actively.

There was quite a colony of Chinese living in Los Angeles; as a matter of fact, it was just about this time—1871—that there had been a very serious conflict with them in the town. Two of their factions were indulging in a tong war among themselves and in resisting arrest shot, not seriously, Jesus Belderraín, a member of the police force. The Chinese were none too popular at the time, and the incident precipitated a savage riot, in which nineteen of the Celestials were shot down or hanged to lamp posts. Most of the Chinese labor activities were confined to cooking, laundering, and vegetable gardening in Los Angeles, and although hordes of them were used in railroad construction, but few of them had found their way to the rural districts as farm laborers.

Known, aside from their internal dissensions, to be very peaceable and having the reputation that, when once shown how to do something, they were practically infallible in its repetition, Father hired twelve of them and moved them to Sunny Slope. So marked were their imitative proclivities that one needed to be careful in his demonstration, lest an unnecessary step be taken, or a false move made, as the Celestial was certain to do the same in executing the new duty.

The arrival of a dozen *Chinos* (Chinamen) created quite a commotion amongst the native laborers, but it was purely curious and not resentful. The two factions soon fraternized and had a fine time trying to teach each other a few words of their respective languages, of which mixture they made a fine jargon.

The Chinamen adapted themselves readily to their new surroundings, were absolutely dependable and honest, rarely losing a day and seldom quitting their jobs, easy to get along with in every particular, housing themselves in quarters that one-third their number of Caucasians would rebel against.

They never quarreled among themselves or with others, but stuck together and resisted, en masse formation, any assault on one of their number by an outsider. On rare occasions a Mexican struck one of them; in an instant every Chinaman in sight or within calling distance—perhaps half a dozen—would be on top of the lone adversary, clawing with might and main. As they were not naturally vicious, their onslaughts did little damage, sufficient, however, to teach the assailant to be sure the next time he started anything with one of them that no other Chinamen were around.

They could be taught any kind of labor. White labor which was used in the horse barns was so undependable that two Chinamen were put to work there to do the cleaning up. They did not know when undertaking the work the proper end of the horse to be bridled; they soon developed, however, into fair caretakers and broke some of the young trotters to harness.

At that date, 1871, there were no bonded warehouses in this section, and, when we wished to make a shipment of brandy, we wrote the internal revenue collector in Los Angeles, who sent the gauger out to check up on the quantity. The gauger made his report to the collector, who then advised us of the amount of tax—ninety cents a gallon—due on the amount. Father sent his check; the revenue stamps were forwarded to Sunny Slope by mail; when received, they were applied to the barrels, and the shipment ready for transit. In his work the gauger made notations on the barrel with chalk, indicating in numerals entire or in fractions how much brandy should be added or taken out to conform with the registered outage, or the small amount of water necessary to be added to reduce the proof to one hundred.

"Hop," an old Chinaman whom we early started as the gauger's assistant, soon learned to make these corrections unerringly, although he did not know the characters. Incidentally, Ivar A. Weid, who at that time considered himself poverty-stricken and bemoaned the payment of taxes on three hundred acres of Hollywood's hills, where he made his home, was for many years our gauger.

Father made his fourth selling campaign to the East in 1872. More gratifying results than those annually attained could not have been asked for. It would quite naturally be presumed that with his income regularly increasing, Father would have enjoyed at least a slight respite from his financial dilemmas. Not so, however. With his unyielding determination to hasten to realization his many visions, it seemed that for each dollar he took in, he had a place to use two, and, during this very period of his financial ascendancy, Father experienced some of his greatest financial worries. True enough, he enjoyed splendid credit with the Farmers and Merchants Bank of Los Angeles for his current needs; not, however, for his apparently limitless expansion. To keep pace with the increasing demand for wine and to more fully reap the fruits of his success with the new varieties of grapes he had propagated by an increased acreage of them, Father had visualized the acquisition of more land.

Though the time seemed most inopportune, he went valiantly to the task of raising money, not only for the purchase price of the land and the great expense of improving it, but also to restore his current credit at the bank in Los Angeles. The tract he wished to purchase was 640 acres of the Santa Anita grant, which abutted against Sunny Slope on the southeast, which he could acquire for $5,000.

At this time on Sunny Slope there were 360 acres of vines in full bearing, two hundred acres of oranges in different stages of production, a hundred acres in English walnuts and fruit trees. The wineries and distillery, though of cheap construction, were ample and in good repair, affording substantial borrowing security.

Father went to San Francisco and called on Lazard Freres, a very powerful private money-loaning firm, and secured from them a loan of $30,000, a momentous sum at that time, with interest at 1½% per month, the loan to be secured by a mortgage on Sunny Slope and the new piece to be purchased with part of the money. The horses, stock of wines, and all movable property were exempt. The land was acquired, and, aside from the costly process of clearing it of brush, another considerable expense had to be incurred at once. To safeguard against jack rabbits and ground squirrels, a rather expensive redwood fence was built requiring upwards of 150,000 running feet of lumber for the four-mile inclosure.

Two hundred and fifty acres were at once cleared and planted the following spring to Blaue Elben and Burger vines. This purchase and the contact it gave Father with Mr. Lewis Wolfskill, who owned Santa Anita at that time, led this same year, 1872, to the largest cash real estate transaction known up to that time in southern California. The Santa Anita grant originally of something over 13,000 acres was granted to Henry Dalton in 1863. Mr. Dalton in turn sold it to Corbitt, Dibblee, and Barker, who used it for sheep grazing. Later Mr. William Wolfskill, who came here in 1831 and to whom must no doubt be given the successorship of the padres as pioneer orange grower of Los Angeles County, bought the grant from Corbitt et al. and presented it to his son Lewis, who had recently wed Miss Dalton, daughter of the original grantee.[17]

The Chapman family, Father, and some others had bought portions of the grant until it was reduced to 8,000 acres—a regal domain, unequaled

[17] Rancho Santa Anita was acquired by Henry Dalton from Hugo Reid (the original grantee) in 1847. Dalton then sold it to Joseph A. Rowe, who in turn sold it to William Corbitt and Albert Dibblee. William Wolfskill bought the rancho in 1865 (excepting the 2,000 acres that had been sold to L. J. Rose). Lewis Wolfskill inherited the rancho from his father.

in all California at that time, and even today there are no 8,000 acres to match it in California. The old adobe ranch house was centrally located near a small lake, with a few acres of oranges and a fair-sized vineyard surrounding it. The property extended from the lowlands in El Monte into the Sierras, embracing within its limits beautiful Santa Anita Canyon, splendidly watered, a wonderful forest of oaks growing on the uplands, and 5,000 acres of it was as level as a floor.

Father was very friendly with H. Newmark and Company, the leading wholesale and retail grocers in Los Angeles, with whom he did all his trading. The price asked for Santa Anita was $85,000, a trifle over ten dollars per acre. Father, with no monetary interest whatever, extolled the virtues of the place at the price, citing in support of his arguments the fact that he himself had paid eight dollars an acre for a piece incomparable to that offered because it was unwatered. The Newmarks were finally convinced and bought the place, paying $25,000 down, the balance to be paid in four equal annual payments.

# *Los Angeles in 1873 - Teams and Iron Horses - Early Banditry*

## I

When in 1873 I reached the age of eleven, my brother and I started to school in Los Angeles, riding horseback the twelve miles in and out daily, rain or shine. Leaving home at a quarter after seven, riding good horses, we would gallop the twelve miles to Durfee & Reichard's stable on Aliso Street in an hour. A quarter of an hour spent sauntering along the streets would bring us to the schoolhouse at eight-thirty, allowing us a half hour of play before school opening.

From our barn the road ran down a lane about a mile between the Titus place and Sunny Slope. Off to the right near by we could see an adobe house, the home of Aunt Susan, an immense darky woman, and her diminutive Mexican husband, Billy. Just north, beyond this, was a glimpse of the little adobe schoolhouse, partially hidden by the oak trees. Beyond in bold relief on a high hill stood the home of Colonel Winston. A half mile farther along on the road, we passed the home of our former schoolteacher, Mrs. Loop. Off to the right a mile or more, high up on the ridge, the pretentious home, San Marino, of Mr. Shorb could be seen.[18] Along on our way we could see the Mulock place, situated where the road turned south to the mission about a mile away.

At this point we were joined by Kewen Dorsey, a boy considerably older than ourselves, who rode to school with us. A little farther along off to the right was the small bachelor home of Edward Hereford, son of the second Mrs. B. D. Wilson by her first marriage.

Immediately across the arroyo skirting San Gabriel on the west, the recently organized Lake Vineyard Land and Water Company, owned by Don Benito Wilson and his son-in-law, J. De Barth Shorb, had placed on sale a subdivision of small acre tracts, on which later rose the thriving city

[18] The Shorb residence was not built until 1877.

of Alhambra. A man by the name of Brown built one of the first houses in this settlement, right alongside the road to Los Angeles; I have gone into this minutia to exemplify the sparsity with which this great outdoors was settled at that time. The vast broad section of flat country passed over for the succeeding five miles, we called "the plains." One could see for miles in either direction, and, unless looking backward toward the mountains, not a tree came in sight until the outskirts of Los Angeles four miles farther were reached. There were three houses seen on the entire trip, these all located on a water-bearing ravine about equidistant between San Gabriel and Los Angeles. Just before reaching these, the roads forked. The lower or main traveled stage road passed by the "Five Mile House," where there was a saloon and watering trough. From here on, this road led through the hills following the present line of the Southern Pacific until nearing the town, where it turned down along the river bank and crossed over the first bridge constructed across the Los Angeles River—a short, covered affair still standing. Just why it was housed in, I've never been able to learn.

On the upper road there was a very old place with a good, homelike adobe house belonging to Rosa del Castillo, a Basque woman who owned large flocks of sheep. Close to this J. C. Newton, son-in-law of our neighbor, L. H. Titus, owned one hundred and sixty acres which he had taken as a government claim. By raising hay, which he sold in Los Angeles, and pasturing livery horses, the place was more than self-sustaining. After Captain Newton's death the property passed to his heirs, who held it until the town of Bardstown was laid out upon it, bringing them great financial gains. An occasional flock of sheep was seen grazing on the hillsides, and hundreds of little brown squirrels, and often a *churrea* (chu-ray-ah), roadrunner, which, if we were not in too much of a hurry, we would run after with our horses and capture. Their periods of flight were brief; they soon became exhausted from running and hid in the grass; we would catch them, then liberate them. There were also many ground owls about the size of a quail, which stood by the holes leading to their underground homes. They always ducked their heads in a sort of curtsy at the approach of danger before descending, or before a short flight to another hole.

I would like to narrate a short story concerning this small bird, which I heard many years ago of my friend Judge Fernald, an effusively polite attorney living in Santa Barbara, not so much of a Nimrod. Going afield with fowling piece in hand, gayly attired as befitted an English nobleman, the judge drew a bead on one of these little fellows, who made his customary bow. The judge lowered his gun for an instant, then again took aim—another bow from the owl, whereupon the gentlemanly sportsman lowered his gun, saying, "I cannot shoot so polite a bird," and moved on.

We met the San Bernardino-bound stage every morning about the same place on our way to school, and I shall always remember the thrill it gave me when it came in sight. Galloping along on our horses in the cool, crisp, air of springtime, over the wide open plains strewn with acres of sweetly perfumed wild flowers, we were perfectly oblivious to all things. In the distance the beautiful low rolling hills were slumberlike in their quietude under their mantles of velvety green, not a single object to mark the landscape, not a sound but the hoofbeats of our horses, when lo! as if by magic, thrust into full view coming over the top of a hill, silhouetted against the blue sky is this gay turnout, teeming with life, the body of the coach painted the reddest of reds, the wheels bright yellow, filled with passengers inside and every available seat taken beside and back of the driver, who, straining every muscle, fairly stands with his right foot on the big brake, all six reins clutched in his left hand, with his right now and then popping a laggard with his long lash, that he may bring down the hill in proper alignment his six foaming half-gentle horses—a spectacle to challenge seriously the artist's skill.

The school we attended was a two-story, eight-room structure, just completed on the hill on which today stands the Los Angeles County Courthouse. There had been several schools in the town prior to this one, but this was the first designated as a high school, and one room of it was devoted to that branch of education.

Prior to this pupils advanced in their studies attended either Professor Lawlor's, located on Main Street at the point where later Second Street was opened through to Los Angeles, or Doctor T. H. Rose's on Bath Street, the latter a public school. The public irrigating ditch, a stream six feet wide and two feet deep, ran through the yard of Doctor Rose's school, and one can gain an idea of how sparsely settled the town was from the fact that the schoolboys bathed naked in this stream unobserved.

The town of Los Angeles at this time claimed a population of seven thousand, but between five and six thousand would have been a closer estimate. The town was but partially sewered, and gas available only in certain districts. The sidewalks of the few blocks of the central business district were of a cheap asphalt structure; aside from these and the entire residential district the sidewalks were of dirt. The streets were no more than country roads, rough and dusty in the summer, and in the winter, after a hard rain, deep in mud. There were no streetcars, a few horse-drawn vehicles for hire, and but one railroad, the Los Angeles and Wilmington, constructed in 1869.

The Pico House, a substantial three-story building erected by Don Pío Pico in 1871 on North Main Street adjoining the Plaza, was the outstanding hotel. The Bella Union, part two and part three stories, and the Lafayette, a two-story brick, standing back from the sidewalk on opposite sides of Main Street near Commercial Street, had previously held sway. The U. S., the "Two Bit (twenty-five cent) House," stood at the corner of Main and

Requena. The Downey Block, a spread-out two-story affair occupying the present site of the Los Angeles Post Office and Federal Building, and Temple Block, situated at the junction of Main and Spring and extending along those thoroughfares to Court Street, were the outstanding office buildings.

Numerous tradespeople, large and small, fairly representative of all branches, most of them occupying one-story adobe structures, were scattered from the Plaza to First Street along both Spring and Main streets and on Market and Court, short streets connecting these two main arteries. Commercial Street from Main to Los Angeles was well tenanted by retailers. The wholesale houses and some of the larger retail establishments were located on Los Angeles Street between Arcadia and Requena. There was some business on Requena, New Commercial, Arcadia, and Aliso streets; also a few business establishments scattered about in outlying districts.

There were several feed corrals on Spring Street, one as far out as Seventh. There were two breweries, one on Aliso Street, the other out on Main just below Third. A small flour mill stood at the junction of Aliso and Sainsevain streets. The post office was on Spring Street between Temple and Court. Wells, Fargo and Company's express, presided over by "Billy" Pridham and Joe Binford, was at the corner of Court and Main streets.

The Western Union was on Main Street near the Bella Union Hotel; Charley Shepherd was the lone operator, and Tom McCaffery was messenger boy and understudy. The county courthouse was a two-story building occupying the very small block bounded by Main, Spring, Court, and Market streets. This block was not over sixty by one hundred and fifty feet in dimension. The sheriff's office and those of most of the other county officials were on the ground floor. The jail, a small brick structure, was on a lot enclosed by a high board fence, corner of Franklin and Spring streets. On the Spring Street side, there was a low one-story adobe in which the jailer lived and had his office.

There were two volunteer fire companies, the Thirty-Eights and the Confidence. A small block where Los Angeles Street terminated on the north was the Chinese quarter. A short street on the east of this block was known as "Nigger Alley," a tough neighborhood. George Gard, a peace officer, later United States marshal, Jesus Belderraín, a city policeman, George Valpey, a painter, and the notorious "Six Toed Pete" fought chickens in the middle of this street regularly, Sundays.

This section was the scene of the riot before spoken of. There were two newspapers—the *Star*, published by Major B. C. Truman, and the *Express*, by Colonel J. J. Ayers. There were two banks, Farmers and Merchants and the private banking house of Temple and Workman. Turnverein Hall on Spring Street was used for conventions and the few barn-storming shows that came to town. Another small hall, The Merced, was on the second floor of a small three-story building adjoining the Pico House. There was a small woolen mill in the outskirts in the southwestern part of the town. There were churches of all denominations, a number of first-class physicians and surgeons, dentists, and brilliant attorneys-at-law.

The American population lived on Main, Spring, and Fort (Broadway) streets, south of First, in very attractive frame houses with a general trend to the southwest. A few occupied old adobes in that section and farther out on Alameda and Los Angeles streets.

A full half of the inhabitants of Los Angeles at that time were Mexican, who lived in that section north of the old Catholic Church, known as "Sonora Town." They were of the middle class and lived in one-story flat-roofed adobes, many of them in solid blocks, built flush with the sidewalk with but one door, and all household supplies were carried through the house. Most of their living was done on a piazza in the rear. There were a few Mexican stores selling fancy work and curios, and fruit stands invariably displaying the sign "Fruta, pasteles y dulces" (fruit, pies, and candies).

Others owning animals had more commodious ground, frequently surrounded by adobe walls. The pretentious adobes built by the grandees many years earlier were located with few exceptions in the southeastern part of the town. Notable among them was that of Don Antonio F. Coronel at Alameda and Seventh, in which the don, still possessed of a fragment of his vast estate, still lived. Three of these famous landmarks still occupied stood in the central part of the town, the most imposing of which was that of Mrs. Colonel Robert S. Baker on the corner of Arcadia and Main streets, a very long one-story adobe built back a considerable distance from the street, with an L on either end reaching to the sidewalk. The site is now occupied by the Baker Block. This pretentious adobe, known as El Palacio (The Palace), was built by Mrs. Baker's first husband, Don Abel Stearns, who came to Los Angeles in 1829 from Massachusetts and shortly thereafter married the young lady who was then Señorita Arcadia Bandini, the daughter of Don Juan Bandini, a member of one of the oldest native families and himself one of the most conspicuous and influential men of his time.[19]

Don Abel—the Don part of which was wished upon him by the natives because of his ready fraternization with them—at once became most aggressive as a stock raiser and landowner. During the time of Richard Henry Dana, Don Abel was one of the leading hide and tallow shippers, and became possessed of tens of thousands of acres of land, his holdings extending from the site of the present city of Long Beach well toward San Bernardino. During Don Abel's early experiences, he at one time incurred the displeasure of the Mexican governor and barely escaped being shot or exiled.

[19] See n. 4 regarding Stearns.

After the death of Don Abel, Mrs. Stearns became the wife of Colonel Robert S. Baker, very prominent in the development of the city and county of Los Angeles and heavily interested with General Edward F. Beale in the sheep business in Kern County. Their immense flocks of sheep grazed over thousands of almost barren acres, now a forest of oil-well derricks, near the location of the present city of Bakersfield.

The remaining two of these old adobe homes were located on the Plaza near where the Catholic Church stands. One was the home of Mrs. Doria Jones, widow of one of the earliest merchants, John Jones, and her family; the other was that of the De la Guerras (of the war), a branch of the famous Santa Barbara family of the same name.[20]

The Bella Union Hotel, for many years the stage office, was on July 5, 1867, the scene of one of the most desperate and sanguinary gun battles in the early history of Los Angeles. It took place at the noon hour while a large crowd was congregated preparatory to taking the stage to the steamer at San Pedro. The stage, lined up at the sidewalk, was taking on the baggage.

Robert Carlisle, a son-in-law of our old friend, Colonel Julian Isaac Williams, of Rancho del Chino, had previously had an altercation with A. J. King, a deputy sheriff, over a murder trial, but friends had intervened. On this day Frank and Houston, brothers of A. J. King, were passing by the barroom of the Bella Union and, seeing Carlisle inside, entered, drew their six-shooters, and began firing at him. Carlisle also drew his gun and shot Frank King, killing him almost instantly. Houston King kept on shooting, and Carlisle, riddled with bullets, staggered to the sidewalk and fell. Houston King, not seriously injured, followed Carlisle out of the door and struck his fallen adversary over the head with his revolver with such force the weapon was broken. Carlisle, a man of iron nerve, summoned his last ounce of strength, raised to his feet, staggered to the wall, and leaning against it, holding his revolver in both hands, took deliberate aim and fired. It was his last shot but found its mark and seriously wounded King. This terminated the fight; Carlisle was carried in and laid on the billiard table, where he expired three hours later. King recovered, was tried and acquitted. During the battle a stage horse was shot dead in its tracks, and seven bystanders had their clothes pierced, and one was slightly wounded by the hail of bullets.

The Lafayette also had its tragedy when on February 14, 1869, Charley Howard, son of Judge Volney E. Howard of San Gabriel, and Daniel Nichols, the son of John G. Nichols, ex-mayor of Los Angeles and a highly respected citizen, met and shot it out. These two young scions of their worthy families, themselves highly regarded socially, had a personal encounter a short time previous to this in which they grappled and wrestled, but friends

[20] The Santa Barbara family of De la Guerra did not have a home on the Los Angeles Plaza; perhaps the reference should have been to Judge Olvera, who did.

separated them before any damage was done. The southern blood of both had been aroused, and at their first meeting, which was that in the Lafayette bar, both drew their guns at sight and commenced firing. Howard dropped dead at the first shot; Nichols also fell and, although at first thought fatally wounded, recovered, and having acted purely in self-defense was exonerated.

After this was all said and done, the three outstanding features of daily life in the dusty little town were Mrs. Doria Jones and her two daughters, who resided in a fine adobe home on the Plaza, with her coachman driving a beautiful team of mules down Main Street for their afternoon airing; the prim, Napoleonic Prudent Beaudry, early identified with the city water works and the pioneer in hillside subdivisions, galloping madly out the same thoroughfare on his bay horse with full Mexican equipment; and the sedate Washingtonian, Doctor Den, one of the earliest arriving physicians, mounted on a large, jet-black horse with black leather Mexican saddle, *tapaderas* (long, leather stirrup coverings) and all, riding stately along after office hours.

Doctor J. S. Griffin, a brother-in-law of General Albert Sydney Johnston, was throughout his life very conspicuous in the development of the town and county of Los Angeles. He was known as the father of east Los Angeles, where in 1863 he purchased two thousand acres of land at fifty cents per acre to be used as sheep pasture. The ability to water the flocks at the Los Angeles River was the force that induced the doctor to buy so large a piece. Fancy one demurring at the purchase of land in the outskirts of a town at 50¢ per acre!

Dr. Griffin was joined in this venture by his nephew, Hancock M. Johnston, and others. This vast acreage carried the doctor's property across the hills in the direction where Pasadena stands, until it all but joined his holdings in the Rancho San Pasqual.

It will be remembered that Doctor Griffin in 1859, under foreclosure of a mortgage for three thousand dollars and a further payment of two thousand, took over six thousand acres of Rancho San Pasqual and all personal property of Don Manuel Garfias.[21] At this time, 1873, Dr. Thomas B. Elliott, a retired army officer of Indiana, conceived the idea of establishing a colony of small acre tracts to be sold to his friends residing in the East. Judge Benjamin S. Eaton prevailed upon Dr. Elliott, J. H. Baker, Calvin Fletcher, and Thomas F. Croft to look at the San Pasqual rancho. The gentlemen were so enamored with the property that they purchased four thousand acres of it from Dr. Griffin for twelve and a half per acre, a fair increment in value from the fifty cents the doctor took it over for but fourteen years previously. The property was incorporated as the San Gabriel Orange Grove Association, with 100 shares at $250 each, but was always spoken of for the first few years as the "Indiana Colony."

[21] See n. 11 regarding Rancho San Pasqual.

The settlement flourished, and Pasadena, said to mean "Crown of the Valley" in Chippewa Indian, was taken as the subdivision's name. During the Mexican War in California, this identical spot was the scene of battle, and both Generals Pico and Flores, rivals in command, had encampments there.

During the same year William Cogswell built a moderate-sized, two-story hotel structure high up on the base of the Sierra Madres, due north of Sunny Slope. This place was called Sierra Madre Villa and was operated by Mr. Rhodes, a son-in-law of Mr. Cogswell. It was the pioneer rural hostelry of southern California bidding for winter tourist trade and continued in popularity until overshadowed by the construction of the Raymond in Pasadena.

The site on which the Raymond stands was known as "Monks Hill," from the fact that the hotel people purchased the property from a young man of that name from Boston, who was visiting Sunny Slope at the time he sold the property to the Raymonds for $12 per acre.

A few years later Abbot Kinney, a globe-trotter of the Kinney Brothers, Sweet Caporal Cigarette manufacturers, married Miss Thornton and built a fine home off to the west and higher up the mountain side than Sierra Madre Villa, christening it with a slight Hawaiian touch "Kinneloa." Nathan Carter, a shrewd Yankee newcomer, also built himself a home off to the east of the Villa and at a greater elevation. In the meantime Messrs. Carter and Kinney had a slight personal altercation, and Carter to taunt his aristocratic neighbor called his place "Carterhia."

## II

General Phineas Banning, who came to Los Angeles from Delaware in 1851, was one of the real empire builders of California's early days. He founded the town of Wilmington, which he named for the city of his birth in Delaware. General Banning was the father of the maritime shipping of Los Angeles County and may well be called the godfather of the Los Angeles and Wilmington Railroad—the first iron horse to invade the county.

General Banning not only led the way to the sea with his tugs, lighters, and steamers, but also braved the desert and penetrated far into the Sierras with his animal-drawn vehicles—operating a stage line from San Pedro to Yuma, Arizona, and colossal freight-teaming outfits over the same route and to the mines in Inyo County. Shortly after his arrival in 1851, General Banning expended thirty thousand dollars for an outfit of fifteen wagons and a hundred animals. At a later date he purchased three hundred and fifty tons of material of which to construct prairie schooners, and once on a few days' notice furnished fifty teams to the first telegraph company entering the field with which to distribute poles in the line of their construction. His regular outfit consisted of twenty twelve-mule teams, each with two wagons, which hauled regularly from tidewater to Los Angeles and outlying districts.

Banning was prominent in every sphere of life; he was a member of the vigilance committee, took part in hunting down desperadoes, was an active politician, and a most genial host. A good whip, he always traveled with a coach and four doing the tooling himself, and I well remember his frequent visits to Sunny Slope threescore years ago when I was a lad, as he invariably gave me a quarter of a dollar, incidentally the first one I ever possessed.

Though Banning was always the leader in his transportation activities, he achieved his position in the face of strong competition. There was always a keen rivalry between the stage lines as to who would make the fastest time. Opposition stages, with six horses carrying twenty or more people, would leave San Pedro on the dead run, I mean running as fast as the animals could, under lash. A change of horses was made at the halfway station, and the thirty-five miles to Los Angeles covered in two and a half hours. Some of the horses were unbroken, others only partially, and none of them any too well. In hitching fresh teams at change stations, it was occasionally necessary to blindfold an animal to get it in place and keep it quiet until the rest of the team were hitched. Often a fractious pair would be snubbed each to a post on opposite sides of the team alignment. As soon as the tugs were fastened, at the driver's command to cast away, the horses were untied simultaneously, and with a pop of the whip the leaders dashed forward carrying along the lunging broncos.

The stage companies catered to passenger traffic, but their main dependence was the mail and express contracts, which were let for only thirty-day periods. Speed was their essence, and if the holder was beaten to town a day or two by the rival company, the contract was taken from him and given his competitor, and the race went more furiously on in an endeavor to regain the coveted prize.

The roads were very rough and full of chuckholes, the driver wore a broad belt around his midsection fastened to the vehicle, and with the passengers it was a case of "Hold your seat, Mr. Greely, and I will get you there on time."

John Reynolds, who later had the distinction of owning the first hack for hire in Los Angeles, was for many years a driver for General Banning. Reynolds was a picturesque character, a wonderful whip, and it was commonly known of him that, when in his seat while the team was at a standstill in front of the office, he could by name attract the attention of any animal and cause it to alter its position by talking to it.

The first railroad in Los Angeles County spanned the thirty-five mile stretch from the city of Los Angeles to Wilmington, where it connected with steamer transportation. This road, financed by a $300,000 joint bond issue of the city and county of Los Angeles, built by Tichnor and Company, contractors of San Francisco, was started in 1868 and, after buffeting all manner of trying ordeals, finally reached Los Angeles late in 1869 and established its depot at Alameda and Commercial streets.

This same year, Charles F. Crocker, Leland Stanford, Collis P. Huntington, and Mark Hopkins completed the Central Pacific from Ogden to San Francisco, out of which construction they made tons of money. A little later the "Big Four," as these gentlemen were called, conceived the Southern Pacific from San Francisco to New Orleans.

A number of years previously, Tom Scott, oil magnate and of Pennsylvania Railroad fame, had made a survey for the proposed Texas-Pacific line, traversing practically the same course as that the Southern Pacific intended to build over. Scott, having abandoned his project, sold his survey to the Big Four.

This survey, after coming out of the San Joaquin Valley and on up over the Tehachapi Mountains, took a beeline from Mojave across the desert to Yuma, leaving Los Angeles a hundred miles off to one side. This contemplated course naturally aroused the ire of the citizens of Los Angeles, and many conferences were had with the railroad magnates, in which General Phineas Banning and ex-Governor John G. Downey took active part. No definite results were attained until in 1872 a public meeting attended by many leading citizens was held in the courthouse at Los Angeles, presided over by Judge H. K. S. O'Melveny, at which a resolution was passed pledging the financial support of the city and county if the railroad was built to Los Angeles within a certain time.

A committee consisting of Don Benito Wilson, W. G. Olden of Anaheim, and my father was appointed to go to San Francisco and confer with the Southern Pacific. As a result of this visit Mr. W. B. Hyde, representing the railroad, accompanied these gentlemen back to Los Angeles. The upshot of these many conferences was that the Southern Pacific agreed to run a new survey from Mojave to Los Angeles, prosecute construction there as diligently as possible, and to begin construction immediately on a fifty-mile stretch of the main line east from Los Angeles via San Bernardino, and also a branch to Anaheim.

In compensation the Los Angeles members of the legislature had a bill passed permitting the city and county to donate to the Southern Pacific the thirty-five mile Los Angeles and Wilmington line. In addition the county agreed to give the railroad $300,000 cash, and the municipality agreed to donate seventy-five acres of land in the heart of the city for railroad shops, to sanction which elections were called.[22]

[22] Los Angeles met the Southern Pacific demands, which included a five per cent

The proposition of bringing in another railroad precipitated a very heated controversy. The farmers throughout the country, on the one side, were bitter in their opposition, under the reasoning that the "iron horse" would destroy the demand for their crops of hay and grain. The Los Angeles merchants and the more enlightened citizens hailed with delight the prospect of speedier transportation. Bitter strife was engendered, and it required a desperate battle and considerable finesse to carry the election.

Partisan lines were tightly drawn, with campaign slogans "For the Railroad" and "Against the Railroad," creating many heated arguments amongst the best of friends. I. W. Hellman, a very positive and somewhat excitable middle-aged man, president of the Farmers and Merchants Bank, was drawn into an argument with Doctor J. S. Griffin, a considerably older man full of the fighting blood of his southern ancestors. The argument got out of bounds, and the grizzled doctor struck his friend Hellman on the head with a light cane—the blow caused blood to flow freely. Mr. Hellman hastened to his home four or five blocks distant and had barely entered his own front door when he dispatched a messenger to summon Doctor Griffin's professional services. The doctor responded immediately, stitched the wound, and the entente cordiale was restored.

At the election, something less than 1,500 votes were cast, the bonds carrying by the merest majority.[23]

The Southern Pacific went before Congress and had a bill passed allowing them to change the course of the road without forfeiture of their land grants. Construction was started on the two lines in Los Angeles County in the winter of 1873-1874.

From this date forward, progress in transportation construction seemed to at once become contagious. In 1874 a party of Los Angeles gentlemen organized the first streetcar line and built from the Pico House down Main Street to the junction at Spring, then out through this thoroughfare to First, then west to Fort (Broadway), south to Sixth Street, then west to the car barns on Figueroa.

Two years later when the Southern Pacific reached Los Angeles from the north, a new station called "River Station" was constructed down on San Fernando Street near the present freight sheds, at which time the one-horse car line was extended down by the station and across the river to the outskirts of east Los Angeles. The same year, another streetcar company was formed and built from Temple Block out Main Street to Washington, thence to Jefferson and on out to Agricultural Park.

---

levy on the assessed value of land and improvements in the county, a station site, and city-held stock in the Los Angeles and San Pedro Railroad.

[23]Actually the vote was 1,896 to 650 in favor of meeting the Southern Pacific demands.

On its long trek into the then very rural districts the Main Street car line passed by Morris' Vineyard—the old adobe house on the property was Frémont's headquarters during the conquest of California.[24]

This same year, 1874, Senator John P. Jones and his colleague, Senator William Stewart of Nevada, flush with recently acquired fabulous amounts of gold from the mines at Virginia City, Nevada, came to Los Angeles and, joined by Colonel Robert S. Baker, purchased the Rancho San Vicente of 1,700 acres lying on the shores of the Pacific. This property was adjacent to Santa Monica Canyon, where Márquez, one of the old-time Mexican dons, lived in grandeur on his cattle ranch. Joaquín Murieta, the crippled bandit leader of the early fifties, frequently availed himself of the sheltering care of his perfectly honorable friend Márquez.[25] The pioneers had not given the great Pacific any consideration as a source of pleasure, and the few who journeyed to the beach for recreation went to Santa Monica Canyon and camped out; there was occasionally a colony there of twenty or more tents. Messrs. Jones, Baker, and Stewart laid out the townsite of Santa Monica and had an auction sale, at which many Los Angelenos bought lots. A comfortable hotel was constructed, and small homes sprang up in rapid sequence. A new sport, seen for the first time in this country, was introduced as a Sunday pastime—a slot such as is used by merry-go-rounds, with two-and-a-half-inch rings protruding from the bottom, was suspended from a scaffold to the height of the shoulder of a mounted horseman. Participants, many of them natives, riding most excellent animals, ran in turn one at a time at full speed fifty yards and endeavored to lance the exposed rings with their six-foot spears. If successful, another ring dropped into position automatically, and the contestant first to lance twelve rings was the victor.

The following year, 1875, Senator Jones built the Los Angeles and Independence Railroad from Santa Monica to Los Angeles, also constructed a wharf at Santa Monica, which afforded competitive freight rates with the port of San Pedro, and the venture did a thriving business. The original plan was to continue this railroad out across the desert into the mining country of Nevada by way of Independence, Inyo County, California. The project was not carried any farther, and the seventeen-mile stretch from the beach was taken over by the Southern Pacific a few years later.

In the meantime the Southern Pacific was steadily threading its steel down the San Joaquin Valley, and, as it drew nearer, the stage line to the new terminus was shortened. It soon crept its way up and over the Tehachapi Mountains. Expectancy became very eager as the road coasted nearer

[24] Frémont's headquarters were at Aliso and Los Angeles streets in Los Angeles, in the two-story Bell Block.

[25] Joaquín Murieta, debunked as a mythical character by Joseph Henry Jackson, was supposed to have been shot in 1853.

with greater speed over the flat Mojave Desert, out through the Soledad Canyon, and established its final temporary terminus at Langs Station, about fifty miles from Los Angeles.

The thousand coolies doing the construction were driven harder; the rails reached San Fernando Mountains; the joyful day in September 1876 had arrived. The big iron horse flashed its way through the 7,300-foot bore and pushed ajar the gates to the first all-rail travel from the outside world to "Nuestra Señora la Reina de Los Angeles"—Our Lady the Queen of the Angels, as Los Angeles was originally named.

My brother and I continued riding back and forth daily to school on our horses for upwards of a year, then, to accommodate our sister Annie, who was taking some advanced studies, we drove for a short time and later lived in Los Angeles for a few months chaperoned by Grandmother Jones.

In the winter of 1874 the Southern Pacific inaugurated its first eastern passenger service of thirty miles to Spadra; and in 1875 we used the train from San Gabriel.

Just previous to this Father bought Jacob Metzger's half interest in the livery business of Ferguson and Metzger—Father had no desire to own a livery business and no time to devote to it and acquired it only because of the prospective value of the ground, which was centrally located, just across the street from the old Don Abel Stearns adobe.

A few years later Father purchased Mr. Ferguson's half interest and built the three-story Rose Building. While engaged in the livery business, Father employed I. N. Moore, a relative of Judge O'Melveny's, a very dependable fine person, to represent him in the partnership. Mr. Moore also kept books for the concern and had bachelor's quarters in a large room next the stable office. Because of Moore's staid habits, Father, thinking he would keep us in bounds, sent Brother and me to room with him in Los Angeles, that we might get in fuller hours at school. During our residence in Los Angeles, we formed many pleasant acquaintances and lasting friendships. J. Downey Harvey of San Francisco frequently visited his uncle, ex-Governor John G. Downey, and on one occasion he was accompanied by our mutual friend James D. Phelan. One evening, while walking in the upper part of town, Phelan, who was quite a sprinter, bantered us for a race around the Plaza. Harvey and I accepted the challenge and were soundly beaten. Both Downey and Jimmy smoked cigarettes, and Downey was always very careful to remove all evidences of tobacco before we approached very near "Uncle John's" (Downey's) house.

In later years, James D. Phelan was elected successively for a number of terms mayor of San Francisco, later United States senator. J. Downey Harvey was commissioned major in the National Guard by Governor Markham. Inheriting a large fortune from his uncle, included in which was the wonderful Warner's Ranch, Harvey embarked in the construction of a railroad, the Ocean Shore, from San Francisco to Half Moon Bay. The venture was fraught with many mishaps, turning out none too well.

We were also very friendly with the Glassell boys, Hugh, Andrew, William, and Philip, sons of Mr. Andrew Glassell, a prominent citizen and one of the leading attorneys; a cousin of theirs, Glassell Patton; and Mayo Thom, son of Captain Cameron E. Thom, also a prominent attorney and onetime mayor of Los Angeles. Often, afternoons, we would drive out with the Glassell team to a stream about three miles from the center of town, off but a stone's throw from the main road to Santa Monica, in which there was a deep pool about twenty feet across known as "Bell's Hole." Another instance of the lack of population—we all used to bathe and swim there by the hour naked, not a soul ever coming within a half mile of us.

In 1875 shortly after the Arcadia Hotel was built in the new town of Santa Monica, we all drove down for a week's vacation unattended by any grown person. The Glassell family had a small cottage down the beach about a half mile from the hotel; near it Major H. M. Mitchell, a prominent young man about town, had a cottage. Mr. Mitchell assisted in the capture of the bandit Vásquez and was later elected sheriff of the county. A number of years thereafter he met a tragic death at the hands of one of his closest friends, Mr. W. E. Dunn, attorney for H. E. Huntington, who on a hunting trip, mistaking him for a deer in the brush, shot him.

The Jones children, two girls and a boy, schoolmates of ours, lived in a charming adobe home on the Plaza, of which I have spoken. We were good friends, and Brother and I spent many happy evenings with them. In later years the elder young lady, Miss Carrie, married the multimillionaire J. B. Lankershim, and I had the honor of being best man.

In the winter of 1875-1876 invitations were issued to the wedding of Miss Lola Whiting and Mr. James J. Mellus, two prominent young society people of the town, to take place in a little old brick church which stood just at the base of the high-school hill. This was when even horse-drawn vehicles for hire were very rare. Mrs. Jones asked Brother and me to come down and walk with her and the girls to the wedding. My father was the best-hearted man on earth and a most generous provider, but in buying things to bring home did not always guess just right as to our sizes. We were not Beau Brummels in our homemade personal attire, and, on his last trip East, Father had brought us each a suit of very nice material, with long cutaway coats. This feature alone would have been bad enough—I had never before seen one, and I doubt if there was another cutaway business suit in the town—but, as a safeguard against our outgrowing the suits, he also had bought them at least two sizes too large. They were the only passable suits we had, and I felt like the devil turned loose the moment I got a glimpse of myself in the mirror. We had to join the Jones family—there was no escape—but ye gods! how I hated to have my sweetheart see me looking as much like a scarecrow as I felt. We walked down to their home and the good Lord was kind to us for a few more minutes. The ladies were not ready, and the servant let us in, deferring our embarrassment at meeting them at least a few moments. We both made for a sofa on the opposite side of the room, facing the door, so that, when the family entered, we would at least for the moment be able to conceal our long coattails. It was the supreme moment of anguish in my young life, but we had to go through with it. The ladies were too well mannered to make any comments, and we managed to survive the ordeal.

While on the subject of my social activities, I will tell "another." The Southern Pacific had rapidly completed the eastern line as far as Colton and installed a daily round-trip passenger service to Los Angeles. In the spring of 1876 they had wound their way beyond Colton up through the Cajon (box) Pass and down onto the desert to a point about one hundred and twenty-five miles from Los Angeles, known as Seven Palms. The first passenger train service was to be inaugurated with a school children's excursion one Saturday. All were on the *qui vive,* fairly counting the hours before the arrival of the festive occasion. My father met me in Los Angeles a day or two previous to the excursion date and gave me a good sound scolding over a report he had from a Mr. Quinn living in El Monte that I had rudely teased his young daughter the Sunday previous at the little Episcopal Church which we attended near San Gabriel, telling me that I must come home Friday night and go to El Monte Saturday morning and apologize. I told him truthfully that I had done nothing. Claiming there must be something, Father was obdurate, leaving no other course open to me. Though grieved at what I knew to be the injustice of the procedure, I got my young head working as to how I would manage not to miss the excursion. Deciding to go home Friday evening and make an early trip to El Monte Saturday morning and catch the train as it passed there, I prevailed on the trainer, Havey, to drive me over to El Monte with one of the trotters on its daily exercise.

Presenting myself to Mr. Quinn, we went to his home to see the aggrieved young girl. She herself did not know what it was all about, could recite nothing specific, going no further than to say that I thought myself "too smart." With which and a proper disavowal on my part I was absolved and the incident terminated. Horrors upon horrors were heaped upon me when I boarded the train and found my new girl sweetheart, Lenore Barclay, a little younger than I, a student in one of the grammar grades, was not aboard. Making the best of it, I paid most of my attentions to my high-school classmate, Miss Frankie McQuaid, four or five years my senior, just blossoming into charming young ladyhood. Her father was a leading lawyer in early San Francisco, in which city the young lady had once lived. She was stopping at this time with her uncle, Colonel James Eastman, one of the brightest lawyers before the Los Angeles bar, who lived out Figueroa Street about three miles from the station. Arriving in Los Angeles after dark, the young lady was somewhat perturbed as to how she would get home. Green as a gourd, with three dollars in my pocket which I wanted to spend, and choosing to be gallant but not knowing how, I made a fine mess of it. Proposing to take the young lady home in a hack (which all those cumbersome, closed, two-horse vehicles with the driver sitting high up in front were then called), she gladly assented. We walked up to Main Street, where I found a vehicle. Handing the lady in and closing the door I mounted the seat with the driver, Johnny Goodwin, and thus we drove away out to Eastmans', the lady riding in state alone inside the carriage. My reasonings were muddled. The first deduction was that my "dulce coeur" would not like it to hear I had driven about with another young lady; the next was, the young lady being so much my senior, I reasoned perhaps I was not a fit beau for the occasion; the resultant effect was that I was a country bumpkin, only fourteen, inexperienced and knew no different, and was over my head before aware of it.

## III

Considering the immense distances people lived apart and the consequent ease of escape, there was comparatively little of organized banditry in California's early days. There were wanton killings and robberies occasionally, but the perpetrators did not last long. The California pioneer was a courageous, two-fisted, red-blooded species of the genus Homo, frowning on lawlessness, and his ability and willingness to punish it even as an individual drew to him awesome respect.

Antonio Garra, who started his reign as *hombre malo* (bad man) just before 1850, and Joaquín Murieta, in the early fifties, were the last *bandidos* (bandits) until in the early seventies, when a number of Mexican sheep-shearers in Kern County crossed the mountains into Santa Clara County with the objective of robbing the pay car on some Southern Pacific construction work. Foiled in this, they proceeded to the town of Tres Pinos, in Monterey County, where they robbed the stores and shot up the town, killing three or four men, some of whom were officers. The bandits made good their escape and were not again heard of until a few months later, when they sacked the town of Kingston, in Tulare County. Fleeing that place under fire they again avoided capture.

The country was so sparsely settled that such a band of horsemen, provided, as they always were, with a little flour, sugar, coffee, and salt, could by going away from the main traveled road a few miles and finding a stream, with plenty of firewood at hand, camp unobserved for days, unless by a lone sheepherder tending his flocks.

They always carried a single blanket in a roll, tied behind their saddles. Horse feed was not a quandary, as their horses were all broken to hobbles or to being staked out. Grass was plentiful, and all but one of the animals would be turned loose, hobbled, the remaining one tethered in good feed near camp.

A year or more after this holdup of the town of Kingston, it became known that the leader of the bandits was Tiburcio Vásquez, a young Mexican raised in Monterey County, and that he and his band of five, including himself and his lieutenant, Chavez, a tough customer, were headed for the southern part of the state. This was at the time Brother and I were riding back and forth daily to school in Los Angeles. Like all young boys, we were very much excited over the fact that the desperadoes were about, wondering with none-too-gleeful thoughts what would happen to us if we chanced to meet the bandits, with no serious idea, however, that such an occurrence could be possible.

One morning about eight o'clock, within three miles of Los Angeles, we met five Mexicans, well mounted, with six shooters slung around their waists. It was not unusual to meet one or two armed men on the road, as practically everyone going through the country went armed. The horsemen spoke to us in Spanish, and we returned the salutation, and, conjuring up in our minds that we had discovered Vásquez, we hastened on to school and created quite a commotion among our schoolmates with our account. The incident was forgotten by the next day; however, we were no doubt correct, for within a week five heavily armed, well-mounted Mexicans appeared at the sheep ranch of Alessandro Repetto, situated in a sheltered valley about two miles back in the hills from the stage road, about five miles from San Gabriel. These horsemen, representing themselves as recruiting an invasion into Baja California, demanded $800 of their unwilling host. Repetto disclaimed the possession of any such amount of cash or the ability to obtain it. However, after having been tied to a tree for some time, repeatedly poked, none too gently, in the ribs with forty-fives and his life constantly threatened, he relented and wrote a check for $800 on Temple and Workman's Bank and dispatched a young employee to bring the money.

Under threat of death if the reason for the drawing of so great an amount was divulged, the young messenger hastened to the bank and, when catechized as to why Repetto needed so much money, would make no reply. The sheriff's office was but a block away; the sheriff was summoned and finally by threats prevailed upon the lad to tell him the facts. The sheriff sought to detain the messenger a short time until a posse could accompany him back to the ranch, but the boy pleaded so earnestly in his fear of what the bandits would do to Repetto if such a course were pursued, he was allowed to depart with the money.

The sheriff hastily formed a posse and followed the messenger, but was just a little late; the boy, arriving a few moments in advance, had given the $800 to the bandits, who, observing the advance of the horsemen, mounted hastily and fled, pursued by the sheriff. With their particularly fleet mounts the outlaws so quickly distanced their pursuers that the fugitives took time to rob Charley Miles, who was working with a number of men on a water pipe near the town of Alhambra, of his gold watch. The bandits camped that night at Piedra Blanca (white rock), now known as Eagle Rock, the fine residential suburb of Pasadena.

No more was heard of the outlaws for a few weeks until Sheriff Rowland received a tip that they were at the home of Greek George on La Brea Ranch. Greek George was a Smyrniot camel driver brought to America by General Beale with the herd of camels, which he imported and used in a transcontinental trip, and later, for an extended period between Fort Tejon and Los Angeles. By sending one of his deputies disguised as a laborer in quest of work, Rowland verified the rumor. There was a reward of $8,000 for the capture of Vásquez, dead or alive, and, knowing the elusiveness of that individual, the sheriff went carefully about laying his plans. Rowland soon found out that Vásquez had someone watching his movements and thereafter made it a point to be in evidence on the streets or his office at all times, day or night. In the meantime he organized a party of eight, consisting of Emil Harris, a detective; Albert Johnson, undersheriff; B. F. Hartley, a policeman; J. S. Bryant, constable; Major H. M. Mitchell, attorney; D. K. Smith, civilian; Walter Rodgers, saloonkeeper; and G. A. Beers, correspondent for the San Francisco *Chronicle.*

To avoid detection, these men went singly at midnight to Jones's feed corral, corner Spring and Seventh streets, where, well provided with ammunition, they mounted their horses and rode to a rendezvous in Nichols Canyon, about three miles from Greek George's.

At daybreak two of the party scouted from a distance and discovered two white saddle horses tied near the house. Just before sunrise two young Mexicans, driving four horses hitched to a farm wagon, came along the road, proceeding in the direction of Greek George's place. The posse commandeered the outfit; all got in the wagon and lay down flat, instructing the driver to go direct to the house, admonishing him and his companion that a false move would mean death.

When immediately in front of the house the officers alighted and surrounded it. Vásquez, who sat at a table eating, seeing the men, made a dash and jumped through a small window opening. The minute his feet struck the ground, he was felled with a charge of buckshot and, being unarmed, made no further resistance. Vásquez and his sole companion, a young man who was found secreted in the house, had carelessly left their revolvers in the holsters on their saddles. Chavez, really the killer of the outfit, could not be located in the neighborhood, and he and the other members of the outlaw band faded from view.

The prisoner was placed on a mattress in a wagon and taken to the jail in Los Angeles, and all of us scholars in the yard just above the jail saw him carried in. Vásquez sought to surround himself with a lot of glamour, with tales of having been driven to his outlaw career because a gringo won his sweetheart from him and mistreated her. At the same time he boasted of his own escapades with an unmarried young señorita near Elizabeth Lake, who had borne him two children.

After a few weeks' incarceration in Los Angeles Vásquez was taken to Monterey County, where he was tried, convicted, and soon thereafter hanged. Sheriff Rowland, well aware that even his nocturnal movements would be flashed to Vásquez, was debarred from achieving his great desire to make the capture personally. Having planned the coup, he received the reward of $8,000, but even this vast sum never fully removed his regret not to have participated in the final stages of the hunt.

# 7

## *Eastern Partnership - The Moor's Family - Santa Anita*

### I

On Father's visits to the trade in New York from 1870 to 1874, he had become acquainted with Charles Stern, of the newly established firm in that city of Perkins and Stern, which had grown to be his best customer. Young Stern, a German Israelite, came to New York from the fatherland in the early sixties, but, as the urge was westward, the young man did not tarry long on the Atlantic Coast, and along in 1864 he was in San Francisco. Kohler and Frohling, who at one time made wine at Anaheim, Los Angeles County, and later in San Francisco, was at that time the leading California wine house in San Francisco, and young Stern, who had been in the wine business in Germany, found ready employment with this firm.

At that time Mr. Richard Perkins, originally of Boston, was postmaster of San Francisco. A very public-spirited man, Mr. Perkins took a keen interest in everything Californian. He spent his Sunday forenoons visiting Kohler and Frohling's cellar, discussing the possibilities of California's wine industry, and incidentally enjoying a glass or two of good port. Young Stern was bottle washer and general utility man; his thrift and energy attracted Mr. Perkins' attention, and their casual acquaintance grew into a sincere friendship. After a number of conferences between themselves, young Stern and his would-be benefactor, Mr. Perkins, evolved a scheme for starting a California wine business in New York to be shared by young Stern with Mr. Perkins' son, Samuel C. Perkins, of Boston, a gentleman socially prominent in his home city.

Kohler and Frohling were consulted and embraced the new scheme with eagerness. The plan was for Mr. Perkins, Senior, to furnish the necessary capital to meet freights and other operating expenses, and Kohler and Frohling to furnish all wines required on credit. Young Stern was to open and have charge of the store in New York, and young Perkins to open and conduct a wine store in puritanical Boston.

A decidedly advantageous arrangement for all concerned—practically unlimited credit for the young merchants and a fine new outlet for Kohler and Frohling. The venture was launched in 1868 and from its inception prospered handsomely, particularly in New York, which was the distributing point. Up to this time all shipments were made by water, some by steamer via Panama—if time was a factor—otherwise by sailing vessel around Cape Horn. Although six months were consumed by the clipper voyage, it was preferred, not only because it was cheaper, but also of the fact that the wine was improved by the constant motion of the long voyage, stirring it around in the casks, causing a very beneficial evaporation of fusel oil, which is the aging process in all liquors.

Stern, at the start of his business career, knew little of its technique, but, possessed of unlimited energy, absolutely straightforward, and knowing the wine business from "A" to "Z", it did not require a great length of time till he had the situation well in hand.

As a means of publicizing the wine business and stimulating the planting of vineyards, Father frequently wrote comprehensive articles on viticulture, giving the public the benefits of his experiments in the line of adaptability, citing the varieties adopted by himself, advertising that he had cuttings of them for sale, and promising to buy any and all grapes delivered at Sunny Slope winery.

In this manner the desired end had been accomplished, and hundreds of thousands of cuttings furnished to various parts of the state. A few years later, when Senator Leland Stanford planted his 2,000-acre vineyard at Viña, about sixty miles north of Sacramento, Father furnished him 1,000,000 cuttings in a single order, which was the necessary number to plant 1,000 acres. These cuttings were sold for $5.00 per 1,000, the labor of making, bundling, and heeling them in trenches, and then getting them ready for shipment consuming about half this amount.

Father was appointed a member of the first State Board of Viticulture and served many years, and, although when he was a beginner there were a few who had antedated him in the business, his aggressiveness and success had given him foremost rank, and he became regarded as the godfather of the industry. It was at this time, 1874, that he was first called upon to make good his promise to purchase grapes from his neighbors. This necessitated further inroads into the money chests of Lazard Freres in San Francisco, who, with the security rapidly enhancing in value, were not loath to make further advances, but the consuming interest rate of 18% per annum was unyielding.

The financial worries were but half the battle; time in which to accomplish his many duties became the absorbing factor with Father. Everything on Sunny Slope was expanding and positively demanded personal attention. With the new vineyard coming along famously, the thousand-acre goal was near at hand. From a handful of ten or twelve laborers, the number had risen to one hundred or more. The orange shipments required his attention in the spring, the summer was all a hustle and bustle getting ready for the vintage, and then all through the fall he attended personally to the wine making. In addition to this, there was the horse business, if such you could call a venture all outgo and no income, which was increasing rapidly in numbers, and, having been created and fostered by his love, he enjoyed being in daily contact with it.

Doing all the bookkeeping and correspondence himself, it easily may be seen that Father had little spare time and, when he started on his annual eastern pilgrimage in 1875, his mind was fully made up to form some connection whereby he would at least be absolved from the sales end of the business. Upon his arrival in New York, he broached the subject to his friend Stern, who was at once very greatly interested, and suggested a partnership. Mr. Perkins was summoned from Boston, the details of the proposition were soon arranged, and the firm of Perkins, Stern and Company evolved. All sales other than those which came direct to the winery were to be made by the firm in the East.

Father turned in his equipment at a nominal rental and agreed to give a general supervision of the business gratis, but exacted an accountant and professional wine maker, the firm collectively to furnish all capital for the proper prosecution of the business, including the purchase of grapes, together with Father's, which were to be turned in at the market price. The firm had only to do with the wine business—grape production and all else at Sunny Slope were Father's personal affair. William Schoelgens, fresh from the Rhine, came out as wine maker, and from this date forward the output grew by leaps and bounds.

On this trip Father had taken Mother east with him, her first visit since her memorable departure from there in 1858. On all former occasions of his absence, Mother had charge of finances, drew all checks for labor and current expenses. On this occasion, although I was not yet thirteen years of age, that duty was delegated to me, and I shall never forget my first banking experience. In need of forty dollars, I went to the Farmers and Merchants Bank and wrote my first check and handed it to Mr. Thomas Rowan, cashier or teller, a very genial gentleman who made it a point to be friendly with children and of whom I was very fond. As soon as Mr. Rowan scrutinized the check, he chided me because of my error in spelling forty, in which I had included the letter "u." I was about heartbroken at such an awful *faux pas,* due entirely to my flurried condition because of my first experience, for with becoming modesty I may say I was a good speller and could have easily spelled forty backward correctly in the schoolroom; at all events, I considered my business career ruined.

The Chinese on Sunny Slope worked for a dollar and ten cents per day, and one of their number settled for all of them every three months. Laborers at the barn, the superintendent, and teamsters worked by the month and drew their wages at their pleasure. The Mexicans worked for a dollar and twenty-five cents per day and came to the front door of the house to draw their pay Saturday nights after quitting time. This was quite an occasion with them, not alone because it was payday and the eve of their Sunday holiday, but also it afforded them a few minutes visit with El Patrón, as they all spoke of Father. As this duty fell to me during Father's absence, I was christened "Patroncito" (little boss).

An outstanding pleasure to the laborers at these gatherings was when there was need for a quarter in change and the supply of that coin had been exhausted, in which case a coin was flipped and the laborer guessed *aguila* (eagle) or *mono* (colloquial: face, image, ape, etc.), their method of heads or tails, the operation accompanied by considerable loud talk and laughter. When all had drawn their pay, the greater number would go by the winery and procure their *botella* (bottle) of *vino* (wine) or a *aguardiente* (brandy) and take it home to the Rancheria, and as late as midnight in the quiet clear air we could hear them over a quarter of a mile away, singing off the effects of their indulgences in their naturally high-pitched, shrill voices. Sunday morning would find them bedecked in their best on the way to the mission to buy provisions, and Monday would find all hands on deck in good condition.

## II

The opportunities of Father's young stallion, The Moor, in his first year of service, 1870, might well be termed a minus quantity, as he served but one mare of any quality, and she, the dam of Billy Buffum, was of unknown breeding. The result of this mating was a beautiful black miss of apparent worth. Her looks belied her, however, as she was little above the average, and the name "Sunny Slope Bell," sentimentally bestowed upon her, was wasted. All other mares sent to The Moor's court were native mustangs, which were later sold for $5.00 per head, but every one of their offspring were good-looking, could all trot creditably, their stamina was proverbial, and they made fine driving animals.

A few which showed pronounced speed were trained, and one of them, Tommy Gates, when five years old, was a near champion for that period in this neck of the woods and took a record of 2:24½. There were two others, Dombey, a white-faced, white-legged colt, which Father presented to my

Uncle Ed Jones, and Becky Sharp, a pony-built black filly, which I called mine. When these two animals were three years old, Uncle and I, then thirteen, worked them together, and it was nip and tuck between them, first one, then the other winning in 2:41 or 2:42.

The second year of The Moor's reign as lord of the harem, a number of the mares brought from the East were sent to his embrace, among them Minnehaha. Father had high hopes from this union, insomuch as it was a forward step in the demonstration of his breeding theory, as Minnehaha was of his espoused Clay tribe, reinforced by the stout blood of Bald Chief, a descendant of the mighty thoroughbred, Mambrino. The result of this union was a beautiful black filly, a high-strung, impetuous little hussy from the time she was foaled; as she grew up, she was mannerly and docile but never overcame entirely her flightiness. Father named her Beautiful Bells for a popular waltz, and, when she was a three-year-old, barring a slight Roman cast in her nose, she was as near equine perfection in beauty and speed conformation as was ever attained. She was possessed of a great flight of speed and her endurance was phenomenal.

Our first trainer, Hurd, broke this filly and continued in her development until she was a two-year-old in 1874. By this time his (Hurd) penchant for strong drink had so mastered him that Father was compelled to part company with him. Bells, as the filly was affectionately called, was positively the apple not alone of one of Father's eyes but of both, and he frequently sat in the deep straw in the corner of her stall feasting them on her symmetry, with hope whispering a flattering tale of her future greatness.

That there should be no lack of skill in her training, Father imported from Detroit Henry W. McGregor, a reinsman of pronounced ability. In 1875 Bells, as a three-year-old, was entered in a stake to be trotted in the fall at San Francisco. Our good friend and neighbor, L. H. Titus, had been doing stud service with his Hambletonian stallion, Echo, and had a three-year-old daughter of his, Echora, which was entered in the same stake as Beautiful Bells.

Everything Father did in the race-horse game was open and aboveboard. Many endeavored to keep the speed of their horses under cover; not so with him. He had constructed a first-class three-quarter-mile track out among the oaks, which were all trimmed so as not to interfere with vision all around the circuit. There was a good cooling-out shed with six stalls, plenty of water, and the track kept properly sprinkled and harrowed. The horses were worked for speed regularly Wednesdays and Saturdays from nine to twelve in the forenoon, and all were welcome to witness the trials.

Mr. Titus was absolutely the other way around, and the rivalry in our horse business always irritated him just a little. He had on his place a half-mile ring where he did his training, and spectators, if not invited, were taboo.

That he might trust no other eyes than his own with reference to what our horses did in their trials, Mr. Titus built himself a crow's nest high up in a massive oak that stood in his yard, from which, with a pair of field glasses, he could see every move that was made at our track, and, by spending his forenoons Wednesdays and Saturdays in his lookout, he knew just what was going on in our speed trials.

Beautiful Bells had shown a trial in 2:37, very unusual speed for a three-year-old then, but was very flighty in negotiating the first turn, often making a break from which it was very difficult to settle her on the trot again. The best Echora had done was a mile in 2:53. In due time both animals were shipped to San Francisco. McGregor took The Moor along and gave him a record of 2:37; he was, however, timed a mile in 2:32 in a heat in which he finished third.

When Father, always sentimentally inclined, reached San Francisco, he ascertained what band would furnish the music for the race meeting and sought the leader, taking with him the music for the "Beautiful Bells Waltz," and gave the bandmaster $100 to have his men learn the music, considering it fittingly appropriate to have it played on the occasion of his filly, Beautiful Bells, winning the race, so foregone was the conclusion that she would do so. The two fillies were summoned for the start, and the word "Go!" was promptly given. Beautiful Bells at once rushed into the lead, and, when halfway around the first turn, made one of her disastrous breaks, stood and danced up and down until Echora was halfway around the track, and, going steadily along about her business, distanced Beautiful Bells. The band, of course, played the waltz, but I am not so sure that Father heard it. The Moor and Beautiful Bells were returned to Sunny Slope. The Moor contracted lung fever on the boat and died a few days later.

In the 1,960 acres ultimately comprised in Sunny Slope, 640 acres were devoted to the horse-racing department; about 40 acres were used for the barnyard, with training barns, hay and implement sheds, roomy paddocks, and stabling for the farm work animals.

There were two fields of one hundred acres each, separated by a half-mile lane running to the race track, with a section of moist land in either field, with clear running water, where there was always enough green feed to nibble on, but the principal feed was the natural grass of California—*alfilaria.* This grass takes its name from the Spanish word *alfiler,* meaning pin because of the resemblance of its seed growth to a bundle of pins, the cluster of seeds at the base being the heads, and the inch-and-a-half-long, tapering spears converging to a common center at the end, the body of the pins. These clusters remain intact until the grass dries in early summer, when they disintegrate into individual, atomlike, irregular-shaped seeds, the pin of which is coiled into the minutest sort of a spiral. This grass is wonderful food both green and dry; the natives in the early days worked their horses both under the saddle and in harness with no other feed. When green in good winter seasons, alfilaria is very luxuriant, growing knee-deep to a horse, and is very fattening. When it dries in the summer, it shrinks into apparent insignificance—not so, however—a field may look quite barren, yet animals will be seen apparently lapping up the dirt. Upon investigation, quantities of these very small seeds and stems of the dried grass will be found, and beef fattened on it will be very firm. There is always a small mixture of burr clover growing with it.

In the farther field of three hundred acres, in which the race track was located, the same feed conditions prevailed. In the first-named fields, there were a few stately oaks affording ample shade. In the latter there was a forest of large and small oaks with quantities of feed which, because of the shady nooks, endured green much longer than in the exposed places.

A fifth field of one hundred acres in another part of the ranch was devoted to raising hay. It may be of some interest to know that our very extensive and pre-eminently successful horse-breeding operations were carried on with no other feed than that growing wild on these pastures for the dam or her offspring until weaning time. The mares were bred in the spring and, with their young foals of the previous year's mating at foot, turned out in one of these fields, allowed to run there until the feed was well gleaned, then transferred to fields and pastures new. This procedure was carried on till October; then the mares were taken up and tied in stalls alongside their little ones until they were weaned and halterbroken. For this period of ten days the mares were fed alfalfa hay. They were then turned out again to roam all winter till foaling time in spring, with not an ounce of artificial feed and no shelter whatsoever other than that of our beautiful blue heavens and the shade trees, and were as fat and far healthier than barn-fed animals.

The young foals were fed alfalfa hay at first and taught to eat grain. They were also taught to lead on a trot alongside of a saddle horse, their feet rasped and well shaped up. In a month or six weeks' time the young colts were again turned out until spring, finding their own feed. They were then taken up and, wearing a bitting harness, turned loose singly in a paddock for a few days, then driven about the yard with no vehicle attached, taught to guide and stand. When they had learned their first lessons well enough, they were hitched double with a gentle, active mule to a light rig and given short drives daily, increasing the length as conditions justified.

The good faithful mule tolerated no mistakes. When the command was to go, the action was precisely what the word implied, and off the mule walked with young Mr. Trotter, a passenger willingly or otherwise. Little or no trouble was experienced; quietness and patience at all times soon gained their confidence. After this lesson was well learned, the youngsters were hitched single to a substantial breaking cart daily until absolutely biddable; then a light training cart was used for a short time, which was the beginning of their first trotting lessons. The theory of their development was lessons early and often, with short snappy brushes and no long sustained efforts. Again turned out and left to run till fall, the colts were taken up for the winter, shod, and driven to a light cart daily on the track. In making speed, care was exercised not to maintain the effort to the tiring point. At first the young trotters were asked to step their best for an eighth of a mile, then the distance was increased to a quarter of a mile. At the end of each trial, their speed was checked down to a sprightly jog, which was continued on around the track, three-quarters of a mile. Reaching the speeding ground again they were driven at top speed for the distance of the trial and jogged around the track again; about three of these efforts daily was their share.

When the distance of their trials was increased, they were hitched to a track sulky and gradually taken along until they could trot a mile at speed, care being taken to tiptoe them only a part of the journey and not to ask this major effort too often. We did not believe in fast mile trials, but in many trials well within the animals' speed; to leg them up was our theory, with short brushes to sharpen their speed. When the distance had been stretched to a half mile or over, they were worked on the track but twice a week, Wednesday and Saturday mornings. Other days they were jogged out over the roads through the country. Along in April a half dozen of the best would be selected with the view of getting a racing prospect or two which would be continued with; the balance, if we had no sale in contemplation, were turned out until fall. In their early schooling the colts were fed alfalfa hay and oats. When their training was intensive, oathay and oats. No hay known compares in fattening and strength-giving qualities with California oathay, so unlike timothy and other eastern hay in its strawlike appearance that eastern trainers bringing their stables here are misled. The animals, however, are undeceived, taking to the hay with great relish, and the tendency is to overeat, not to their permanent injury. In the vernacular of the race track they "fill up" and, like one after a hearty meal, are not ready for a severe effort. Trainers immediately detect this condition and feed more sparingly.

In our western racing experience occasionally a horse bled from the nostrils, nine cases out of ten of which were the result of allowing the horse to eat too freely of this California oathay. No great harm results from these purely local nosebleeds, though it is a most distressing spectacle to the spectators. This condition is altogether different from bleeding from the lungs, which is constitutional and serious, the distinguishing feature being that in the latter case the blood is frothy and filled with air bubbles.

After Beautiful Bells's miserable showing and the death of The Moor,

Father parted company with McGregor and hired Richard Havey, who as a lad came from the East with Norfolk and rode him in his memorable matches with Lodi. All of Havey's previous experience had been with runners, but as he was known to be a good conditioner, alert and of good habits, Father felt quite positive he could be no worse than the trainers he had previously employed.

The mare Lulu Jackson, which was purchased with Irene Harding, had produced to the cover of Woodburn the filly Nina R. This filly was now two years old, and Havey brought with him to break her Walter Maben, a sixteen-year-old lad of Los Angeles, who had achieved a worthwhile local reputation as a race rider. Nina R. developed into a fair runner and won a number of races.

In his horse swapping Father acquired Camilla Urso and Annette, both royally bred running mares, each with a foal at foot. Annette's colt was by Hubbard; Camilla Urso's, a beautiful black which we called Raven, was by Monday. As a two-year-old we sold Raven to Henry Schwartz of San Francisco, who raced the colt successfully in the East on the flat one season, then put him to obstacle racing, and he became one of the best timber toppers in America at that time. Father bred Camilla Urso to imported Creighton; this produce was the filly Armida, who a few years later, when Lucky Baldwin entered the racing game, was sent East with his string and won a number of races.

There was also a year's crop of something like thirty yearlings to be broken, and young Maben, a first-class horseman, began his later spectacular harness-horse career while teaching these young things to trot.

At the same time there were about twenty-five two-year-olds, the crop of 1874, prominent among which were Sultan, Sable, and A. Rose. Sultan was the son of Sultana, a highly prized filly brought in the second shipment from the East. Sultana had shown a lot of early speed when first arriving, and because of our meager training accommodations at that early date was sent to Barney Rice, a prominent trainer in San Francisco. Sultana developed a spavin and was returned to Sunny Slope, and her first mating with The Moor produced Sultan, three days after whose birth she died, and the young king-to-be was raised by a foster mother.

Sultan was a very flashy, fine-looking colt with many ideas of his own—far from biddable—and it took a lot of patience and perseverance to get him to trot. He could trot well enough but without reason would break into a run frequently, and he was a four-year-old before he was raced. Sable, a very speedy, somewhat overgrown daughter of Gretchen, of which our hopes were particularly high, would not stand training and was sold later, becoming a famous matron. The third of the trio, A. Rose, was the original she-devil—headstrong, self-willed, and in harness such a vicious kicker that she could never be driven unless the rear end of her was securely strapped to the shafts.

On July 4, 1876, a day's racing was given at Agricultural Park, Los Angeles, and A. Rose, a two-year-old, was started in a two-mile heat race—mind you, two-mile heats for a two-year-old—against the five-year-old gelding Cade. Young Maben drove A. Rose, hitched to a sulky, walking and jogging her slowly alternately fourteen miles from Sunny Slope to the Los Angeles race track in the forenoon of the race, cooled her out, put her in a stall, and fed her. In the middle of the afternoon, Havey drove her in the race, winning both heats in identically the same time, 5:20, at the rate of a mile in 2:40 for each of the four miles, when such speed for a single mile was far from common in aged horses, to say nothing of a two-year-old.

Along toward evening, the filly was jogged back to the ranch and was as notionate at the end of this trying day's ordeal as she was when it began.

In August of the same year, 1876, Havey took Bells and A. Rose north to race, and also a few younger ones to gain experience. Bells was started a number of times, and managed to win a race and took a record of 2:37, not within a dozen seconds of her speed. She would invariably make a break going around the first turn, and then it became solely a matter of how long she would jump up and down before settling again, and then she would fairly fly, trotting the last half in 1:10, but generally so far arear when beginning one of these marvelous spurts of speed that she could not overhaul the leader.

The filly A. Rose attracted the attention of Mr. Newland, of Newland and Pomyea, livery stablekeepers in Oakland. Father priced her at $2,250. Mr. Newland had seen her in harness quite often, knew she was a bad kicker, and the last word said to him when he led the filly away was never to drive her without a kicking strap. Mr. Newland had lost the sight of one eye, and, heedless of this admonition, a few days later while driving A. Rose without the precautionary measure, she took one of her kicking spells, demolished the sulky, all but killing Mr. Newland, and destroying the sight of his one good eye. After this catastrophe A. Rose was put to breeding and became the dam of some useful horses.

## III

The activity in railroad construction and the founding of the towns of Alhambra, Pasadena, and Santa Monica in 1873, 1874, and 1875 had focused the notice of people in other sections of the state on the potentialities of the southland, and early in 1876 E. J. (Lucky) Baldwin drifted into Los Angeles.

Baldwin, who was keeping a livery stable in San Francisco, got a tip on

Ophir mining stock when it was very cheap and invested in it all the money he could raise. When the rich ore strike was made, the stock skyrocketed to such an extent that Baldwin cleared up $5,500,000.

Baldwin's attention was called to the 8,000-acre Santa Anita Ranch, recently acquired by H. Newmark and Company, and he made a number of examinations of the property. The road to Santa Anita passed immediately by the long orange avenue at Sunny Slope, and on each of his trips of inspection Baldwin drove in to see Father, who became as great a factor in the sale of the property to Baldwin as he had in the purchase of it by the Newmarks. I well remember the first time I saw the suddenly famous Croesus. He was standing high up on a long ladder, placed against an orange tree, that he might pluck his first orange.

Baldwin wore—as was his custom for many years—a black slouch hat, a single-breasted, long-tailed, black broadcloth coat, a cross between a cutaway and Prince Albert—an insult to either—gray striped trousers, and high-top boots. In later years "Lucky" moved a few notches higher in the standard of his attire and donned the conventional high silk hat and regulation frock coat.

The Newmarks priced Santa Anita at $200,000. Baldwin made up his mind at once to buy the property; but thinking he could beat the price down by "making money talk," accompanied by his attorney, Reuben H. Lloyd of San Francisco, Baldwin marched into Newmark's store and after a little bargaining opened a satchel he carried, in which Mr. Newmark always averred there were millions of dollars in currency.

Baldwin counted out $150,000 and slammed it down on the desk, saying to Newmark, "I will give you this for your ranch, and not a damned cent more." The offer was refused, and Baldwin in a huff started with his attorney down the long storeroom to the front door. Before they had reached the street, Lloyd, the attorney, remonstrated with Baldwin, cautioning him, insomuch as he really wanted the place, he had better trade at once, or the price would be raised. Whereupon Baldwin rightabout-faced, reopened negotiations, and made a deposit of $12,500 to bind the trade at $200,000—a profit on Father's advice to the Newmarks of $115,000 in less than four years.

Baldwin took charge of Santa Anita at once, planted extensive acreage to oranges and vines, built a large winery and distillery, and later made fine wines and brandy from his own grapes.

The winter of 1875-1876 was one of the recurrent very dry ones experienced in early California days within each decade. With no irrigation for crop production, the sole dependence for feed for the immense herds of stock was the native grass on the hills and plains, renewed each season by the winter rains, and during these droughts with positively no grass whatsoever the death loss was tremendous, amounting almost to extermination. The private bankers Temple and Workman were big stockmen themselves, counting their flocks of sheep, herds of cattle, and bands of horses by thousands. The stock business was the backbone of the country; the clients of these bankers were mostly ranch owners, whose sustenance was derived alone from their sales of stock, in the absence of which they were unable to meet their financial obligations.

Security in the way of chattel mortgages was rarely asked; moreover, in a case of this character it would be valueless. The death loss suffered by Temple and Workman themselves was in itself ruinous, to say nothing of their easy-going friendly methods of allowing their hearts rather than their heads to dictate their business policy. Disaster was inevitable and overtook them in the last days of 1875, and they were forced to close their bank.

Temple and Workman negotiated a loan of $225,000 from Baldwin, with interest at 1¼% per month compounded monthly—offering as security a mortgage on Workman's 40,000-acre ranch at La Puente and the Temple Block in Los Angeles. This immense amount of security was not enough for Baldwin, and Juan Matías Sánchez, a princely old don, to accommodate his friend "Templito" (F. P. F. Temple) purely as a matter of kindness, with no other consideration than affection and faith, included his three properties—La Merced, Potrero Grande, and Felipe Lugo—comprising 12,000 acres, in the mortgage.

Temple and Workman reopened early in 1876 but failed again within the twelve months. Failure to realize on their assets, lax methods, and extravagance were their undoing. Baldwin did not foreclose until just before the statute of limitations would run against him, by which time the mortgage, interest, taxes, and legal expenses amounted to $500,000. This regal domain of 52,000 acres then passed into the ownership of "Lucky" Baldwin; and F. P. F. Temple, his father-in-law, William Workman, and their confiding friend, Juan Matías Sánchez, were left homeless and penniless. All of them maintained large households, with armies of people living upon them. The shock and loss was so severe in their advancing years that they weathered the calamity but a short time before passing—in almost squalor—to the Great Beyond.

This very act of Juan Matías Sánchez is truthfully typical of the friendship and the manner of doing things between the early settlers in this wonderful country, where the good Lord had bestowed so much upon them that they considered the supply limitless.

It is likewise a fair sample of the childlike faith, wonderful generosity, and self-imposed jeopardy of the native Californians, and one can readily realize their certain destruction at the hands of unscrupulous schemers, of which there were many.

Oil was struck on all of these different properties; thousands of derricks with wells of great production still adorn them; and Baldwin's heirs and others who purchased some of the land from Baldwin have received millions of dollars from royalties or their own production.

Shortly after purchasing Santa Anita, Baldwin went into the running-horse business. He sent East and purchased the stallions Rutherford, a golden sorrel, and Grindstead, a solid brown. Both of these stallions were of the choicest strains of breeding, and tried and true great race horses. At the same time he purchased a number of two-year-old fillies, among them Clara D. and Jennie B., both great race mares, the former by Glenelg out of The Nun, a sister of the mighty Lexington. The offspring of these mares immortalized their dams with their racing triumphs. Later Baldwin bought, along with others, a gray mare, which he sentimentally named Ophir. She did not amount to much as a race mare but covered herself with glory in later years by producing an American Derby winner. Baldwin also brought to California Lexingtor, said to be the last son of Lexington. If he was, his looks belied him, as he looked more like a small-grade draft horse than a thoroughbred.

Baldwin had as his mentor Luther Martin, an admittedly astute horseman, judging by the wisdom of his selections, as, from the nucleus with which he started Baldwin in business, a family of horses grew, who for their numbers have never been equaled in any man's land.

## *Near Catastrophe - State Fair - Stern and Rose*

I

BY THIS TIME, 1876, there had been two additions to the Rose family, Maud Amanda, who was born in 1873, and Mabel Rose, the tenth of Mother's babies, who was born in the spring of this year. With these young recruits, the children of the household numbered eight, and the cramped, plain old house constructed in 1862 was remodeled and enlarged; and, although not pretentious in scope, it was transformed into a commodious, comfortable, and very attractive country home. Its broad expanse of piazza and glass doors reaching the floor, giving it a bright and cordial appearance, fitted it perfectly into the serenity of nature's unadorned beautiful landscape.

With scores of laborers of all denominations coming and going by the house, strange peons traveling through the country by day and by night, and streams of visitors passing through the grounds daily, the doors of the house at Sunny Slope were never locked, not even in the 60's, when the country was in a truly primitive state. Cordiality and trust were the dominant characteristics of Californians, and on many occasions friends from San Francisco, finding the family away, entered the house and refreshed and rested themselves.

In August of this year my brother and I were sent away to boarding school at Benicia. It was an Episcopal military academy, operated by the Reverend J. H. D. Wingfield. The military discipline under Major Hackett was of the best, and the scholastic attainments qualified one for the University of California. There was no railroad open to San Francisco at this time, so we took the steamer Mohonga from a new 4,600-foot wharf recently constructed by the Southern Pacific near Santa Monica, called Port Los Angeles. We had never been so far from home before, nor had we ever seen a steamer, and I'm free to state we were a couple of very green young men from the country. Though San Francisco was the destination, and, with the Mohonga's lack of speed and the numerous stops she was to make, it would take the greater part of three days to reach there, I was no sooner than aboard when I commenced to worry for fear I would be carried by San Francisco, where to, I had not yet figured.

We had supper and were soon on our way. Our first stop would be Santa Barbara; we retired and were sleeping soundly when a blast of the whistle awoke us. Hurriedly dressing, we went on deck and I was greatly relieved to learn we had not yet gone by San Francisco.

We remained in San Francisco a few days—this was at the period when Denis Kearney, the agitator, and the sand-lot hoodlums were holding sway. They were a very tough gang, and holdups and beatings were of very common occurrence in almost any locality of the city. We stopped with a McGregor family on Eighth below Mission. We got off a car, corner Market and Eighth, and there was a long high pavilion on the corner. I won't undertake to say how long it was but will say it seemed miles in the darkness, as we walked along the side of it down to Mission Street, with visions of the sand lotters garroting us any minute.

Brother and I soon branched out as financiers; signs were displayed in many show windows offering $21.20 in silver for $20 in gold. Each, having in addition to a few dollars in change three $20 gold pieces for our semester's spending money, took the bait like trout; suckers would have known better. The weight of the silver nearly pulled our clothes off before we got back to our lodgings, and then we had this bulk of coin on our hands to carry with us to boarding school to hoard there for months as weekly spending money. We were not, however, going to part with that $3.60 premium we had each made, so we went through with our financial coup.

The Palace Hotel, built by Mr. William Ralston, one of San Francisco's leading citizens, a gentleman of great wealth and ability, had been completed the year before. Mr. Ralston had an estate down the peninsula at Belmont and drove back and forth daily to the city about thirty miles with his coach and four fast trotters, horses that could trot in 2:30, changing teams midway at another of his places. A lavish entertainer, no crowned head did things in better taste or more grandeur. Mr. Ralston had as his guests such notables as Adelina Patti, Christine Nielson, Booth, Barrett, Jefferson, and scores of others. Mr. Ralston was one of the really big men of California, an indefatigable worker when at work and a cheerful player while at play. He was interested in many gigantic projects and had barely finished building the Palace Hotel in 1875 when San Francisco's leading banking house, The Bank of California, of which he was president, failed. This public calamity heavily weighed upon Mr. Ralston, who was a very high-strung gentleman. The assumption was that he sought surcease from his worldly sorrows in a watery grave. At all events, the great man drowned while taking his regular afternoon swim at North Beach in San Francisco Bay, and the whole West was stunned and mournful.

The Palace Hotel building was a remarkable structure, wholly of lumber, six stories in height, covering an entire block. The main entrance was on New Montgomery Street, where all vehicles, including tallyhos, drove in to a circular drive around an immense palm tree in the center of a rectangular court extending to the roof in uniform design.

On each floor there was a promenade ten feet in width, supported by large round pillars and bordered by a heavy banister, surmounted by a panel of plate glass to the height of six feet, as a matter of safety and yet not destroying visibility. There were numberless, opaque, white, clustered, round globes for gas burners, the only lighting system in those days. The rooms were enormous, with ceilings twelve feet in height. Though the architecture was purely on straight lines and severely plain, the general effect in its massiveness was wonderfully attractive, particularly at night, when illuminated.

The court was roofed-in with glass and was so high and ample that one had the feeling of being out-of-doors when seated there, enjoying the reflected rays of the sun. The Palace was opened by Warren Leland of the famous Leland Brothers, hotel men of New York City, Albany, Saratoga, Springfield (Illinois), and elsewhere.

In those days, purveyors to man's thirst were men of some quality, were respected and fraternized with in their spheres. One of these was Ned Fay, head barkeeper at the Palace Hotel, a square gambler, champion live-bird shot, good horseman, well liked by everyone, and no story of San Francisco's early life would be complete without mention of his name.

At that period because of the river of gold flowing there from the Comstock Lode in Virginia City, Nevada, San Francisco, though not a fifth the size of New York City, was fully as well known and equally metropolitan. No city boasted of so many high-class restaurants, all under French management. The Poodle Dog and Marchand's were famous from Paris to Yokohama, and the Palace Hotel was second to none in America. The best theatrical troops and opera stars came to San Francisco, and no notable that crossed the Atlantic felt that he had seen America until he saw the Golden Gate.

On the third or fourth day after our arrival in San Francisco, Brother and I took an ancient stern paddle-wheel river boat running to Sacramento which stopped en route at Benicia, forty miles up the bay, where we arrived at eight in the evening and were soon installed in our dormitory at St. Augustine's. Benicia, located on the straits of Carquinez, was the second capital of California.[26] It was here that later the largest ferry boat in the world conveyed in a single trip three or four loaded passenger trains across to Port Costa, en route to San Francisco.

[26] During the American period Benicia was California's fourth capital; San Jose, Vallejo, Sacramento, Benicia, and Sacramento were the capitals in the order named.

There was a United States Army arsenal at Benicia and three boarding schools for young ladies, St. Mary's, under the same management as the military academy we attended, Snell's Academy, and a Catholic convent. We enjoyed a very pleasant social life at occasional functions, which the young ladies of St. Mary's were allowed to attend. There was one young lady residing in Benicia with her family, to omit whose name from anything glorious or beautiful that could be spoken or written of California's wondrous early days would be unforgivable.

Miss Minnie Mizner—at once the sweetheart and sister of practically every cadet in St. Augustine's—was the daughter of a distinguished politician and attorney doing business in San Francisco, and her mother was one of the most charming of women. There were five boys in the Mizner family, two of whom were our schoolmates at St. Augustine's. One of the two younger ones was Wilson Mizner, the well-known author, actor, and *bon vivant* of New York City.

At the end of the semester Brother and I returned to Sunny Slope for our Christmas vacation. On this occasion we traveled on the Southern Pacific railroad, which had reached Los Angeles a few months earlier, September 1876. During the last days of our vacation a near calamity befell us which all but wrecked the Rose family.

The day before our intended departure for Benicia, a man peddling live quail drove up to the house. Mother, desiring some quail for the table and a brace or two particularly for a lunch she was going to prepare for our trip, purchased a number. My younger brother, Guy, about nine years old, conceived the idea that he would like to keep the live birds as pets and bargained with Mother that Harry and I would go out that afternoon and bring in two dozen dead birds in exchange for the live ones. Shortly after our noonday meal, Harry and I started, each carrying a gun. Guy went along just for the sport. The day was warm, and we stopped and lay down in the shade of a large oak at the Rancheria. Whilst we were lying there dozing, Guy, who had not yet been allowed to shoot, had been busying himself practicing putting in and ejecting cartridges from Harry's Remington. Childlike, the poor little fellow forgot and left the gun loaded. After our siesta, when the air was a little cooler, we started for the hunting ground. Not dreaming it was loaded, Harry handled his gun carelessly, and it was discharged, striking dear little Guy in the face. By the grace of the good Lord, the charge of bird shot struck him at an angle just missing his mouth on the left side, tearing away all the flesh from his chin to the upper part of his lower jaw. He was not over ten feet distant, and the charge of shot had not scattered. Horrors of horrors, as he fell I rushed to him and almost got my hand in his mouth, when I in my frenzy clasped it over the wound. It was more than a quarter of a mile to our house. How we got the little fellow there without his bleeding to death I cannot imagine. I cringe this moment when I realize the shock it must have been to our dear mother. There were no pets in the family, but this lad was of different temperament from Harry and me. Of a studious nature, very fond of books, knowing nothing of nor caring for horses, he kept in close contact with my father in the evenings, who was also a great reader. Whereas with Harry and myself it was just the other way around. Guy was such a sweet, retiring little chap that it really made it seem much worse happening to him. Flour was used in staunching the flow of blood. Dr. Steinway, twelve miles away in Los Angeles, was the leading physician and surgeon in the county. A man was dispatched on horseback to call him.

There was a young doctor from the East who had recently located with his mother in San Gabriel about two miles away. He soon was on the scene and did the necessary things pending the arrival of Dr. Steinway. The young doctor may have been quite a medico, but his appearance, which was more that of a piano tuner, did not inspire much confidence in us when the case was turned over to him by Dr. Steinway. After the wound had been properly dressed (the wound, though too gaping to permit of stitching, was clean cut), there was nothing to do but apply suitable, soothing, and antiseptic preparations. No bones were broken or teeth destroyed, though later a little bone did slough off from the lower part of the chin.

Dr. Lathrop came daily to remove the bandage and dress the wound, pronouncing the progress satisfactory. After a few days, Guy became quite restless and complained of great pain. Father, realizing that even slight pressure from a bandage on a wound frequently caused it to throb and ache, decided to give fresh air under proper sanitary safeguards a chance, removed the bandage, and painted the wound freely with crude petroleum, just as it came from the well, laying a soft piece of gauze over the wound to keep the dust and flies away. The child was at once more comfortable, and Dr. Lathrop's services dispensed with.

The daily applications of crude oil stimulated the growth of new flesh, and in the course of six or eight weeks the wound had healed, leaving a deep line scar from the base of the jaw down to the chin, the left half of the flesh of which had never grown, leaving a bad depression about the size of a silver dollar.

It was a providential recovery; Guy's health was in no way impaired, and he was manly enough not to be sensitive about the scar, which in manhood was entirely hidden by a full beard. You may have wondered why the use of the crude petroleum. In our extensive horse rearing, there were frequent cases of lameness from both bruises and open cuts, and the only remedy we ever used was crude petroleum; a light coating of it daily would cause a speedy closing of an open cut and restore the hair. In an inflamed condition of a tendon or a bruise or an enlargement from a kick or other causes, by rubbing the oil in lightly a slight blister would be produced, similar to but not so severe as by the use of cantharides, and in virulent cases of distemper its use was very efficacious in producing suppuration of swollen parts. Moreover, we had frequently—and in all cases of sore throats in the family—applied it to the affected parts with a fine brush or swab. Why should it not have been possessed of curative virtues (though we were unaware of the fact at that time) as the base of Vaseline, Listerine, Creolin, and a dozen or more medicinal by-products?

While lying prone on his back, Guy developed artistic tendencies; he began to sketch and to use a small box of water colors. When up again and about and ready for school, the die for his future had been cast; his mind centered entirely on painting. His early literary schooling was had at San Gabriel and Los Angeles. When the time arrived for him to study in art, he went to San Francisco, where he remained until 1888, studying under the very eminent masters, Virgil Williams and Emil Carlsen. His sincerest thanks always went to Carlsen in spite of the fact that he spent three years in the Julian in Paris under such famous painters as Doucet, Constant, and Lefebvre.

The rating of the upper classes at St. Augustine's was the same as that of high schools, and, when I returned there after the summer vacation in August 1877, I entered upon my senior year—my brother Harry was one grade lower. There were seven in my class, to wit: Harry Reed of Chico; Frank Carolan and Julian McAllister of San Francisco; Fred Autenreith of Yreka; Isaac Fleischner of Portland, Oregon; Henry Durner, a frail, physically imperfect from birth, day scholar residing in Benicia; and myself.

Reed was the nephew of General Bidwell of Bidwell's Bar fame, who owned immense pear, prune, and almond orchards near Chico, a very progressive and influential personage, closely identified with California early history. We are indebted to the general for the introduction into this country of the delightful casaba melon. Carolan was the son of James Carolan, of the pioneer firm of Carolan, Cory and Company, competitive and contemporaneous hardware merchants in Sacramento, with Huntington and Hopkins and Stanford and Crocker, before they became the multimillionaire "Big Four" of the Central Pacific Railroad. Young Carolan later married Miss Pullman, daughter of the sleeping-car magnate, and built a beautiful home in Burlingame. McAllister was the son of Hall McAllister, a famous lawyer during San Francisco's halcyon days. Autenreith, when last I heard of him, was conductor on a passenger train in Siskiyou County. Fleischner at last accounts was a partner in the large wholesale house of Fleischner, Mayer & Company, of Portland, Oregon. And poor little Henry Durner, who graduated at the head of our class, succumbed to his physical infirmities shortly after graduating. St. Augustine was patronized by sons of some of the real "Gringo Grandees."

The Reavis boys, James and William, were the sons of D. M. Reavis of Chico, who in a single year sowed and harvested 90,000 acres of wheat. Henry Miller, named for his father, was the son of the Miller of Miller and Lux, cattle barons of the West, who owned 14,000,000 acres of range fully stocked with cattle, situated in California, Nevada, Utah, Oregon, Montana, and Wyoming, and could ride on horseback, or in a horse-drawn vehicle, from California to Montana and sleep each night in one of their own ranch houses. The Glenn boys, Charley and Frank, were sons of Doctor Glenn, the creator of Glenn County, California, who owned the greater portion of it, which he devoted to wheat raising. Harvesting a big crop one season, Doctor Glenn shipped the grain to San Francisco on barges to be loaded on vessels for the Atlantic ports. Finding a combination of freight rates existing against him, the doctor bought a fleet of steamers and moved the grain himself. The boys, Charley and Frank, were truly wild "Injuns," and in their later life, when visiting even the metropolitan city of Sacramento, the news would soon be heralded that "the Glenn Boys are in town."

The home ranch of the Glenns was near the small settlement of San Jacinto; their trading was done at Willows, a fair-sized town, and Willows was also the scene of their local parties. At a dance there one night, when the party broke up with the early morning well on its way to daybreak, the Glenn brothers extended an invitation to all to drive out to San Jacinto ten miles away to a ham-and-egg breakfast in the commodious ranch cookhouse, and many accepted. The country was all open with unfenced roads along section lines considerable distances apart. Country road construction was an easy matter there by plowing a strip of ground and smoothing it down; then the first good rain that fell would make it firm and up to the general standard of roads. These wretches, conceiving this devilishness in advance, had made some new roads and by cutting off some corners created a veritable maze. The guests were started off in the van and soon were away out in the great wheat fields on the mixed-up roads, driving around in circles until daybreak and but little nearer San Jacinto than when leaving Willows, where the hosts had remained awaiting developments.

## II

During the winter of 1876-1877, Senator Leland Stanford started a trotting-horse breeding farm at famous Palo Alto, purchasing to head it the Hambletonian stallion Electioneer, who beyond doubt was the greatest progenitor of trotting-horse speed during the score of years which he lived.

Senator Stanford bought at the same time the stallions General Benton and Piedmont; they were of secondary importance as speed producers but rendered valuable support through their daughters as matrons to the embrace of Electioneer. Electioneer's dam, Green Mountain Maid, was of the fainthearted Clay tribe, as a means of fortifying which the senator espoused a thoroughbred dam theory and purchased many high-class running mares in this country, and also imported from England mares of their finest strains, regardless of cost. The best of California running stallions were crossed on trotting dams also in the production of matrons for the mighty Electioneer, and the wisdom of the expenditure in expounding the theory gloriously manifested in later years. The senator was an ardent devotee of road driving in his earlier life and owned fast roadsters, one of which, Occident, a California-bred gelding, created a great sensation when he took a record of 2:19½, a spectacular performance for a California-bred trotter at the time. The senator was not only a horse lover, but also a student of the co-ordination of their anatomy and action. In furtherance of his desire in this research, Senator Stanford promoted at great expense the first demonstration of what was then known as instantaneous photography and now known as motion pictures. Photographs of horses in action were made by an Englishman named Muybridge along about 1880, at which date I had the pleasure of seeing the pictures. There was no continuity of motion shown, simply single, different poses, caught during the transitory trotting action, which were unbelievable in appearance. At times the animal seemed to have thrown a foot away or to be striking the ground stiff-legged, and in no instance was there any pronounced degree of curvature shown in their motion. Senator Stanford's hobby was the earliest possible development of the trotting gait; to promote this an original and novel method was introduced. An eighth-of-a-mile ring was constructed enclosed by a high board fence with a three-foot rail on the inner side. When the foals were only a few months old, they were brought with their dams from the field and one at a time taken from their mothers and turned loose on the miniature race track, in the center of the oval of which a groom was stationed. The first impulse of the young things was to start on a gallop around the ring, in which instance the groom shouted "whoa!" to them until they sobered down somewhat and struck a trot, whereupon the attendant urged them onward by clucking. It required but a few lessons for the little babies to understand what was expected of them, and they bounded around the circuit like old trotters, with apparent relish. The lessons were of short duration and repeated every second or third day. That the theory was a sound one was yearly demonstrated, as at one time Senator Stanford held every world's colt record and all older records, except that of a stallion, in which his animal failed by but a quarter of a second.

To our great delight Father gave my brother and me permission to go to the State Fair at Sacramento. This was in September 1877. We got a week's leave of absence and took the Sacramento River stern-wheel boat, Stephen M. Whipple, leaving Benicia at eight o'clock Saturday evening and due to arrive at Sacramento at six or seven Sunday morning. The boat had a steam calliope, with which she livened things up occasionally. She was loaded to the guards, and we were of course unable to secure any sleeping accommodations. Many persons in different stages of inebriety were stretched all over the floor, positively all the chairs were occupied, and many of us stood on our feet the entire night. There was a bar on board, faro and poker games were in full blast, and confidence men were quietly at work on the more unsophisticated, and an occasional fight stirred things up. Along about three o'clock the boat stopped with a thud, and we found we were stuck on a sand bar. At this season of the year all California streams are at their lowest ebb. The snows of the Sierras have long since melted, and the winter rains do not commence until a couple of months later. These sand bars were a continual menace, and being stuck on one was no uncommon occurrence. Because of the shallowness of the water the entire width of the stream, it took us some time to wiggle ourselves loose; in fact, we about churned ourselves out with our old stern paddle wheel. We got into Sacramento along about noon, went to a French restaurant known as the Arcade, where Father had secured rooms, got ourselves freshened up presentably, had a mighty good breakfast of nice cold cantaloupe, fried chicken with Long Branch potatoes, sliced tomatoes, and some good red wine—mighty fine in contrast to the mutton stew, applesauce, and warmed-over fried potatoes of our mess at school. We were not as verdant as we were a year ago, but this was "big league stuff" to us.

It was a very warm day and Father was resting in dishabille in his room. Mr. Killip of the pool-selling firm of Killip & Co. came in and handed him a statement and $11,400 that he had won on Beautiful Bells and other horses the week before at Chico.

All betting in California at that time was by auction pools. The firm of Killip & Co., composed of J. N. Killip and Sam Whitehead, did practically all of the pool selling in the state, as there was no conflict of dates, and they had a fine organization and were both men of sterling character. Well-known persons who wagered large sums did business on a credit basis and settled at the conclusion of each meeting.

At this period fairs with racing of a week's duration were held at San Francisco, Oakland, Marysville, Chico, Sacramento, Stockton, San Jose, and Los Angeles. The one at Sacramento, the State Fair, was a gala event, and everyone interested in racing and many distinguished people from San Diego to Del Norte County made it a point to attend.

The racing was of the very best. Many did not start their horses prior to the State Fair, in the meantime getting a line on those of others starting at the preceding meetings, keeping their own animals under cover as much as possible for a killing. Those that had been racing also covered up as much of their horses' speed as they could without running afoul of some judge's ire, with the idea also in mind of making a clean-up at Sacramento. Many bitter contests were waged; many "good things" went wrong with corresponding monetary losses and disappointments.

Father, who was as well known as any man in California at that time, was a member of the State Board of Agriculture. Everyone liked him, and Brother and I naturally shone a little from the luster of his popularity and came in for a full measure of attention. We had the entree for the sumptuous luncheon in the director's room at the track. The pavilion in the center of the city was a brilliant affair—by far the most magnificent I had ever seen.

We met many of the prominent men of California, with whom I enjoyed splendid friendships throughout their lifetimes. Havey was there, with Beautiful Bells, Sultan, and a few young colts. Bells had won two races, one at Marysville and one at Chico, and had lost two, one each at Oakland and San Francisco. At Sacramento she won the best race of her career from a time standpoint, taking a record of 2:29½, thereby entering the then charmed 2:30 circle. It took seven heats to decide the race. If it accomplished nothing else, the contest demonstrated her indomitable gameness. The exhibition was far from satisfactory; the same old story of her flightiness and breaking, then fairly flying to avoid being distanced, trotting the last half mile on three occasions in 1:08, and it was only this terrific flight of speed that enabled her ever to win a heat. The race she won at Marysville was also a seven-heat affair; the one at Chico was five.

From Sacramento, Bells went to Stockton, where she won a five-heat race, and another of the same length at San Jose the following week, giving her five victories in seven starts. One morning at Oakland after Bells's defeat, there in an endeavor to teach her to negotiate the first turn without breaking, Havey scored her one hundred times. Of course the scores were not at full speed, but in the neighborhood of forty miles was covered by them with almost negative results. The mare was in no way distressed, ate her food contentedly, did not tuck up at all in her body, and her legs without the use of bandages were as cool as cucumbers the next morning.

Father was naturally disgusted with the shattering of his idol; he appreciated her great individuality and blood lines, but, as it was his plan to place his dependence in the paternal line and use only his own stallions, Bells's close kinship precluded her use as a matron at Sunny Slope. A gentleman sought to purchase her, and, having her dam and three of her young sisters, Father reluctantly decided to part with her and traded her for mining stock valued at $10,000, which, however, proved absolutely worthless.

At this time, the running horse was rapidly coming into his own in the northern part of California. Mr. Theodore Winters, who brought from Kentucky Lexington's mighty son Norfolk, because of lack of competition for them, worked Flood and Connors, two of Norfolk's magnificent sons, with their colors up one afternoon at this fair. The great Molly McCarthy, by Monday, also raised by Winters, was just attaining her greatness, and from thence forward Winters soared to the loftiest height as a breeder of thoroughbreds. Mr. Pritchard, of Sacramento, also had some good horses by his stallion Leinster at the same meeting. There were many others of lesser note who had good horses that later attained turf prominence.

## III

In the late fall of this same year, the lamentable tidings of the death of Father's partner, Mr. Samuel C. Perkins, of Boston, was flashed over the wire. Mr. Perkins, a gentleman of high attainments socially and intellectually, in the very prime of life, liberally surrounded by the Lord's blessings, had but recently attained the coveted honor of being elected alderman of Boston. The California wine business in New England had thrived handsomely under his management.

Father was greatly distressed by Mr. Perkins' untimely taking away; the two years of his partnership with Perkins and Stern had been the first period of relaxation Father had enjoyed since leaving Van Buren County, Iowa, with his elaborate covered-wagon outfit in 1858. The arduous task of wine making had been stricken from the roster of his numerous daytime duties, and the tedious rote of accounting and correspondence spared him during the hours of his evening reveries, thus enabling him to give freely of his time to his hobby, horse breeding.

Every afternoon after his siesta he spent a couple of hours strolling among the horses in the large wooded pastures, communing with lovely nature, wandering about formulating new breeding crosses, until each one of the widely scattered hundred or more animals had been personally inspected. In the evening twilight hours after supper, Father invariably spent an hour or two seated in the open at the barn, talking horse, an inexhaustible subject, with the trainer and grooms.

Though the death of Mr. Perkins or naught else within the range of human possibilities would be allowed to interfere seriously with the horse business, the absorbtion of his interest in the firm became at once a momentous financial problem.

A few months later, May 29, 1878, I graduated from St. Augustine's College, with no other honor than that of being the youngest cadet ever to have graduated at that institution. I was just a few days under sixteen; the other members of my class were twenty or twenty-one. Father had always intended that I should study law and had calculated on my continuing my studies at the University of California at the conclusion of the summer vacation.

Mr. Stern and Father had absorbed Mr. Perkins' interest in the business, and the firm was now Stern and Rose, and as an afterthought Father concluded that, insomuch as he had not been in personal touch with his business in the East since entering the firm of Perkins, Stern and Company, it would be of value to him to have my firsthand impressions of the general trend of the firm's business in New York City, Boston, and Chicago. Furthermore, knowing the travel and a year's sojourn in the metropolis actively engaged in business would be education invaluable to me, he decided to send me East and defer my entering college a year.

Father had also taken somewhat into consideration my youthful advancement in my studies with some misgivings as to whether it might not be injurious to my health to continue under the existing status. This, however, was a needless solicitude, as I was in no wise studious, but, having the faculty of grasping things quickly and blessed with a very retentive memory, study was never a hardship.

My brother and I arrived at Sunny Slope from Benicia a few days after my graduation. We had a number of camping, hunting, and fishing trips, and were fooling around breaking some two-year-old colts Father had given us. I was scheduled to leave for New York August 28, 1878. On the 27th I was helping Harry break his colt Reveille to harness, and he was doing the driving. We had the colt hitched to a long-shafted breaking cart, and it got out of hand, ran over the top of a large pile of manure, in coming off of which we were upset, and I landed on my ribs on the edge of a long watering trough. I was well shaken and my side pained me, but, as my mind was set on my eastward departure the next day, I made no complaint, fearing that I might be the means of delaying my leaving.

I was on my way the next day. At that time one had to go by way of Sacramento, and it took seven days to reach New York. The weather was intensely hot, and I suffered a great deal of pain from my side; an examination upon my arrival in New York revealed that one of my ribs had been fractured. Mr. Stern called an old German doctor, who doped me freely within and without, but with my physical ailment, the great unaccustomed heat, and some homesickness I was truly miserable.

The Stern family lived in Hoboken and were of the Jewish faith. Mr. Stern was a phlegmatic German, and Mrs. Stern, of French birth, his direct antipode in temperament, full and overflowing with the vivacity and *élan* of her nationality. She was about the best and busiest little body one ever met, and, although the mother of seven bedlamite youngsters, ranging in age from fifteen to two years, Mrs. Stern was still attractive in appearance to a degree that bespoke rare beauty in her maidenhood.

In their kind solicitude the Sterns decreed that I should live in Hoboken and had secured me a large back room in the regulation twenty-five-foot front four-story brick structure boardinghouse, and I carried my modest luncheon across the Hudson each morning.

Thunderstorms were unknown in California, and it was while domiciled in my Hoboken quarters that I experienced my first electrical storm, and, perfectly satisfied that my end had come, almost suffocated myself by closing all windows, shutters, and curtains and drawing the shades.

With becoming modesty, I do not hesitate to state that both Mr. and Mrs. Stern were very fond of me, and the dear little woman in sweet solicitude appointed herself my guardian on shopping expeditions. In her foreign way of doing things, Mrs. Stern constantly embarrassed me in her manner of bargaining with tradespeople in my behalf. I started out in life with the fool notion which has stuck to me throughout my career and been the greatest factor in keeping me from owning half of California of buying first and inquiring the price afterwards.

Stern and Rose had a fine large basement and subcellar at 14 and 16 Vesey Street, New York, directly opposite the cemetery, back of the church on the corner of Broadway and Vesey Street. There was a fine glassed-in office. Mr. Stern gave me charge of the books, and as I got my bearings I became the general utility man, made the bank deposits, went for bills of lading, and did some collecting. The original Astor House of New York stood on the Broadway corner of the same block in which our place of business was located, and its large high-ceiled, gorgeously decorated rotunda, famous for its luncheons, was the noon-hour rendezvous of the elite from Wall Street and adjacent business districts. One glance at this sumptuous spread of edibles weaned me from my cold Hoboken sandwich, and I cautiously felt my way among the spectacular throng.

Gradually the verdancy of my boasted native grasses of California faded from my manner, and I edged myself from under the protecting care of my good friends the Sterns. I moved to the metropolis and took quarters in a fashionable boardinghouse, kept by Mrs. Perry, at 16 East 23rd Street, Madison Square. Here I became acquainted with many nice people, among them some Columbia law students, one of whom, Robert Gilbert, whose family founded Gilbertsville, New York, was my dearest friend. His brother, James Blackman Gilbert, was at the time an understudy in the office of Doctor Gurnsey at 10 West 23rd Street, then the "Grand Daddy" of the homeopathists of the country.

Mr. Stern had his racial characteristic of saving—a trait of which I had not given any evidence—and I am sure that when my father turned me over to him the uppermost thought in his mind was that I would be taught the value of money. His instructions to Mr. Stern were: "Let Leon have what money he needs." Candidly, I thought this would anchor me along about $25 per week at the utmost. Board and lodging at that time were very reasonable. I had a hall room on the fourth floor facing directly up Madison Avenue, with excellent table, for $12.50 per week. When in need of pocket money I would ask for five or ten dollars as the occasion demanded. Mr. Stern would give it to me, and I would charge it to myself against Father's account. This occurred two or three times a week, and one day Mr. Stern, who had dropped the "n" off from my name, said in answer to my request for money: "When you want money, Leo, take it out of the cash drawer, put a tag in for it, and at the end of the week we will charge it to Father's account."

The circle of my friendships, all with fine young men five to ten years my senior—possessed of *savior-faire*—expanded readily, and through them lady friends were met, and a dress suit, my first, was at once indispensable. I went to the best shows, learned to play a cracking good game of billiards, sat in poker games with the Columbia College young men, and fortified with my barnyard-acquired knowledge of the game, from sharper gambling heads than theirs, was perfectly able to take care of myself.

I hobnobbed with the trade, frequently took one of them to lunch, occasionally splitting a bottle of Cliquot, created a good impression, and made new customers. Although all of these accomplishments were not essential to the business, they fitted nicely in the day's doings, and I availed myself of the propitious occasion and drew money freely. In candor, I must admit a strong feeling of transgression with serious forebodings for the day of reckoning; these, however, I gladly cajoled myself into dispelling under the subterfuge that frugal Mr. Stern allowed it.

Even in this premise I was taking an unfair advantage, for, as a matter of fact, I can say with positively no egotism my mentor had grown positively so weak in his admiration of my youthful ability that I believed he could not bear to correct me. Whether this deduction or the fact that I had been generally helpful and somewhat of a factor in developing trade caused him to allow me to use money so freely was never discussed, and the practice continued during my stay in New York. Be all this as it may, after the fireworks my Father set off when he heard of the matter, I had no desire to ever again open up the subject.

I had the pleasure of a very friendly acquaintance with Reverend Henry Ward Beecher, who had previously visited Sunny Slope and came regularly to the store every fortnight and ordered a gallon of port wine for sacramental purposes. The jovial friendly Reverend enjoyed my stories of California and would sit and chat with me for fifteen or twenty minutes, sipping a small glass of wine betimes. I also knew Professor Felix Adler, who on one of his trips to California had lunched at our house, and the acquaintance was renewed in New York.

As positive evidence of my high standing with Mr. Stern, I offer the fact that for the first time in his business career he was going to take a vacation of a month and make a trip to California and leave me in absolute charge of the business. After Christmas he left, and I ran the business without a hitch until his return.

On April 1, 1879, about four o'clock in the morning an alarm of fire was sounded in our boardinghouse, and from the amount of smoke issuing up the stairway I decided it was no place for me, so I, boylike, rushed down and out into the street with little but my sleeping clothes on me—with no shoes on my feet. It was a rather cold squally morning, and though it took but a few minutes to control the fire in some trash, I got chilled and took a severe cold, unlike any other I had ever had; it settled on my lungs, and I could not shake it off. My good young doctor friend, Jim Gilbert, advised Mr. Stern to send me south to a warmer climate. I had made several trips to Boston on business and had availed myself of the opportunity to become acquainted with the Monks family, wealthy people who lived on Chester Square. It was one of the sons of this household, Henry, who had visited us at Sunny Slope and sold the hill that still bears his name, on which the Raymond Hotel in Pasadena was later built. His brother George, about ten years older than I, was contemplating a southern trip, and, when he came on to New York, I joined him and we sailed on the steamer Isaac Bell for Virginia, where we put in two delightful weeks between Richmond and Norfolk. Unable to shake off my cough, I returned to New York, and my good friend Mr. Stern in his genuine solicitude sent me home to California.

The annual statement was made up July first. Father paid no attention to eastern details, only when the trial balance was taken. He quite naturally inquired of me as to my eastern expenditures, and, when I showed him the statement where I had used $3,300 in a little over eight months, I surely set off a lot of firecrackers. He was as liberal a man as ever lived and spent money extravagantly in various ways. In my case, however, it was a matter of principle, and he was very provoked. As a matter of retribution, the next day I was provided with a pair of $1.10 overalls and a denim jumper and put to work at thirty dollars per month, and work I did. If because of real indisposition I laid off a day, I was docked a dollar and fifteen cents and took a fair-sized lecture as well.

In returning from the East I had come by way of Benicia and witnessed my brother Harry's graduation, and he was put to work along with me. We did everything from rough carpenter work and barrel making to washing bottles.

The new distillery and building for the steam crushers were just being installed. Being small and active, it fell to me to crawl in all the manholes and under everything that needed fixing from underneath.

Upon the completion of these units in the summer of 1879, we had the most complete and capacious wine-making establishment in southern California, if not the state. From an insignificant, peon, foot-tramping concern of half a dozen vats surrounding a large oak tree, the business had grown in fifteen years into an imposing cluster of buildings with daily capacity in excess of the original seasonal capacity of five thousand gallons. One of the buildings was a two-story brick, 100 x 150 feet on the ground floor, in which there were tiers of storage casks of 2,500-gallon capacity, thereby insuring a uniform carload of wine. The upper story was used as a storage warehouse for brandy. Another brick building was three stories in height, 75 x 150 feet, the ground floor used for storage room, and the second floor was used as a fermenting room, with large five-thousand-gallon vats placed in double tiers, connected with an overhead sluice box, which received the crushed mass of grapes from the floor above, which was used as a crusher room, to which the grapes were carried by a canvas elevator.

Adjoining this structure was another fermenting room, 100 x 100. This was a wooden building of but one story except for a twenty-five-foot strip running the length of it, which had an additional floor, in order to accommodate another crusher at an altitude from which the crushed product would gravitate into the fermenting vats located on the ground floor. All these fermentation vats were connected by an underground sluice box with the distillery, and, after the juice had been drawn off, the residue or pumice was flushed with water and run down into the stills to be converted into brandy.

The new distillery and boiler room were at the lowest level; in fact, all the structures had been so arranged as to take advantage of the force of gravity. There was a three-chambered wooden still in which the pumice was treated with direct injection of steam; the gases evolved escaped through the upper chamber on out through a copper pipe down through a water-cooled coil. There were two copper stills through which, as a matter of further purification, the product of the wooden still was redistilled or "doubled," as the term is. In this the heat was from a fire beneath the large kettles, and the evolution was from boiling. This product was almost chemically pure, of about one hundred and eighty proof, which means that one gallon of it diluted with pure water would make practically two gallons of good merchantable brandy—cognac, the French call it.

The buildings I have described were all new and had replaced smaller structures. However, there were a number of other large old wooden ones still used for storage of sweet wines, which were rather improved than otherwise by the warmth within the buildings from their exposed position in the sun. These, with a large cooper shop, and the wine makers' cottages, completed the group. The office was in one corner of the brandy warehouse. It was a very large high-ceilinged room, finished in California white pine, with panels of laurel, with a fine sideboard and furniture of like material.

Father had continued to make good his promise to buy all grapes delivered at the winery, and at this time we were using at least 75% of all the grapes raised in Los Angeles County. We were paying $23.50 per ton for them, and some were hauled from Los Angeles twelve miles away. The grapes from our place and from those near by were delivered in 50-lb. boxes, which the driver and helper lifted up on the apron, from which they were fed into the crushers, which were run by steam. From afar the grapes were hauled in bulk and forked up to the apron with large many-tined forks. We crushed 200 tons of grapes per day for thirteen or fourteen weeks and produced 500,000 gallons of wine and 125,000 gallons of brandy annually. The internal revenue tax on that amount of brandy amounted to $112,500. When the vintage started, my brother Harry was apprenticed to Schoelgens, the German wine maker. I was given the job of weighing the grapes.

## 9

# *Distinguished Visitors - Mackay's Generosity - Wine Salesman*

### I

SUNNY SLOPE was now in full flower; the immense thousand-acre vineyard was in bearing, the orange orchard had reached the peak of production, the horse business had finally attained paying proportions, and all nature was lavish with her smiles.

The house was somewhat centrally located, with the winery less than a quarter of a mile in one direction and the barns about a half mile in the opposite. A fine large lawn on two sides, the same confined little stream of clear water that had been running without an instant's cessation for nineteen years rippled merrily over its pebbled bed, within ten feet of the front step. The sapling eucalypti, weeping willow, and pepper trees planted in 1860, now grown to massive size, took turns with the changing orbit of the sun in casting a cooling shadow upon the house.

The half-mile-long avenue leading to the front door with two rows of orange trees on either side was the most attractive feature about Sunny Slope. The trees were pruned high enough to allow a mule to walk under them in cultivating. In irrigating, a basin twelve and a half feet square and about ten inches deep was thrown up with shovels around each tree; the water, carried in an S-shaped ditch, included five trees in each turn of its serpentine journey. Beginning at the lower end, the water was cut into a basin at a time, and so on up the line. In the course of two or three days, after irrigation, just before the land commenced to bake on top, men with single mules and cultivators broke down the basins, and after a couple of times over it the land was left level and as mealy as a flower bed.

Seated on the front porch on a summer's afternoon, fanned by the gentle cool breeze which came up daily about two o'clock from the Pacific thirty-five miles away, one could enjoy a beautiful panorama at a glance—the symmetrically shaped orange trees, their foliage of darkest green thickly jewel-studded with their golden fruit, closely flanked on either side by hundreds of acres of vines standing in a solid mass about four and a half feet in height, with their lightest shade of green feathery-tipped foliage nodding faintly to the breeze. The stream of water coming from the shade into the sunlight at the edge of the roadside on its winding way sparkled like diamonds. Countless birds twittered and flitted about. In the distance eight and ten miles away respectively the gently rolling hills of La Misión Vieja and La Puente stood out in such bold relief in the clear atmosphere they did not appear to be over a third of that distance. The broad level plains in the foreground boasted of but an occasional oak, and there were but two or three habitations in view in the distance to dispute nature's sole possession under California's eternally blue skies.

It was under these glorious happy conditions during vintage time in 1879 that my two older sisters, Nina and Annie, who as tots had passed through the Indian massacre, were given in marriage. Nina, the oldest child of the living number, married John V. Wachtel, teller in the Farmers and Merchants Bank of Los Angeles, and took up her home in that city. Annie, the second daughter, married E. H. Sanderson, who was in the grocery business in Los Angeles, and she also went there to live.

As early as 1870, when all travel reached Los Angeles by water, Sunny Slope had become famous not because of its physical attainments at the time but because of the magnitude of its outline. Travelers from all over the world, reaching Los Angeles, always included in their sight-seeing a trip there, and rarely a day passed than an old-fashioned hack or two, drawn by four horses, did not drive through the place.

In later years, as its glories increased, people came in droves. Conventions came en masse, and as high as two and three hundred visited us in a single day. A trip to Sunny Slope was on the itinerary of eastern excursion companies as one of the sights of southern California, and no notable came to Los Angeles that did not pay homage to her. We had the honor of entertaining celebrities from far and near. I have spoken of Reverend Henry Ward Beecher and Professor Felix Adler of New York. The Honorable Rutherford B. Hayes lunched at Sunny Slope after vacating the White House. Colonel Robert G. Ingersoll was a personal friend. Helen Hunt Jackson graced our portals when she was collecting data for that gem of romance, *Ramona*. Senator Leland Stanford, Colonel Charles Crocker, Mark Hopkins, and Collis P. Huntington, the mighty railroad barons, were close friends of Father's and never failed to call when in Los Angeles. John W. Mackay, Senator Fair, James Flood, and William O'Brien, Croesuses of the Comstock Lode, were likewise friendly and attentive, as were also Senator George Hearst and the never smiling James Ben Ali Haggin.

Sunny Slope was daily host to all Los Angeles, and no one ever came to pay her a visit that was not showered with hospitality. Everyone was given all the wine they cared to drink; they were shown through the winery; and, when reaching the barn, the horses were led out for their inspection. This was all gratis. The crowning delight with many was to pluck an orange from the tree. For this they were charged fifty cents per dozen for really luscious oranges, as an offset to the trouble and expense of a Chinese laborer placing a ladder to enable them to reach the fruit.

Even so, Father's energy was ceaseless; the terrifying toll of passing through an Indian massacre, a score of years of the hardships of the pioneer had left no imprint on his zeal. Although the mortgage on Sunny Slope had now reached the stupendous amount of $90,000, carrying the consuming interest rate of 18%, even this crushing impost weighed lightly on his shoulders, and visions of still further great achievements hovered in his mind.

In the matter of borrowing money, he was fully as persistent as the most profligate, uncalculating old dons, aside from the fact that he was a punctual and cheerful interest payer. Determined in his desires for expansions and betterments, he went ahead regardless of intermediate circumstances. The same results could have been attained in the end by a more moderate course of procedure, but Father's ambition knew no bounds, and his financial obligations, though stressed to the limit all through his life, instead of worrying him, added stimulus to his endeavors.

Walter Maben, the lad who came to work at Sunny Slope with Havey in 1876, was now an active understudy at the barn, under Donathan. Maben's people were of the worthy pioneers; he was a fine boy, and all of the Rose family regarded him with kindred love, and, as he was just between the ages of my brother and myself, he was a fine recruit in our deviltry.

Country dances of the "hoe down" variety were of frequent occurrence in San Gabriel Valley, given usually by some homesteader in a room about sixteen feet square in his rustic home. These affairs, attended by a motley mixture, frequently took place in isolated districts, ten or twenty miles from Sunny Slope, up a canyon or in the dense woods.

Whenever we heard of one of these "shindigs," distance meant nothing to us, though the means of getting there was often a serious obstacle. With a hundred horses or more at Sunny Slope, it was very much the case of a shoemaker's family going barefoot. We were supposed to ask for an animal for night use and were refused many times, under the pretext that all stabled animals had been used that day. The true reason, however, was Father's desire to curb our night escapades.

Public balls were given by Dodson, proprietor of the hotel at El Monte, and incidentally a dance there was not a bit like a Methodist social, and was no place for a fainthearted chap. The "Monte-ites" were the last clan in

Los Angeles County to tame down, and no ball there was a complete success without a vicious fight, and, while I was yet a young lad, I kept a man from killing Donathan by almost decapitating the assailant with a heavy beer mug.

A necktie party, not of the long-rope, short-shrift variety, in which, however, the Monte people were very active participants in the middle 50's, but of a milder nature, was advertised for April 1, 1880. This nomenclature for the occasion arose from the fact that each lady attending made a small bow tie of the material of her dress and sealed it in an envelope. The envelopes were numbered serially, admission was $2.50, and, when a male attendant paid the price, he received an envelope, enclosing a tie. When the envelope was opened, the wearer of a dress of that material was sought out; she adjusted the tie to the buyer's collar and became his partner for the first and last dance of the evening and supper.

We had in our employ as foreman at Sunny Slope at the time James E. Dickey, who incidentally a few years later filed a homestead on 160 acres of then San Bernardino County land, on which Lake Elsinore was located and upon which the town Hot Springs and the resort of that name stand today.[27] Dickey rode a gray saddle mare, belonging to himself, around the ranch during the day, attending to his duties. On this occasion, Walter, Harry, and I were stalled for an animal to use to drive to the party, every driving horse on the ranch being in some way engaged, so it fell to us to slip Dickey's gray mare out of the back door of the large barn. We hitched her to a heavy breaking cart and were on our way to the ball.

All went well; the Monte young ladies were fine dancers, and we schottisched, varsovienned, waltzed, and quadrilled till three in the morning, at which hour the heavens had fairly opened and a torrential rain was falling. We were unprepared for such weather and realized at that season of the year it was but a heavy passing shower. We, therefore, acceded to landlord Dodson's suggestion and went to the hotel parlor to have a few winks of sleep, with the positive assurance that he would awaken us at 4:30. This would enable us to reach the ranch by 5 A.M., before Dickey went for his mare, and he would be none the wiser. Dodson forgot to call us, and when we awoke it was seven o'clock, and the cordial April sun was well above the horizon.

Be assured the half-hour spent in reaching Sunny Slope was a tough one; Dickey had reported the matter to Father as soon as he was out of bed, and, when we reached the barn, Father and Dickey were pacing up and down. No time was lost in calling the convention together, and its business was succinctly stated. Brother Harry sidled away to the winery; Walter took up

[27] This was then San Diego County land, not San Bernardino.

his duties at the barn. Feeling that we were alike guilty, I resented being more severely upbraided than the others and decided not to return to my work. On my way to our sleeping quarters adjoining the office at the winery that evening when passing the house, Mother counseled with me over the matter. I was on hand for breakfast early next morning, and the entente cordiale was restored.

## II

Aside from those of The Moor's get I have mentioned, no colts of unusual importance had been developed. There was an increase in foals yearly, but with a desire to have only the best the less promising ones were disposed of. The young animals were all fine looking, and those of them that were raced were better than the average, won their share of contests, and as road horses they all were fast enough and no road was too long for them.

When The Moor died, his only entire son of sufficient age to do stud duty was Silver Threads, a handsome gray fellow, the son of a half-thoroughbred dam. Silver Threads's success was negligible, his only worthwhile laurels accruing to him through siring Lady Mackay, which we sold to go to Kentucky, where she achieved great renown as a brood mare, as the dam of Oakland Baron, one of the stars of his period. Sultan finally succeeded to the coveted station as lord of the harem, and the first of his get were now yearlings.

On January 1 of this year, 1879, our trainer "Dick" Havey took a position in the northern part of the state, and we hired our former running-horse trainer, Billy Donathan. When Father sold Irene Harding to Charley Thomas in 1872, Donathan, who had trained her, forsook running horses for trotters. Donathan had not had any experience with harness horses previously, and his first essay as a reinsman was with his white-faced runner, Maneater, who at the time was six years old, had never had a harness on him, and had not a drop of trotting-horse blood in his veins.

Donathan kept at the task and fairly hammered the gait into Maneater and got him to trot a mile in 2:40. Later he had another cold-blooded buckskin-colored livery horse, Don Elipha, the property of James Billings and Aaron Smith, livery stablekeepers, that he gave a mark of 2:30.

During the centennial year, a trotting meeting was held at Philadelphia, and our friend L. H. Titus—the first Californian to make an invasion of the East with harness horses—hired Donathan and took Echora, Belle Echo, and Joe Hamilton, all by his sire Echo, across the continent and brilliantly upheld California's prestige by winning with all of them.

Joe Hamilton, of this trio, bred by our old friend Fin Slaughter, was out of Belle Mason, Slaughter's great early-day running mare, and Echora was the animal that so upset Father's sentimental calculations with his waltz music, when she beat Beautiful Bells back in 1875. After this eastern triumph Echora was consigned to the breeding ranks, and to the embrace of Monroe Salisbury's great stallion Director, producing the champion Direct, who paced a mile in 2:05¼ and himself founded a family of great trotters.

It is indeed fittingly singular that the two mares Echora and Beautiful Bells, daughters respectively of Echo and The Moor—two stallions whose breeding was at such great variance in the early standards for success—should each mother a family of champions.

Donathan, who had developed into a famous reinsman, was a resolute fellow, just the proper type to battle with the erratic Sultan, and Father was glad to have him back at Sunny Slope in his new capacity. Donathan took Sultan and Del Sur, the latter a beautiful black four-year-old son of The Moor and Gretchen, to the State Fair at Sacramento in September and gave each of them a record of 2:24. Sultan's record was no measure of his speed. Naturally of flighty temperament, this fault had been greatly aggravated by a runaway, and he was hard to keep at a trot. Del Sur, however, was as steady as a cock, a dingdong, constant sort of trotter, a little shy, however, on staying qualities, but acquitting himself creditably.

Senator Stanford had hired as his trainer Charley Marvin, an easterner, who was very much in the limelight at the time, having wrested Goldsmith Maid's long-held world's record of 2:16 from her by driving the Kansas-bred stallion Smuggler a mile in 2:15. None of the senator's own breeding were old enough to race, and he sent Marvin to the races with Captain Smith, a California-bred horse which he had purchased, and this horse and Del Sur met four times. It was a battle royal on each occasion they met, first one, then the other winning, leaving honors easy at the end of their meetings in the north.

The ensuing year, 1880, the filly Sweetheart, Sultan's first foal—incidentally, out of Minnehaha—was two years old and had fully lived up to her promise as a yearling. Father sent Donathan with her to Sacramento to race in a colt stake at the State Fair in the fall of 1880. She won the stake in straight heats and in doing so trotted to a world's record for two-year-olds of 2:26½. Father's hopes had always been very high for Sultan's success as a sire, and to have him thus glorify himself by giving to the trotting-horse family of America a record-breaker in the first scion from his loins was a matter of great delight. In this achievement Sultan had vanquished his worthy sire The Moor. Minnehaha's first and best foal by The Moor was Beautiful Bells, who took a five-year-old mark of 2:29½, and along comes Sultan's baby daughter Sweetheart, out of the same dam, who at the tender age of two years takes a record of 2:26½.

Edward S. Stokes of New York, who killed Jim Fisk over the latter's mistress Josephine Mansfield in the Grand Central Hotel in New York, came to California after being liberated from four years' imprisonment for this spectacular tragedy. Stokes was a magnetic fellow, and, while living at the Palace Hotel in San Francisco, became very friendly with John W. Mackay of Bonanza King fame, who with his friendship and great wealth made it possible for Stokes to amass an independent fortune. Stokes, who was a good reinsman and great lover of trotters, was at the fair and witnessed Sweetheart's great triumph and at once sought Father in an endeavor to buy her. Father refused to price the filly, saying that she was not only Sweetheart in name but was his Sweetheart for the time being in her great renown. Stokes was very insistent and offered as the reason for his ardor that he wished to present Sweetheart to Mr. Mackay, who he said was "getting a little horsey" and to whom he was greatly obligated. Finally Stokes proposed that Father put a price on Sweetheart, which, if not out of reason, he would pay in full, and they would jointly present her to Mr. Mackay. Stokes elaborated enthusiastically on the probable benefits that might accrue to Father from a closer friendship with Mr. Mackay, which must necessarily follow so magnificent a gift. This procedure was agreed upon, and Stokes paid my father $14,000 for the filly, and the presentation was made.

Mr. Mackay was visibly affected by his emotions, and Stokes's forecast was absolutely correct. Although Mr. Mackay and Father were friendly in a general way—as a matter of fact, Mr. Mackay had at the time three choicely bred mares at Sunny Slope, which had been bred to Sultan—this episode created a much closer contact at once and was the cementing bond of a friendship of rare sincerity.

At the conclusion of the State Fair, Stokes came to Los Angeles to visit us and look over the young stock. I met him there and drove him to Sunny Slope. I was driving a very spirited team, and he complimented me on my reinsmanship, promising me a drive behind his team if I ever came to New York. He purchased three colts from us, and they were shipped to New York. He quite fell in love with my baby sister and sent her a beautiful pair of solitaire pearl earrings upon returning East. He was the best-looking man I ever saw, having physique enough to rob his good looks of effeminacy: heavy through the heart and shoulders, tapering from these to the tips of his toes. A well-shaped, honest-to-god, well-kept brown moustache, and his chin, nose, and ears were as clean-cut and symmetrical as though of marble. He wore the finest of clothes, which seemed to rest easily upon him, and he never appeared overdressed or foppish. It was no wonder he was a Lothario.

Mr. Mackay's interest in the horses increased, and he came on different occasions to Sunny Slope for a short visit. John W. Mackay, who was the father of Mr. Clarence Mackay of the postal telegraph, had been a toiler himself in early life, knew all sides of living, and was a two-fisted, square-shouldered, big-hearted fine man, just about my father's age, and of very jovial disposition. They were two old boys together, and I have seen them on more than one occasion sprint down the road twenty-five or thirty yards. On one of his visits Mr. Mackay asked my father if he could not be of service to him. Father was hesitant. Mackay then said: "Let me loan you some money; you owe the Lazards a lot of money on which you are paying 18% interest, which is outrageous. You'd better owe me. I will let you have all you want at 6%." Such a liberal proposition out of a clear sky quite took Father off his feet, causing him a feeling of delicacy, and he told Mr. Mackay so, who then said: "Don't be mealy-mouthed; how much do you want?" Father finally said he would take $100,000, whereupon Mr. Mackay said: "Oh! hell, take $200,000 and you'll have some extra cash to play with." The mortgage of $90,000 at 18% per annum to Lazard Freres was transferred to John W. Mackay for $200,000 at 6%, and for the first time in more than a score of years my father's nose was eased away from the grindstone.

This is what I choose to call California friendship. How many men are there in the world today capable of such kindness? I should like to see just *one* again.

Within ten days after Sweetheart's triumph further joys accrued to the Rose family. While my brother and I, who had spent the evening in Los Angeles, were on our way to the livery stable about midnight to get our team to drive to Sunny Slope, we met a doctor friend who informed us our sister Mrs. Wachtel had just given birth to a son.

This was her first child and incidentally the first grandchild in the Rose family, and we hastened home, eager to inform Mother of the great event. In walking from the barn to our quarters at the winery, when we reached the ranch house, we met another doctor, who was just leaving, after confining Mother. This child was also a boy, the eleventh and last of Mother's children.

Father himself named this youngster Roy, the Chief. As a child he was a great acrobat and, when yet in his teens with no preparation, conceived the idea of swimming the channel, twenty-two miles across from San Pedro to Catalina Island. Accompanied by friends in a power boat, he swam fourteen miles, until, becoming very chilled, he abandoned the effort.

H. Slotterbeck, an old-time Los Angeles gunsmith, kept a shop on Main Street in Temple Block, and on the sidewalk beside his door he had as an advertisement a 1,000-lb. dumbbell. All the hornyhanded sons of toil took a try at lifting it. My brother Roy at twenty-one, weighing but 160 lbs., lifted it repeatedly an inch off the sidewalk.

Mr. Hancock M. Johnston, a son of General Albert Sydney Johnston, also embarked in the breeding of trotters. Purchasing the half-thoroughbred gray stallion A. W. Richmond and the thoroughbred imported Creighton, from the fusion of these two strains in later years he produced some high-class horses. Mr. Johnston purchased Barbara and Gretchen from Father, and from the former to the embrace of Richmond produced a fine-looking, ordinary gray horse which he named Len Rose for Father. Gretchen produced to Richmond's cover Joe Romero, also a gray, a really high-class trotter, who took a record of 2:19½. Johnston was a handsome man of engaging manner, strictly of southern type; inoculated with the chivalry and extravagance of his natal land Virginia, he was an easy prey for the easy-come and easy-go financial methods of early days. At one time he owned in partnership with his uncle, Dr. J. S. Griffin, all of east Los Angeles and with William Rowland owned much valuable oil land in La Puente. When in his cups—as were many of us in those days—Johnston was a profligate spender and dangerous with his shooting iron. He had in his employ a native-born Mexican, Joe Romero, who always accompanied him as a bodyguard. Romero was a powerful, well-mannered man who often had his work well cut out for him in protecting his patron.

I met them one night in the old Reception Saloon in the Temple Block in Los Angeles. Johnston had forty $1,000 bills, waving them in his hand, willing to bet them on any proposition, and was insistent upon loaning them to me. He would have given them to me had I asked and would not himself have called the matter off the following day.

Romero was himself a character, raised by Mrs. White, a charming southern lady, the mother of Mrs. Colonel E. J. C. Kewen, who, true to her native tradition, had taught Joe good manners in his servile capacity, and as he was of good "address" he grew to be a factor in local life. Romero took an active part in the Chinese riot in Los Angeles in 1870. He was a great wing shot, and for many years hunted quail for the market, and tales of his exploits make my game stories sound commonplace. He frequently killed 25 and 30 dozen quail in a day, himself alone. When game grew scarce, Joe, a great horsebreaker, went to work for Hancock Johnston, handling the young trotters and attending to the breeding of the mares.

During this fall, 1880, Romero, who had left the employ of Hancock Johnston, came to work at Sunny Slope and took charge of breeding operations and lived in a cottage with his young family near the barns. I have mentioned his skill as a Nimrod; he had done his own cooking for months at a time on his hunting trips and acquired a good knowledge of the culinary art, which made him a valuable addition to our hunting expeditions and a worthy ally in our midnight revelries.

During occasional absences of Joe Romero's wife, Maben, my brother, and I would, when returning from a dance or a poker party, slip in during the small hours of the morning and awaken him, then scurry to the nearest chicken roost for chicken. We were privileged characters, paying in full for our ravages through loans that were never repaid and countless other accommodations. By the time we had purloined the fowl, Joe would have a good fire going, the dough ready for biscuits; the chicken was soon dressed and in the frying pan. In the meantime, one of us would have made a hurried trip to the cellar for a half-dozen bottles of white wine, and the feast was on— and such a feast. Sitting around the stove smoking for an hour or two afterwards, with the coming of daylight and another cup of coffee, we were on our way to our sleeping quarters to don our working togs and take up the daily grind.

## III

During the summer of 1880, Stern and Rose bought a thoroughly up-to-date distillery and winery on the bank of the Los Angeles River, just opposite where Cudahy's packing plant was erected later. It had been constructed at great expense but was operated only one year by the first owners. I was put in charge of the campaign that fall, and Mr. F. Bachman, a fine old gentleman and a good friend of my father's, was employed to weigh the grapes and to live with me and be a check valve upon me. We had a fine old adobe house just across the street, a good Chinese cook, and we lived like nabobs. I made all the contracts for the purchase of grapes, drew all checks in payment for them, and kept the books. Everything went as if by clockwork, the campaign was thoroughly successful, and my management was very gratifying to my father.

In the winter Mr. Stern came from the East, and I was slated for a return to New York with him. We left early in January via Sacramento, Ogden, and Omaha. I was none too well and was taken down with diphtheria on my arrival in New York. I put up at the Hoffman House, which was kept by Cassius M. Read & Co. (Stokes and Mackay were the company). I called my good friend Dr. James B. Gilbert, who speedily checked my malady. I was soon up and around, and Stokes took me for a number of sleigh rides behind his team, Kittie Wilkes, a brown mare, hitched with a very flashy cream-colored horse with a white mane and tail.

Despite his shooting trouble, Stokes was very popular with all the wealthy road drivers, who usually congregated during the afternoon at Case's on the Harlem speedway. Through Stokes I met Mr. William Vanderbilt, Mr. Robert Bonner, and Mr. Frank Works, who owned the fastest horses on the road. Mr. Vanderbilt was then driving Aldine and Early Rose, which he drove a mile in 2:16½ to his light top buggy. The following year Mr. Vanderbilt bought Maud S., and, after that peerless trotting queen had dethroned J. I. C. by taking a record of 2:09¾, drove her double with Aldine a mile in 2:13¾.

I soon went to work, and Mr. Stern sent me on the road as a salesman.

My first efforts were through New Jersey, Pennsylvania, and Maryland. A little later, in the spring of 1881, because of my knowledge of Spanish, I was sent down to Mexico and went to Chihuahua, then the terminus of the Mexican Central, on one of its first trains. Kettleson and Degetau were the leading wine merchants. They were buying superior wines laid down from France for less than I could offer mine in the states, and as a consequence I did no business but drummed up some trade on my way back to New York, in El Paso, Texas, and New Mexico points.

That fall I went to Kansas City, St. Joseph, Omaha, Cheyenne, Denver, and on down as far as El Paso. Denver was a great burg at this time; Leadville was in full swing. H. A. W. Tabor had just made his millions. The Windsor, the best hotel, was kept by Tabor's son Maxey and Bill Bush. George Krug, a German salesman for Anheuser-Busch, was introducing their bottled beer in the West. He was a perfect steam engine. There were many high-class people in Denver from all parts of the United States. I formed a fine acquaintance with a Mr. Ingalls of New York and Harry Fowler of Philadelphia. Colorado Springs and Pike's Peak were at the height of their glory and drew many tourists.

From Denver I went to Las Vegas, N. M., where I fell in with two salesmen from San Francisco. I had not met them before but was naturally pleased to see anyone from California. Albert Wilzinski sold cigars for Englebright and Fox, who had a factory in San Francisco. I remember his leading brand was "Judge Sloat." The other man, Hynman, sold blankets for the Golden Gate Woolen Mills of San Francisco, of which his people were proprietors. The principal firm in Las Vegas was Otero Sellar & Co., a gigantic concern which sold everything from a needle to a threshing machine.

Finishing our work in Las Vegas, Hynman entrained east, Wilzinski and I west to Santa Fe and Albuquerque. This was the first time I had ever visited Santa Fe, and I greatly enjoyed looking over the old Fonda Hotel, where Father got his new start after the Indian massacre.

In Albuquerque we put up at the Armijo House, named for a family then very prominent. Wilzinski and I had a customer in common here, a man by the name of Talbot, a mighty fine fellow who gave us each an order. We started for El Paso, Texas, but because of a washout on the railroad we were sidetracked at Socorro, where there were also passengers detained from other directions. The town hotel was a one-story adobe affair, where three or four strangers slept in the same room with no locks on the doors nor facilities for washing oneself. I am happy to say the hotel was full, or we might not have fared so well. Wilzinski knew the Judah brothers, who kept a dry-goods store, and they very kindly provided us with comforts and blankets and allowed us to sleep on the counter in their store. We had at least plenty of fresh wholesome air and could help ourselves to water from the pump in the back yard. By foraging around, we fared well enough gastronomically. Our hosts were good fellows, and we got some pleasure out of our enforced vacation. After a day or two the tracks were repaired, train service resumed, and we were on our way again. Wilzinski went to San Francisco, and I headed for New York.

When I reached New York, one of the first men I ran into was Mr. William Ingalls, whom I had met in Denver, a very spectacular gambler—a fine-looking, polished fellow, twenty-five years my senior, an immaculate dresser, and always wore a high silk hat. I should not use the harsh term "gambler." Ingalls knew all the big men around New York, was a club member, and confined his card playing to the wealthy Wall Street brokers and businessmen, and more than likely he would not sit in a card game once a month, but when he did he was very apt to win twenty or twenty-five thousand dollars. He was a fine billiard player, and it was through him that I met Jimmy Rowe, who for many years up to the time of his recent death had charge of Mr. Harry Paine Whitney's great racing establishment. We met every evening at George Slosson's billiard room on Fourteenth Street just off of Sixth Avenue and played a few games of billiards. Ingalls taught me a lot about billiards and card playing, and gave me much fine advice in other lines.

I went to the races occasionally around New York. The Lorillard brothers, George and Pierre, were at the height of their glory in the race-horse firmament. Most of the racing was done on the Jersey side. Long Branch was particularly popular. Mr. Withers had a beautiful track, Monmouth Park, near there. I saw Parole run before his successful invasion of England.

I wound up my affairs and left for California, December 15, 1881, to spend the holidays. I had made good as a salesman, and again the past was forgotten. There were the usual joys of a large family at Christmas time.

# 10

## *Double Queen - Sporting Events - Fannie Fargo*

### I

THERE WAS great glee in the horse department of Sunny Slope. More luster had been added to the escutcheon of Minnehaha. The year following Father's valueless sale of Beautiful Bells, she passed into the hands of Senator Leland Stanford of Palo Alto Stock Farm. She was sent to the court of Electioneer in the spring of 1879, and the result of this union was a sprightly miss, foaled in 1880.

As a compliment to Father, Senator Stanford named this little lady Hinda Rose for one of my sisters, who died in infancy. This filly was now a year old, and a few months earlier, on November 24, 1881, she electrified the trotting-horse kingdom by establishing a world's record of 2:36½ for yearlings.

Father was enraptured, and his cup of joy was overflowing with delight to have his first—and I believe his greatest—equine love, Beautiful Bells, so cover herself with glory with her first baby. He could not have been prouder of the phenomenal little Hinda Rose had he bred and owned her. In this mighty achievement Bells had atoned handsomely to him, and the many disappointments and heartaches she had caused in her erratic career as a race mare were forgotten, and greater became his faith in and solicitude for pathetic little Minnehaha.

No animal ever more forcibly illustrated the fallacy of judging an equine matron by appearances than Minnehaha. When purchased as a yearling, though she was somewhat undersized, aside from a Roman cast in her nose she was well proportioned and attractive, but, when Minnehaha had attained her growth, she was as common looking as an Indian pony. She stood about 14½ hands high; her body, shoulders, and hindquarters were of the best but were of sufficient size for an animal 16 hands high, which gave her a squat, ill-proportioned conformation, and the Roman cast in her head had grown so pronounced that it looked like a deformity. She had developed a spavin—an incurable bony solidification of the hock joint—on each hind leg and, to make this pathetic combination still worse, was permanently lamed by rheumatism; withal in ensuing years she took rank as one of America's most famous brood mares.

I left Sunny Slope again for New York in January 1882 and made my customary canvass of the Texas trade, then went to New Orleans, from there up the Mississippi to St. Louis, then to the Missouri River points as far as Omaha, then to Chicago and on east. I was back and forth as far as Denver and the intermediate country twice during the year and again returned to Sunny Slope for the Christmas holidays of 1882.

Great as had been the ado there the winter previous over the record-making performance of Hinda Rose, it was naught by comparison to the hubbub that was going on at the barns on this occasion. There were something like twenty two-year-olds by Sultan which were being trained, and, although they all showed speed, two of them, Ruby and Neluska, stood way out in fleetness of foot. Ruby, who belonged to Mr. John W. Mackay, was the first foal of his Hambletonian mare Fleetwing to the embrace of Sultan.

The mutual attachment between grooms and their charges is very marked; the animals are very responsive and evince far more thinking powers than horses are given credit for. The attendants are ever ready to champion the cause of their favorites in arguments or with their brawn if necessary, and there was a continual battle royal—of words at least—between the respective partisans of Ruby and Neluska. There was added zest to this controversy from the fact that these fillies were both entered in a produce stake for two-year-olds, to be decided the ensuing fall at the State Fair of 1883.

Our friend Charley Durfee was gradually climbing the ladder of success, and Father sold Del Sur to him on credit for $5,000—a considerable amount at that time—to be used as a public service stallion. The horse had raced creditably enough, had taken a record of 2:24 (in no wise to be despised for the period), was a flashy looking individual, and of Rose's stock, then a mighty attribute. As a consequence, his book was soon filled, and the money Del Sur earned was a great factor in Durfee's financial uplift.

I left Sunny Slope again early in January 1883 with the delightful knowledge that this was to be my final selling campaign. I was soon to celebrate my twenty-first birthday, had caused Father no worries for a couple of years, and was to return early in summer to be on hand for the vintage and again to reside in glorious California. Although I was kept busy during the interim, traveling all over the eastern country, it seemed that summer would never roll around. My life in the East—particularly around New York City—had been fraught with many pleasures, but throughout my absence my heart was constantly yearning for California, a feeling of which death alone can deprive those who were born here.

I reached Sunny Slope again in the middle of July 1883. The vintage was fast approaching, and everything and everybody was in a hectic rush, but this momentous occasion was a matter of secondary consequence—at least as a conversational topic—in comparison to the approaching contest between Mr. Mackay's filly Ruby and Father's Neluska.

Another long-cherished desire of Father's had materialized; he had dispensed with Donathan's services and placed Walter Maben—whom he had been grooming seven years for the position—in complete charge of the training of the horses. Maben was just rounding out his majority, and to him belongs the greater portion of credit for the wonderful later development and triumphs of our trotting horses. His feeling for Father was almost a filial one, and, although a keen observer himself and a close student of the horses, he realized many of Father's theories were correct and did his utmost to expound them.

Despite his youth, Maben at once took rank as one of the country's foremost developers of early speed, and, in correcting a horse's action by proper weight adjustment in shoeing, had no peer. Maben's pet theory was to infuse the young animals with the idea to move quickly. That is to say, when leaving the barn, as soon as the colt had adjusted itself to the harness and shafts, Maben would get it into active motion as quickly as possible without taking chances of its jumping on itself. The colts were taken to the track at a good brisk gait, jogged, and returned in like manner, keeping their thoughts on trotting all the time, never allowing them to loll, loaf, and scuff along, walking.

Our strain of horses were a hot-headed lot if stirred up but responded amiably to gentle treatment. Maben was endowed with a wonderful even temper and mastered them so completely that none of them was ever improved by different ones of America's best reinsmen after leaving his care.

Maben conditioned both Ruby and Neluska for their contest, and late in August they were shipped together to Sacramento. According to the rules governing racing, horses starting in the same race must have been in charge of different trainers at least one week prior to the date of the contest. Ruby was accordingly turned over to John A. Goldsmith—the greatest trotting-horse reinsman I have ever known—a son of Alden Goldsmith, who developed the illustrious Goldsmith Maid. Mr. Mackay was very much interested in the approaching battle between the young kinswomen, and Father told him repeatedly that his (Mackay's) filly was the better and would win the race.

The contest took place in due time, and, although it was spirited, Mr. Mackay's filly won the race, greatly to his delight and also to his surprise. Such fair and square dealing in connection with a horse race was not altogether in accord with Mr. Mackay's concept of the game.

A very short time after this happy occurrence, Mr. Mackay and Stokes

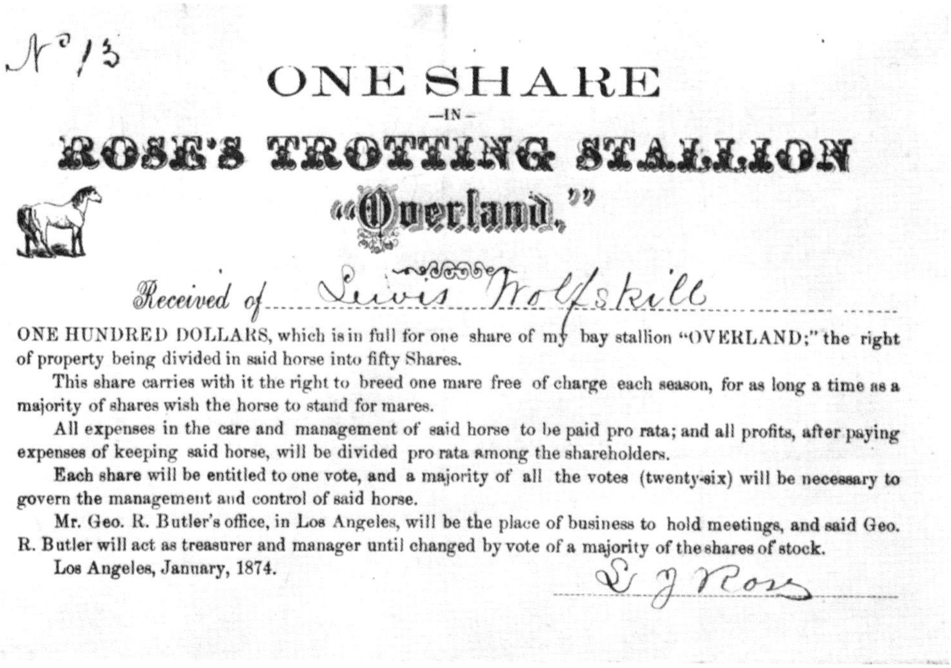

No 13

# ONE SHARE

—IN—

# ROSE'S TROTTING STALLION

# "Overland."

Received of Lewis Wolfskill

ONE HUNDRED DOLLARS, which is in full for one share of my bay stallion "OVERLAND;" the right of property being divided in said horse into fifty Shares.

This share carries with it the right to breed one mare free of charge each season, for as long a time as a majority of shares wish the horse to stand for mares.

All expenses in the care and management of said horse to be paid pro rata; and all profits, after paying expenses of keeping said horse, will be divided pro rata among the shareholders.

Each share will be entitled to one vote, and a majority of all the votes (twenty-six) will be necessary to govern the management and control of said horse.

Mr. Geo. R. Butler's office, in Los Angeles, will be the place of business to hold meetings, and said Geo. R. Butler will act as treasurer and manager until changed by vote of a majority of the shares of stock.

Los Angeles, January, 1874.

L J Rose

*Overland, one of Rose's first breeding horses, was in the historic first shipment of horses by rail across the Rockies.*

*Rosemead Stock Farm. At a New York auction in 1890 Rose realized $238,800 from the sale of 86 of his race horses from Rosemead (see illustration of catalogue). Courtesy of J. V. Wachtel, Santa Barbara.*

# California Trotting Stock.

## GREAT CLOSING-OUT SALE

OF THE

# Entire Rosemeade Trotting Stud,

THE PROPERTY OF

MR. L. J. ROSE, Los Angeles, Cal.

## Wednesday and Thursday, March 5 and 6, 1890,

**Commencing at 10 o'clock each day at the**

## AMERICAN INSTITUTE BUILDING,

Third Ave., bet. 63d and 64th Sts., New York, by

**PETER C. KELLOGG & CO., Auctioneers.**

Office: 107 John Street, New York.

---

**ALL THE BROOD MARES, STALLIONS AND YOUNGSTERS BY STAMBOUL 2:12½, AND ALCAZAR 2:20½, THE SON OF MINNE-HA-HA AND HALF BROTHER TO BEAUTIFUL BELLS.**

---

Read the list of brood mares about to drop foals by those great Stallions. You will find them by Electioneer, Guy Wilkes, Director, Nutwood, Alcyone, Arthurton, The Moor, Sultan, Almont, Dictator, Kentucky Prince, Del Sur 2:24, Simmons 2:28, Echo, Indianapolis 2:21, Strathmore, Santa Claus 2:17½, Sweepstakes, Whipple's Hambletonian, and other great sires.

---

Affording an opportunity to buy the best, and such stock as no one can buy at private sale at any price, being the wealth of the most successfnl Stnd in the world, considering number of head and period of existence.

---

SEND FOR CATALOGUES TO

PETER C. KELLOGG & CO.,

**Auctioneers and Commission Agents in Improved Live Stock,**

OFFICE: 107 JOHN STREET, NEW YORK.

*Title page from catalogue for Rose's widely publicized auction sale. The printer's error in the spelling of Rosemead was fortunately not perpetuated in naming the town of Rosemead. Huntington Library Collections.*

fell out over a financial transaction in which Stokes took advantage of Mr. Mackay's confidence to the extent of something like a million dollars. The huge amount of money involved did not annoy Mr. Mackay half so much as the shattering of his faith in Stokes, of whom he was very fond.

Stokes had been the means of Mr. Mackay's starting in the horse business, and their disagreement robbed Mr. Mackay of all the pleasure he had had in it and decided him to get rid of his horses. Early in the spring of 1884 Mr. Mackay met Father at the Palace Hotel in San Francisco and very abruptly inquired the amount due for pasturage and stud services on his mares at Sunny Slope. There had been three mares originally, and with their foals of different ages there were now ten head. No charge had been made up to this time, and, because of Mr. Mackay's magnanimous generosity, Father did not intend ever to make any charge and so informed Mr. Mackay very positively. Thereupon, Mr. Mackay said such a procedure was not fair, that there must be quite a bill against the horses, and asked if it would be agreeable with Father to take the lot of them and call it square. Father responded that the animals were worth twenty times as much as a correct bill on them would amount to and offered to buy them. Mr. Mackay was obdurate, would have the matter settled in no other manner, and Father became possessed of the lot, one of which was Stamboul, just entering his two-year-old form. Mr. Mackay gave Ruby and his champion Sweetheart to some friends and washed his hands of the memories they brought him of Stokes. On October 10, 1883, at Lexington, Kentucky, the great little yearling queen Hinda Rose, now a three-year-old, earned another laurel wreath by taking the world's record for that age, trotting a mile in 2:19½. And thus further rose the star of glory in the trotting-horse firmament for this doubly crowned young queen, her mammy, Beautiful Bells, and her grandma, Minnehaha.

This fall at the County Fair at Los Angeles we had raced two nice three-year-olds, one, Center, a gray by Sultan out of Belle View Maid; the other, Don Carlos, one of the few colts by Del Sur out of Sunny Slope Bell, who was the first foal The Moor sired. Don Carlos was a very flashy light sorrel, with four evenly marked white legs and white face. As indicated by his pedigree, Don Carlos was inbred; and both his sire and dam were as black as the ace of spades.

## II

On one of Father's trips to San Francisco in 1882, he met Mr. J. E. Bowe, an English subject, who had previously visited Sunny Slope and was greatly impressed with its magnificence. Mr. Bowe was soon returning to London and was so confident of his ability to place the property with some of his countrymen that he prevailed upon Father to give him a year's option at $750,000, subject to a commission of 10%. The trotting horses and all wine on hand were not included in the transaction.

Mr. Bowe came and spent considerable time on the property. Father went into every detail with utmost minutia and candor, and when Mr. Bowe left he took with him a voluminous array of statistics that should suffice for all time. From my personal observation in the later stages of this same transaction, I became thoroughly convinced there was nothing a prospective buying English syndicate liked better than a report—aside from a number of them—with absolute disregard, however, of the caliber or aptitude of the person furnishing it.

Mr. Bowe had been in London but a few months when in the spring of 1883 he cabled Father that a Mr. Porter was sailing for America to make a report on the property, and in due time the gentleman arrived.

I have always regretted that I was not of the committee that entertained Mr. Porter; nonetheless the matter was attended to with proper decorum. As I have stated, we had a beautifully appointed spacious office at the winery. It was nicely equipped with a fine fireplace, easy chairs, and a sideboard with a half-dozen different kinds of excellent wine and fine brandy, that were just as free as water to visitors.

Walter Maben, my brother Harry, and I had splendid sleeping quarters adjoining the office, and evenings that we happened to be at home some of the men from the barn or employees in other departments dropped in and had a drink or two, and, if there was a quorum of the proper coterie, we played poker. Mr. Porter was a good sort, became very fond of the "bloody good port, you know," and Maben, my brother Harry, Joe Romero, and O. H. Burke, who was the Southern Pacific station agent at San Gabriel, put on a poker party for him. He said he had never played poker but was very agreeable to taking a hand and, after a few deals in which he won a little, was delighted with the game because it was so similar to one called "nap" in the "old country."

The port wine flowed freely, and, when those highbinders were through with Mr. Porter, he did not have a thin dime left. There were two of the stable boys who had been watching the game and making themselves useful in serving drinks. The night was dark; Mr. Porter was staying at Father's house about a quarter of a mile distant, to reach which the road passed along a very shady row of large olive trees. When the game broke up at midnight, the guest was somewhat "overboard," and one of the devilish party, speaking in Spanish, told the men who had not been in the game to leave and secrete themselves along the road and, when Mr. Porter came along, to hold him up. After a nightcap or two Mr. Porter departed for his sleeping quarters, and, when he reached the row of olive trees, the deputized highwaymen stepped out and took his watch and chain and pocketknife.

Father was a man of so few words and so pensive in manner that he created an austere impression not characteristic of him and, although he would not have subscribed to the holdup part of the devilment, would have considered the poker episode as purely incidental to the experience of a tenderfoot. At all events, Mr. Porter, who had made considerable racket in lighting himself to bed, considered silence prudent and made no report of his contretemps. He did, however, recall very suddenly the next morning that traveling in America was far more expensive than he had anticipated, and he would be greatly obliged if Father would cash his draft for a hundred dollars.

In a few days, after the poor fellow was just about exhausted from repeating the story of his terrible experience, his watch and knife were returned to him with harrowing tales of brigandage and felicitations on his narrow escape. For the remaining few days of his sojourn, as soon as darkness approached, Mr. Porter sought the comfort of the family fireside at Father's house.

Though Father had no control of the social entertainment, he would tolerate no foolishness in the business end, and, although Mr. Porter showed no amount of aptitude for the matter in hand, he left for London reinforced with data on the property and somewhat qualified as a wild westerner.

When after my return from New York this same summer, 1883, I had become settled at Sunny Slope, a number of us organized a poker party, consisting of O. H. Burke, of whom I have just spoken, "Ikey" Cooper, whom I mentioned earlier as living with his widowed mother on the Don Benito Wilson property, Otheman Stevens, and Charley Wilson. Otheman Stevens, who had recently come to California with his sister Mrs. Halstead and her invalid husband, lived with her on a nice ten-acre tract in Alhambra, about three miles from our place; later he was society editor of the Los Angeles *Examiner*. Charley Wilson, who was the son of the parson of the Episcopal Church near San Gabriel, kept a very small tin and hardware store near the Southern Pacific railroad station at San Gabriel and lived alone on a five-acre tract also in Alhambra, where because of its seclusion we had most of our sittings.

Our sessions endured for a number of months, during which poor luck pursued the parson's son, and at the windup of them I was owner of the small safe, which was about the only thing left to adorn his small store, moved it to Sunny Slope, and sold it to Father.

While residing in New York, I had seen John L. Sullivan in two short exhibitions in the old Madison Square Garden, one with Tug Wilson, the other with Charley Mitchell, the crafty young Englishman who in appearance at least was a child compared to Sullivan. Notwithstanding this apparent frailty, he knocked Sullivan down, which led to their matching and terminated in their fiasco at Chantilly, France. I had never met Sullivan, and imagine my surprise when he turned up as a visitor at Sunny Slope in the fall of 1883. He was making a triumphal tour of the country, accompanied by Robinson as a sparring partner in exhibitions. He, like the rest of the hegira from the East, found his way to our place. I do not remember clearly whether it was immediately prior or subsequent to John L.'s visit that Mr. William Muldoon, present member of the New York Boxing Commission, who was then the champion wrestler of the world, called upon us in company with John Peck. This is a long time ago; I am certain, however, that should Mr. Muldoon chance to see this he will remember the instance. Sullivan with his party sampled many kinds of wine—and had a fine time. Nothing would do but that Harry and I should come in to Los Angeles that night and see his act with Robinson. We drove in after supper, and after his exhibition we all went to a variety show at the Club Theatre, kept by Perry Brothers on North Main Street near the Pico House, where the Stanley Sisters did a dancing act. They were Los Angeles-bred girls. Their name was Henderson, and their father, a respected citizen, was for a number of years jailer of Los Angeles County. They were thoroughly good girls, young and attractive as well as popular, and those of us who knew them and patronized that class of show had sort of a civic pride in them.

Our party took a box on the second floor, which brought us very close to the stage. As an act of high appreciation it was customary to throw coins upon the stage at the conclusion of a turn. Sullivan, Robinson, my brother, and I had liberally provided ourselves with silver dollars. When we unloaded our first volley, it sounded like machine-gun fire as the coins fell upon the bare boards. We repeated the performance for two encores, and I assure you the young ladies had use for a good, strong, fair-sized box to carry their plunder home.

## III

My brother Harry had become very much interested in raising and fighting game chickens. Albert Cooper, the good-natured colored trainer for Lucky Baldwin, had been his preceptor and adviser. They fought a main every Sunday with Los Angeles people right out in the open in The Mission, as San Gabriel was always spoken of. The Mexican people were very partial to the sport, many of them owning cocks, keeping them tied during the day in their front yards and at night in their houses. Their method of fighting was atrocious, even to the hardened American chicken fighter. They used for heeling a single *navaja* (razor), quite appropriately anglicized as "slasher," a sharp-pointed, double-edged blade half an inch wide, four inches in length, sharpened to a razor edge. At the first fly it frequently cut off a head or wing, or laid a cock wide open. This was absolutely a matter of chance and no test—the real one—of gameness. Nacho Belderraín and Pedro Dornaleche of Los Angeles were my brother's regular adversaries. Their mains were all with the regulation 1¼-inch gaffs. Wagers were high. In particularly exuberant mood, we would fill two soft Stetson hats of the same size with silver dollars, uncounted, agreeing mutually as to whether they were equally filled. The hats were then placed on the ground at the edge of the imaginary ring, formed by the spectators standing around in a circle.

I had never cared much for this class of sport, but this winter, 1883, I went to the fights occasionally. At one of them a very distinguished rotund gentleman of about sixty years, bearing every evidence of much high living, slapped me on the back, accompanying the action with the words: "By God, Rose, how are you? I'm glad to see you." I returned the salutation in kind although I had never laid eyes on him before. I inquired who he was and learned he was C. F. Fargo of San Francisco, who had recently purchased a place about a mile from the old church from an English gentleman by the name of Aspland. Fargo was very cordial in his invitation to me to come by the house and have a drink and take dinner, making the invitation doubly attractive by the information that "the girls" were there—meaning his nieces from San Francisco. He was a bachelor and had purchased this place as a home for a younger brother and his wife. The Fargo family were originally from Batavia, New York. C. F. Fargo was a forty-niner, who when embarking from New York City had been carried aboard the sailing vessel, a supposed consumptive weighing one hundred and eighteen pounds. At the end of the six months which it took to make the trip around Cape Horn, he weighed over two hundred and was as well as the day he was born.

C. F. Fargo's first business in California was in the operation of a burro (donkey) pack train to the mines, in which he was associated with "Colonel Jim" Dickey. After a year's experience in the pack train business and an occasional try of his luck with a pan and outfit in some newly discovered diggings or in grubstaking some prospector, Fargo settled in San Francisco and went into the wholesale whiskey business. Fargo's partner, Colonel Dickey, became a Boniface, and his fame as a purveyor to man's thirst and gastronomic desires soon spread far and wide.

Senator Stanford and Colonel Dickey were very close friends, and, when the senator built the famous Bay District race track, he fitted up a beautiful bar and cafe in the clubhouse and gave Dickey the tenancy of it.

No city in the world boasted of a more magnificent drive than that through Golden Gate Park to the Cliff House, standing out on a jutting cliff on the edge of the Pacific. The road was flanked on either side by beautiful stately pines and cypress, countless blossoming shrubs, and myriads of brightly colored flowers. The roads were of the very finest natural macadam, well cared for and splendid alike in summer and winter. With these alluring conditions most of the free-spending sport-loving San Franciscans kept fine horses, and hordes of them drove to the Cliff House daily. The Bay District track was only a block off the main drive. Colonel Dickey was of southern birth, and what he did not know about fried chicken, chicken gumbo, corn bread, small biscuits, etc., was not worth while; a late breakfast or a luncheon at the colonel's was quite the proper thing, and road drivers always stopped there for their afternoon toddies.

The first exclusive running-race meetings in California were inaugurated at Bay District by the Pacific Blood Horse Association early in the 70's. The Blood Horse Association was an organization of high-class gentlemen sportsmen, who raced their horses for the love of the sport, and profits from the club were not the paramount consideration. Colonel Harry I. Thornton, a polished southern gentleman and attorney of renown, was for many years president of the club.

Their biennial race meetings of six alternate days each were social events; San Francisco's elite turned out en masse; and the clubhouse was a bevy of beauty, resplendent in fashionable attire.

Mr. Fargo's wholesale whiskey business prospered famously, and he invested freely in San Francisco real estate, among his earliest holdings being the building, corner of Bush and Dupont (later changed to Grand Avenue) streets, which housed the original Poodle Dog French restaurant, an old landmark in San Francisco and for almost a half a century the rendezvous for *bon vivants*.

Fargo had also been successful in mining deals, and in 1867, though not yet at the half-century post of life and still unfettered by marital ties, he decided to wind up his business affairs, go on to New York state to visit his mother, and on across the Atlantic for an extended stay in Europe. At that time Mr. Fargo had in his employ two young men, C. Wilmerding and E. Kellogg. To these young men Fargo presented his business, consisting of good will, stock, fixtures, and accounts, which could have been sold in twenty-four hours for $40,000—another bit of California friendship. Fargo was a very high liver and heavy drinker. With Paris as his destination he shipped to himself there five barrels, of forty-five gallons each, of the best whiskey he had in stock. Fargo returned to San Francisco from Europe in 1880, after an absence of thirteen years, and took up his residence at the Union Club, corner Montgomery and California streets.

It was but a few years later that Mr. Fargo drifted down to San Gabriel and bought the fine country estate of which I have spoken; and, when he extended to me the effusively cordial invitation to visit his house, upon learning who he was, I at once realized he had made a mistake by confusing me with my brother Harry, whom I closely resembled. This, however, did not deter me from driving by the following Sunday to pay my respects and meet his niece and her lady friend, and I enjoyed a very pleasant afternoon. He was a wonderful host. I never have known a more profane man or a bigger-hearted one. He soon realized his mistake in my identity, and though exceedingly cordial I felt I could see a bit of skepticism in his manner as to my desirability as a friend for his young ladies. My earlier escapades had earned for me the name, "the wild one of the Rose boys." My conduct when enjoying his hospitality was at all times decorous, and we parted the best of friends when he and his party returned north.

Later in the year along toward winter he returned with the same niece, Miss May, of the former visit and another, Miss Fannie, cousins, being the daughters of different brothers. I was a frequent visitor and became very much attached to Miss Fannie. Their stay was cut short by a decision to go to Hawaii. The young ladies were to be joined by Miss Minnie Webster in San Francisco, the party to be chaperoned by Mrs. J. W. Brown, one of the leading society matrons of that city. They sailed away and spent a glorious six weeks in Hawaii. This was during the reign of King Kalakaua and Queen Liliuokalani. Mrs. Brown took letters of introduction to them. The king, a fine-looking, well-educated gentleman, was lavish in his entertainment of the party with native fetes and demonstrations, receptions, brilliant balls, and wonderful banquets. He made of them practically his own guests, which created a long enduring friendship.

It was during this year, 1884, that the first boom started in Los Angeles. Money was very plentiful. The town was like a mining camp, and speculation was rampant. Subdivisions were put upon the market, and any old lot could be sold. I remember one instance in particular. A Mr. Bayard Smith purchased some acreage a few miles southeast of Pasadena on the Don Benito Wilson property, naming his subdivision Oak Knoll. Positively no reason existed for the subdivision at that time, as enough lots had already been platted to supply the demand for years to come. The lots—small ones—in this subdivision were $1,500 each, and, as an inducement to buy, a lottery element had been introduced. On two of the lots nice $5,000 bungalows had been erected, and one did not know which lot he would receive until the drawing was had. I believe there were about fifty of us who contributed. The drawing took place; I know I was not one of the lucky ones, and, as was the case with many others, I had never seen the subdivision, nor did I ever go to see the lot that befell me or ever think of it again as an asset. Twenty-five years later the same property, having reverted to the original owners, was purchased in acreage tracts by newcomers, and today some of the finest homes in the vicinity of Pasadena grace it.

Paper profit money was so easily counted the tendency was to overbuy, and there was a sorrowful day of reckoning when the bubble burst about two years later. In the meantime we all flew high, with poker as our pet diversion. I sat in a game every Saturday night, made up from among Will Kingsbury, John Gaffey—I name them first as they were about the best players—Charley Watts, Sid Lacey, Downey Harvey, Guadalupe Estudillo, Juan Forster, Tommy Rowan, Jimmy Martin, Billy Carlisle, Walter Moore, and Walter Maxwell—with an occasional guest dropping in. Mervyn Donahue of San Francisco, whose father owned the Union Iron Works and a railroad running up into Sonoma Valley, was ever a welcome guest. Not very adept, he always left considerable new money floating around. The sittings were quite protracted. The game would start in the late afternoon Saturday, and I stayed until 4:30 Monday morning, which allowed me just time enough to reach Sunny Slope at six o'clock to begin my day's work. Our meals were served in the cardroom, part of us eating while the others kept the game going.

Though I did not know it at the time, these were the last of my untamed sprees. Late in the fall my young lady friend Miss Fannie Fargo returned to San Gabriel alone. She was a little indisposed with a cold that had fastened itself upon her, and was making a visit to her Aunt Olive and Uncle Duane. By this time I had acquired a fine Brewster side-bar buggy, to which I drove my wonderful road mare Margaret, by Sultan. I was not long in seeking the young lady again, called quite often, and, with thanks to Aunt Olive, who was good enough to squeeze in with us in the narrow buggy, we had many wonderful moonlight drives. Her uncle C. F. Fargo soon came from the north. He sat evenings in an easy chair on the vine-covered porch of his beautiful home. He always retired about nine o'clock, and I have vivid recollections of the way he would shuffle his heavy ranch boots on the floor as a signal for me to take my departure. Even yet he was not so sure of my intentions. I, however, was decidedly in earnest, and in time Miss Fannie had promised to be mine. Naturally she at once communicated the knowledge to her uncle. This did startle him, and he wanted to know if she did not think we should be married at once. He himself was such a roué that he suspected everyone. All his fears were finally allayed. We were married about two months later on January 14, 1885, at my wife's father's home at No. 1310 O'Farrell Street, San Francisco, and are still together after forty-six years.

Our wedding was a quiet family affair with but few close friends attending. My father, mother, and my young sister Daisy were the only members of my family present. We were married in the afternoon and took the train shortly after for San Gabriel, where we were to make our home in a cottage built a few years before for my sister Nina and her husband, J. V. Wachtel, who had been in charge of the wine business and had resigned and resumed his position with the Farmers and Merchants Bank in Los Angeles.

I now had charge of the executive part of the wine business, and my brother Harry of the production. Between us we gave a general supervision to everything about the place except the horse business, which had ever been Father's hobby, giving to it a lot of earnest study and every hour of personal contact that he could contrive. Business affairs of various nature took him from home considerably. While at home, however, he never failed to take his customary walks through all the pastures and notice each individual animal.

Mrs. Rose was the second daughter of Jerome B. Fargo, a younger brother of C. F. Fargo. He left Batavia, New York, and moved to Wisconsin, where he trapped and hunted bear for their pelts. Later he married Miss Martha True of Janesville and lived there till 1864, when, with their two daughters, Jennie, aged ten, and Fannie—my wife—five, they left for California by way of the Isthmus of Panama and settled in San Francisco, where Mr. Fargo conducted a wholesale liquor business for thirty-two years.

A few years after their arrival in California, a third daughter, Lulu, was born to them, and later a son. Martha Fargo died from the effects of this child's birth, and the infant, the only male Fargo of his generation in this family, succumbed a few months later.

Mrs. Rose grew up with the Crockers, Floods, Fairs, Shreves, Sharons, Blandings, Hookers, Durbrows, Boswells, Lents, Schmiedels, Peters, Tevises, Pachecos, Sperrys, Websters, and the children of other pioneer families. Upon graduating from Clark's Institute in San Francisco, she went to Europe with Mrs. Boswell and her daughters May and Edith and spent two years studying music, painting, and languages.

## II

# *Alcazar and Sultan - Sale of Sunny Slope - San Buenaventura*

## I

OUR YOUNG trainer had been north to the races the preceding fall with Le Grange, a four-year-old son of Sultan; Neluska, now three years old; and Stamboul, one of the number of horses presented to Father by Mr. Mackay. Stamboul was a two-year-old, and this was his first bid for racing honors. He started four times, was twice victor, and took a record of 2:37. Neluska had become unsound but managed to scratch out a record of 2:30¼. Le Grange raced creditably and took a record of 2:23½.

The horse business had grown to such proportions that Maben needed an assistant, and we hired Andy McDowell, a sensational driver recently arrived from the East, who could get up behind a strange horse and drive him a single mile faster than anyone I ever knew, but I did not regard him highly as a race driver because of this very qualification. The astute race driver will always manage to have a little reserve left, whereas McDowell would take it all out of a horse in one whirl around the ring.

In 1885 Maben went north again to the races, taking with him Stamboul and Kismet, another three-year-old by Sultan out of an Arthurton mare, and Alcazar, a two-year-old, brother of the great Sweetheart. Stamboul again found as his staunchest foeman Apex. There were others in their races, but these two stood out, and in all their races they were the only heat winners. These races were hammer-and-tongs affairs, in a number of instances requiring five heats to settle their singlehanded contests. They met each week at the successive fairs, six or seven of them, winning about alternately. Apex was the steadier, whereas Stamboul had the most stamina. Any heat in which Stamboul was fractious and broke repeatedly Apex would win, but if the race went beyond three heats Stamboul usually wore him down. Stamboul wound up the season with the very fast record for the period of 2:26½. Kismet won two races, took a record of 2:25, and showed himself to be a much better horse than Stamboul. Our hopes were very high on him; we were most unfortunate, however, for he contracted lung fever on the way home and died a few days later. As a compliment to his young prowess we had bred Minnehaha to him that spring, and a little filly was the issue the following year. She died when but a few days old, and all trace of the blood of her apparently significantly named sire, Kismet, vanished.

Alcazar found a couple of *bêtes noirs* on his travels, Del Norte and Valensin. Their races were all spectacular, and none of them decided in straight heats. The colts were very evenly matched, and occasionally each won a heat which carried the contest into a fourth, very strenuous racing for two-year-olds.

Alcazar was of the dynamic, bull-dog, do-or-die type and kept on doing his best under all conditions—the gamest colt I ever saw. He won the lion's share of his contests, taking a record of 2:29½, thereby adding another jewel to the richly studded diadem of his dam, Minnehaha. Alcazar's valiant racing courage endeared him greatly to the racing public, and he had ten admirers to Stamboul's one, although in individual appearance there was positively no way of comparing them.

Alcazar was of the leggy, greyhound type, and, although not to a degree of faultiness, his conformation was in no manner so pleasing to the eye as that of Stamboul, who at this immature age of three years had every fine quality a critic could seek and at maturity developed into equine perfection. There was scarcely a straight line in Stamboul's body, and I have no better means of describing him than by saying he had the substance of a draft horse with the finish of a thoroughbred.

It occurs to me that the records I am furnishing may sound childish to the uninformed, but to those who know and to those who then lived—a half century ago—they were wonderful, and the fame of the obscure-bred Moor and his mighty son and successor, Sultan, had spread even to that breeding hotbed, Kentucky.

In that long ago the trotting gait was still an acquired one; prepotency had not been instilled into the breed by numerous successive crosses of individuals that had acquired great speed at the gait. The standard then was the 2:30 performer, and a stallion's worth was measured by the number of his get that took records of 2:30 or better. The Moor in his short span of life did not sire more than fifty colts; more than half of them were from mustang mares; withal he had five within the charmed 2:30 circle, an average of one in ten.

This statement becomes particularly significant when one takes into consideration that Rysdyk's Hambletonian—in reality the father of the trotting-horse family of America—then at the height of his glory, serving only the best of mares, was the sire of twelve hundred foals and had but seventy

2:30 performers, an average of but one in seventeen. Moreover, one of The Moor's first crop, Beautiful Bells, had in her initial essay in the field of maternity given to the trotting family the doubly crowned record-breaker Hinda Rose and by this time, 1885, had added to the galaxy of her aristocratic offspring two young sons—Chimes and Bell Boy—both of great speed—the latter selling for $51,000, the first trotter to sell for more than $50,000. And these were but forerunners of Beautiful Bells's greatness as a matron. In her long years of service at Palo Alto she became the dam of seventeen, every one of them famous, and at her death was ranked as one of the three great brood mares of America, along with Green Mountain Maid, dam of the mighty sire Electioneer, and Lady Russell, dam of the peerless trotting queen Maud S.

Now to take up the achievements of Sultan, at that time in his eleventh year. He was the sire of sixty-odd foals of racing age and had nine on his roll of honor, Sweetheart, Eva, Alcazar, Le Grange, Center, Kismet, Ruby, Margaret, and Stamboul, one in seven, if you please—all of them stellar performers for the period, and the very first from Sultan's loins was the record-making, two-year-old Sweetheart.

Lastly we come to Minnehaha, who unfalteringly on her road to fame had added to her royal family of record holders another daughter, Eva, a full sister to Sweetheart and Alcazar, with a record of 2:23. Augmenting these three, all by Sultan, with her famous daughter Beautiful Bells, Minnehaha was the dam of four within the mystic 2:30 circle and stood forth one of the greatest brood mares of all time.

Father had been in correspondence with some people in Chicago and others in Kentucky with regard to the sale of Sultan, whom he had priced at $15,000. In January 1886 W. H. Wilson of Cynthiana, Kentucky, and Percy Talbot of Lexington arrived at Sunny Slope to inspect the horse. Though not of the show-horse type from the connoisseur's viewpoint, Sultan was an animal of very striking appearance, had a splendid crest, carried his tail high, and would attract attention at all times by his animated manner and agility of action; when led out to show, he came forth with the fire of a Roman charger.

He far surpassed the expectations of the Kentuckians—a very unusual occurrence when inspecting a horse on the description of a vendor. They were enraptured with him and were generous enough to admit it. If there was any lingering doubt in their minds with regard to purchasing, it was instantly dispelled a few hours later, when they walked among Sultan's get in the pasture.

The living picture presented by Sunny Slope at this time—midwinter—as contrasted with the snow-covered fields left behind in the East was irresistible. The stately mountains in somber repose, apparently within walking distance, the balmy air, the cloudless blue sky, the cordial sunlight were a fitting beginning. Then enter upon the mile-square domain of the equine Sultan and his harem and stroll leisurely among the beautiful, choicely bred brood mares, with their satinlike coats glimmering in the sunlight. Every line of their conformation revealed their aristocratic ancestry, as they browsed in the knee-high native grass amid stately oaks and sycamores and wild flowers fragrant and colorful. Numbers of young foals gamboled about, and yearlings and two-year-olds followed around, nudging the visitors with their muzzles in their desire to be petted. Could anything be more exquisite? A slight tinge of color might be added to the lily when a few steps farther along you pluck for yourself a luscious orange, which you enjoy with a glass of Sunny Slope port, that would tickle the cockles of the heart of a saint.

The deal was closed, the gentlemen bought Sultan for $15,000, purchased a few young animals, and soon thereafter Sultan and a number of his tribe were on their way to their new home in Cynthiana, Kentucky, and Stamboul ascended to the throne of The Moor—in the third generation—as master of the breeding court.

In the summer of this year, 1886, Mr. Bowe, of whom I have spoken as negotiating the sale of Sunny Slope in London, sent over another emissary—the third since the highly entertained Mr. Porter—for a further report on Sunny Slope. I mention this in justification of my previous statement anent the love of an English buying syndicate for reports. During the intervening three years from 1883 up to the present, cables flew so thick across the Atlantic asking extensions to enable Mr. Bowe to hobnob still further with His Highnesses and Her Ladyships that the probable consummation of the sale of Sunny Slope became a great joke with Father. Nothing was lost in the matter, however, as the property was paying handsomely, and with each extension there was an advance in the price.

On the 11th of August of this year, 1886, our first child, a daughter, Martha True, was born to Mrs. Rose and me.

During this same summer J. F. Crank and his associates from the East, who had been quite active in the installation of cable streetcar systems in Los Angeles, started construction on the Los Angeles and San Gabriel Valley Railroad. The survey of the road crossed Los Angeles River near Elysian Park, then out through the Arroyo Seco to Pasadena, then due east through Monrovia and the foothill country to Pomona, and onward as far as San Bernardino.

In its course the survey cut off a narrow strip from the north end of Sunny Slope. Father added a piece of the same size to the south side of the survey and placed a subdivision on the market, calling it Lamanda Park, and it soon grew into an active suburb of Pasadena. In choosing this name, Father combined the first letter, "L," of his given name, Leonard, with that of my mother's given name, Amanda.

The Los Angeles and San Gabriel inaugurated passenger service over this line as far as Monrovia the following year, and within a few months the system was taken over by the Atchison, Topeka and Santa Fe and became their main-line entrance into Los Angeles.

## II

Early in the spring of 1887 the least expected of all things transpired. Mr. Bowe cabled that all the M.P.'s, lords, and ladies had been corralled, and Sunny Slope had been sold for £207,000. The occasion was naturally a most momentous one, and, although the idea of selling had grown to be a desire, when the matter had become a reality, every one of the large family from Father down was filled with sorrow.

If ever there was an Edenlike spot on the surface of the earth, Sunny Slope was the one—a domain all of our very own of 1,960 acres. There was everything there that heart could desire—trees and fruits in lavish quantity and flowers in gorgeous beauty, babbling brooks, balmy air, eternally blue skies, a perfect climate, and perpetual sunshine. In the heart of a sportsman's paradise, with quail, dove, rabbits, and all sorts of waterfowl at a stone's throw from the front door, and within a few miles' ride there were trout in the streams and deer in the mountain canyons. There were scores of America's famous and beautiful horses, and excellent wines. To stimulate one's mind, there was the zest of a great industry in the raising of the vast acreage of oranges and grapes, manufacturing the wine and marketing it and the orange crop.

There was no room for lonesomeness; we were a village unto ourselves, with a hundred or more Chinamen, thirty Mexicans, and twenty white men. There was no dearth of changing scenes or lack of new faces to gladden the eye; swarms of eastern tourists paid homage daily to Sunny Slope, and friends of the family were legion. If there is aught to challenge the happy freedom and romantic grandeur of such a country estate, it is beyond my conception to visualize it.

The price of $1,035,000 did not include the horses or wine on hand, and it required three or four months to ship the wine and remove the horses.

Some time previously, Father had purchased 500 acres of moist, waterbearing land three miles south of Sunny Slope near Savannah in the El Monte district. This had been drained with tiling, and a portion of it seeded to alfalfa. Two fine barns, each 50 x 150 feet, were built with ten box stalls and twenty single ones and loft room in each for three hundred tons of hay.

In his usual sentimental way Father conceived the idea that a fitting manner in which to dedicate the new place, which had been christened "Rosemead," would be by the introduction of a new bird family into California and imported two dozen skylarks from England for the occasion, and I journeyed there to witness the joyous event. The birds had been housed for two months in a large aviary at Rosemead. On the gala day for their liberation, with the peal of their chorus as they rose to wing all but ringing in our ears, the aviary door was opened, and upwards soared in silence the two dozen skylarks out of sight. As far as Rosemead and the Rose family are concerned, they may still be soaring, as we never saw or heard of them thereafter.

In the sale of Sunny Slope Father had reserved three acres of water-bearing land where artesian wells were easily available, with a perpetual right to drill thereon. A number of wells were put down, a pipe line was laid three miles to the new place, the wells were capped, and the water never saw daylight until it emptied into the reservoir at Rosemead.

A three-quarter-mile track was built, a fine two-story house for Maben, a ranch superintendent's house, and mess hall for the men. Father bought four hundred acres adjoining, which were planted to figs, peaches, and pears the following season, and, although Father was in his sixty-first year, he was back in harness again in a new venture.

By the middle of summer 1887 the money was paid over for Sunny Slope. Mr. Bowe was paid a flat commission of $125,000. Father paid C. White Mortimer, the English consul, $7,500 for his friendly offices in the matter and presented his lifelong dearest friend, T. D. Mott, $7,500.

Father purchased the lot 40 x 160 feet on the southwest corner of Spring and Sixth streets in Los Angeles for $400 per front foot, greatly to the alarm of his friends because of the high price. There was a drugstore on the corner and a small dwelling in the rear on Sixth Street, where Father and Mother, the three younger daughters, and the youngest son took up their temporary abode. The fears of Father's friends were ill founded. A few months later he sold the lot for $600 a front foot, clearing $8,000. In a few years a large building was erected upon the lot in which the Southern Pacific had offices, and the value finally rose to $10,000 per foot.

The English syndicate, known as the "L. J. Rose Company, Limited," sent over as manager for the property Captain Pavey, a retired seafarer upwards of seventy years of age, who I am quite certain was never previously on a ranch, and, true to the clean-sweeping-new-broom tradition, the captain at once inaugurated an era of changes. Captain Pavey was accompanied by his very estimable wife, and it was quite natural and proper that alterations in the old home should have been desired and made. But why roads strictly for ranch use, that had stood the test of usage as to their desirability for twenty-seven years, should be changed seemed quite unreasonable.

The year previous, a pest known as the white cotton scale had attacked the orange groves of Los Angeles County. It was a serious affair requiring vigilant attention, for, if left alone, it would soon sap the vitality and kill the tree. The scale multiplied with alarming rapidity, and when mature was crustaceous in appearance, about an eighth of an inch in thickness, very white, and absolutely covered the smaller branches. The sole means of combating its ravishes at that time was by spraying with a chemical solution.

When Captain Pavey arrived and for months previously, two spraying outfits, each drawn by a pair of mules, manned by two Chinamen, one of whom drove and the other operated the pump, were busy daily, driving through the orchards treating the infected trees.

There was no secret about the affair—a blind man could have sensed it—moreover, Father had discussed the matter impressively with Captain Pavey. There were some low swales in one of the pastures where wild mustard grew very luxuriantly every spring, and in his meanderings the captain had discovered the seed had ripened. He conceived the idea that it would be a frugal stroke of business to reap of nature's bounties and harvest the seed. He thereupon instructed the ranch foreman to cease spraying operations, offering the gratuitous advice that it was a needless expense insofar as the first good shower of rain that fell would wash the scale off.

The men working at the job with a half-dozen others were set to work garnering the wild mustard seed, of which ten men would not gather one dollar's worth per day. This and kindred operations continued, matters rapidly went from bad to worse, and at the end of five years the formerly rich-paying, wonderful Sunny Slope—L. J. Rose Company, Limited—was on the rocks, with a deficit of £57,000. Some sort of a settlement was arranged wherein the more fortunate stockholders were allotted acreage for their stockholdings, which was peddled about during boom deflation periods for $250 and $300 per acre to local people, and all traces of the English syndicate vanished.

San Gabriel Valley, with her glorious vistas and superb climate, was not to be denied, however, and today the once mighty domain of Sunny Slope is dotted with palatial rural residences on acreage tracts, which in their bare state are now—1931—held at $2,500 per acre.

Shortly after taking up his residence in Los Angeles, Father purchased the lot 100 x 100, corner of Grand Avenue and Fourth Street, about the highest point in the residential district. In order to conserve its altitude, a very massive, high, retaining wall of granite was built around the lot, and a palatial residence was built upon it. The house was complete in every detail, the ceilings beautifully done by an Italian artist of note, and the hardware throughout was of solid silver.[28]

[28] When this house was wrecked in 1937, some of the heavy interior paneling was salvaged by the Twentieth Century-Fox Studios for use in their period spectacle "In Old Chicago."

*Stamboul the Great, 1887, champion trotter (2:07½) and thrice winner of best in show at Madison Square Garden. Courtesy of Miss Hinda Rose, San Diego.*

*Rose house at Fourth and Grand, Los Angeles, 1888, was built at a cost of over $100,000. Interiors were later used as sets for Hollywood. Courtesy of J. V. Wachtel, Santa Barbara.*

*L. J. Rose, 1892, from a painting by his son, Guy Rose.*
*Courtesy of the Los Angeles County Museum.*

The outlay for this was $110,000, a great amount for the period, and the home was one of the most elegant in Los Angeles, and Father presented it to Mother. He also presented my sisters, Mrs. Wachtel and Mrs. Sanderson, and my brother Harry and myself with $25,000 each. Mr. Wachtel invested his wife's money in the furniture business. Mr. Sanderson put that of his wife in a draying business; my brother joined Refugio Belderraín and purchased the St. Elmo Hotel business.

Personally, I was undecided as to future action, and my first venture was in connection with my father and my cousin Henry O'Melveny, whom I mentioned early in this narrative as the son of Judge H. K. S. O'Melveny, who had so generously succored my father upon his return to Santa Fe after the Indian massacre on the Colorado River in 1858. Henry O'Melveny, though not yet thirty years of age, had risen to prominence as an attorney in Los Angeles.

My father, young O'Melveny, and I purchased the eight-acre homesite of J. Downey Harvey on Figueroa Street for $24,000 for subdivision purposes. This was at the fag end of Los Angeles' first boom, and the investment did not prove a lucrative one; we, however, managed to dispose of the property without loss.

During the preceding fall, 1886, Maben had made his customary annual trip to the northern race meetings, taking with him Le Grange, Stamboul, and Alcazar. Stamboul found Apex, his foe of the previous year, ready for the fray, and they had a number of dingdong battles, sharing honors about equally, Stamboul taking a new record of 2:23.

Alcazar met his antagonist of the year previous, Valensin, and no two three-year-olds ever waged such battles for supremacy. Most of their contests were singlehanded, and, as their races were three-in-five affairs, it frequently required five heats to return a victor. Valensin was a worthy foeman, and honors were about even; Alcazar, however, secured the faster record of the twain, trotting in 2:23. In this achievement he had added great luster to himself by tying the record of Stamboul, who was a year his senior.

Stamboul, now in his five-year-old form, 1887, was again taken north by Maben, but our champion, Alcazar, had fallen lame in one foreleg and was left at home. Stamboul was raced at San Francisco, Oakland, Petaluma, Santa Rosa, Sacramento, Stockton, and San Jose, concluding his season at Agricultural Park in Los Angeles, and gave a most splendid account of himself. His hardest battle was in the Los Angeles race, where he was combined against by two horses from the north, Lot Slocum, driven by Mike McManus, and Como, driven by George Bayliss.

Lot Slocum was a constant-going, fainthearted trotter and could beat Stamboul the first two heats. After that, however, Stamboul was his master. Como, the other entrant, was a hop-skip-and-jump fellow, and, after Slocum had won two heats on his own resources, Bayliss with Como proceeded to herd Stamboul all over the race track by breaking his horse into a run, cutting across in front of Stamboul, impeding his action, and carrying him wide on the turns.

As was generally the case at the race meetings of the fairs, the judges—prominent citizens or politicians, who served gratuitously—were possessed of positively no knowledge of the rules and, shameful to say, often bet on the races. In this instance they allowed Bayliss to do all but upset Maben throughout the seven heats it took to decide the contest. Slocum won the first two heats; Stamboul won the third. Como, by running and all other means, won the fourth heat. Slocum, who had been conserving himself for a couple of heats, staggered in and made a dead heat with Stamboul in the fifth, in which Stamboul took his record for the year, 2:17½—incidentally, the second best for a five-year-old stallion. Stamboul won the sixth and seventh after as rough a voyage as any trotter ever had.

This same fall a wonderful laurel wreath was dedicated to the glorious memory of The Moor. Sable, the two-year-old daughter of Gretchen by The Moor, who went wrong as a two-year-old when Havey was training for us in 1876, had found her way to Corbitt's San Mateo Stock Farm and in 1883 had been bred to the great Guy Wilkes. The following spring Sable foaled a black colt called Sable Wilkes, who was now three years old. The great John Goldsmith had nursed this promising young animal from infancy with paternal zeal for a shy at Hinda Rose's world's three-year-old record of 2:19½, and one sunny fall afternoon at the Bay District track he set the trotting-horse world afire by trotting a mile in 2:18. Father again, by reflection, quaffed freely of the joys of victory in having the son of a mare of his own breeding wrest the three-year-old crown of championship, although in doing so he had nullified the achievement of another of the same clan.

During this same year Nick Covarrubias and Charley Durfee bought a bay pacer from Alfonso Den of Santa Barbara, called Arrow, paying for him $1,000. The horse was bred by Hancock Johnston of Los Angeles and was the happy blending of the blood of the two sires with which Johnston started his breeding ventures, being by A. W. Richmond out of a mare by imported Creighton.

Nick Covarrubias, who discovered the horse, was one of the most picturesque native Californians of his time. Born and raised in Santa Barbara, he was son of the original grantee of Catalina Island and the Rancho Castac in Kern County.[29] He was of very striking appearance and commanding personality, was sheriff of Santa Barbara County for a number of terms, later

[29] The original grantee of Santa Catalina Island was Thomas M. Robbins, who sold it to José María Covarrubias in 1850.

United States marshal of the Southern District of California. Keeping a livery stable most of his life, he was a great horseman, and his exploits with horses were numerous. He always traveled between Santa Barbara and Los Angeles—110 miles—with a double team, never taking over twelve hours for the long trip. No one could hitch a span of horses to show to better advantage than he, and when in the saddle he was positively statuesque, appearing to be an integral part of the animal. Covarrubias, who often led festal parades, was a genuine Mexican cavalier, a past master with his riata, and very playful even in his advancing years. I once rode as one of his aides at the Tournament of Roses in Pasadena. We spent the morning riding along the street before the parade had formed, chatting and planning some deviltment. If a horseman—not to the manner born, but much in earnest to the occasion—came galloping toward us, Covarrubias with his rope ever ready, with no apparent effort whatever, would lasso the gentleman's horse—stopping it, of course—rudely jarring the rider's body and his dignity as well. Instantly approaching the suddenly detained person, hat in hand, speaking always with a slight Spanish accent which for the occasion was exaggerated into crude broken English, Covarrubias would very apologetically offer the explanation that he thought the horse was running away. This is but one of the many devilish pranks that he would pull off, always talking himself clear. One day while he was seated in a barber chair in a shop on Main Street, Los Angeles, his face all covered with lather, quite a commotion was created by a team passing, running away with its driver. Leaping from the chair, running hatless to his saddle horse tied in front, Covarrubias mounted, was away in a jiffy, and lassoed the team before it had gone two blocks farther.

## III

Father had always been greatly enamored of the farming country in Ventura County, in which San Buenaventura, beautifully located on the ocean with a population of 3,500, was the only town of any size.[30] During the hectic movement in all other portions of southern California in the preceding three years, scarcely a single transaction in real estate had taken place in this slumbering little burg.

No section of California is more fertile than Ventura County, and none so well adapted to growing lima beans, in which branch of agriculture it was then pioneering and in which it today stands supreme in the United States. Visualizing for the town a certain great future because of the great productiveness of the contributing country, Father advised me to move there and offered to join me in an endeavor to boom the place.

[30] The county seat of Ventura County was formerly called San Buenaventura, after the mission, and later shortened to Ventura.

The Southern Pacific railroad was at the time building a branch from Saugus on the main line to San Francisco, which went down through the Santa Clara Valley of the south via Camulos, Piru, Sespe, Santa Paula, Saticoy, San Buenaventura, Rincon, and Summerland, with Santa Barbara as its objective for the time being.

In the meantime all land travel was by private conveyance or a 55-mile stage ride from Saugus, paralleling the railroad construction. The stage, a very rickety affair, left Saugus at three in the afternoon and dragged its way wearily along until midnight to cover the fifty-five miles. My advent in the somnolent little hamlet was a momentous occasion to many of its residents, whose hopes of selling their meager holdings were moth-eaten with despair. Father was very optimistic in the matter and put no limit on the amount to be invested, 75% of which was to be for his, and 25% for my account. In the course of a week I purchased thirty parcels, most of them vacant lots, on the main street and one business property of 100 feet, improved with a one-story, shantylike building, which housed the post office, at an outlay of $128,000.

I returned to Los Angeles and gathered together my little family, consisting of my wife and infant daughter, the nurse, and my hunting dog; and with them, whom I could not subject to the tiresome, dusty stage ride, I took the steamer to Santa Barbara.

Mrs. Rose's uncle C. F. Fargo, of whose great mistrust of me prior to my marriage to his niece I have spoken, by now was my stoutest adherent, and, although forty years my senior, we were great pals. Learning of Father's and my extensive investments in San Buenaventura, he made the trip with my family and me on the boat, and together we all were driven by my friend Major Durfee behind his fine span of horses the beautiful thirty-mile stretch of country to San Buenaventura. Mr. Fargo was greatly impressed with the outlook and wired Father, asking to be in on the deal. Father conveyed to him a third of his holdings, which placed Mr. Fargo on the same status as myself, a fourth owner.

I took up my residence in the Palace Hotel—the only one in the town—a small two-story brick building in the Mexican end of the town, belonging to the Schiappa Pietre brothers, very wealthy land and sheep owners, and operated by A. I. Wagner.

As soon as I got my bearings in San Buenaventura, I discovered the water-supplying system was both inadequate and antiquated, and Father, Fargo, and I decided to install an up-to-date system, purely as a matter of bettering the community and with positively no desire to become monopolistic.

Captain A. J. Hutchinson of Los Angeles, with the same idea in mind, a number of months previously purchased a flour mill about three miles up Ventura Avenue, in order to secure the fine water right it possessed. Realizing the importance to us of the property, the captain very generously transferred it to us for just what it had cost him, $14,000.

Early in the spring of 1888 I started operations toward the construction of the system. Desiring a reservoir site, I sought to purchase one from A. D. Barnard just across the avenue from the mill. Mr. Barnard was better than a green hand at trading, and, realizing I needed the piece of ground—about an acre—insisted upon my taking twenty acres at $250 per acre. The land was planted to two-year-old walnut trees and well located, and I purchased it. I paid Frank Sifford $500 to build me a cheap reservoir, and shortly the cat flew out of the bag.

We had offered to buy the existing water works, which belonged to the Bradley sisters of San Jose, and had offered them more than it was worth on its earning capacity. They were decidedly unreasonable, and we could do nothing with them; however, no serious objection had manifested itself from any source to our completing our system. The intake for the Bradley water was not well placed, and as a consequence occasionally during freshets in winter it went out. At such times the Bradley Company had been diverting the water which ran our mill into their reservoir. Not feeling it incumbent upon myself to thus foster their competition, I proceeded to cut the water from my mill wheel back into the river. Strange as it may seem, my operations in the little town had engendered a lot of jealousy among some of the old-timers, notwithstanding that my purchases had in many instances lifted people from poverty, from which they had long ceased to hope for escape. I had at all times been considerate, liberal, and conciliatory.

This act on my part brought my enemies from cover, foremost of whom was Mr. Chaffee, a resident of many years and member of the leading firm of dry-goods merchants. He, with his attorney, L. C. McKeeby, enjoined me, had me arrested on a trumped-up charge of trespass, and advanced other trivial contentions. I could have defeated their action; this, however, would have entailed protracted litigation, and, rather than have me thus harassed and make enemies, Father counseled me to drop the matter of a new water system.

Not choosing to be bothered with the care of a young walnut orchard, I sold the twenty acres back to my friend Barnard for $225 per acre, losing $500 on that part of the deal, and the $500 paid for making the reservoir. Today the twenty acres is thickly dotted with producing oil wells.

I became acquainted with Robert Orton, a miller by trade, as fine a person as it has been my good fortune to ever meet, and he prevailed upon me to finance the flour-milling business, he to give it his entire attention and I to furnish all moneys necessary for buying wheat and the conduct of the business. We made an arrangement with Father and Mr. Fargo on a leasing basis and conducted a thriving business for three years.

In no wise daunted by my experience as a public benefactor with my water company, I decided to build a gas works and brought Mr. Sims, an expert in that line, from San Francisco and had him construct me an up-to-date plant for a town of ten thousand people. San Buenaventura had but 3,500 at that time. Early in the spring I had enlarged and renovated a house on a piece of our property, centrally located, and shortly thereafter on June 30, 1888 the second of our children, another little girl, Hinda Alice, was born to Mrs. Rose and me.

As I was without a driving team, I took a trip to Rosemead and purchased from Father, Inez, a twelve-year-old bay, daughter of The Moor, and San Mateo Maid, a sorrel daughter of the same age by Whipple's Hambletonian. Among the scores of good teams I have owned, this pair was a standout.

When I took up my residence in San Buenaventura, there was incarcerated in the county jail an early resident of Los Angeles, Joe Dye, whom I had known in my boyhood. Dye was a Kentuckian of the mountaineer type and although of friendly disposition had a most violent temper. Some years previous he had killed two men, one of whom was William Warren, town marshal of Los Angeles. Dye at the time of the shooting with Warren was a deputy under him, and their quarrel was over a hundred-dollar reward for the apprehension of a stolen Chinese woman. Dye was tried and acquitted, moved to Ventura County, and took up a government claim in Sespe Canyon, and in the early 70's, in connection with Stephen Mott, Captain Wesley Roberts, Hancock Johnston, and my father, made one of the first oil discoveries in California.

Dye was being held in jail under a stay of execution pending an appeal to the higher court and had as his attorneys Henry T. Gage, the leading criminal lawyer of Los Angeles, who a few years later was elected governor of California, and Stephen M. White—a young man of great eloquence and ability—who was subsequently elected to the United States Senate. With this formidable array of legal talent, Dye was granted a new trial and acquitted.

The Southern Pacific branch from Saugus had been completed to Santa Paula, and passenger service inaugurated to that point. All travel from Ventura to Los Angeles was by stage to the railroad terminus. During the preliminary proceedings at Dye's trial Gage made frequent visits to Ventura, and, as I often went to Los Angeles on business, I made it convenient when Gage was returning there to drive him to Santa Paula with my team.

This slight attention on my part made of Gage one of my greatest friends throughout his life, and one of his first official acts upon his election as governor of the great commonwealth of California was to appoint me a member of the State Board of Agriculture.

Despite all the money we had spent in our effort to advance the growth of San Buenaventura, the name of which at this time had been shortened to Ventura, the town remained at a dead standstill. In addition to our gas works and street railway, a sewer system had been installed, and sidewalks laid in all directions, our share of the latter alone amounting to $12,000. In addition to all this, Mr. Fargo had joined G. W. Chrisman in a new water system, toward which he contributed $30,000.

Early this same fall, 1888, a number of citizens called on me seeking to prevail upon me to build a good hotel where people could stop, if they did come to Ventura, as the only solution of the existing dearth of visitors. Father and Fargo finally consented.

Ventura, like all country towns, was a one-business-street burg. In our purchases we had acquired a little over half of a mile of frontage on that portion of the main artery still occupied by small residences. Four of our lots were on the corners of an intersecting street but two blocks from the business center. I was living on one of the corner lots and selected the one just across the street as the hotel site. I at once let a contract for a building of pressed brick, with terra-cotta trimmings, 65 x 150, three stories high, to cost $57,600.

I had William Curlett, one of the leading architects of San Francisco, draw the plans, and the structure was the last word in excellence—at the time—with extra touches for its convenience costing $7,500. The ceilings were very high, all the rooms in suites, the floors throughout of solid oak and walnut, and enough colored glass in the windows and gingerbread trimmings without to satisfy the most fastidious.

We had not laid the foundation when a clique of leading citizens and businessmen clubbed together and built a three-story wooden firetrap down in the center of the town, which they called the Anacapa Hotel, and had it tenanted and opened before our building was completed. There never before had been business enough to support one hotel. As a consequence of this piece of base civic ingratitude, we were left with a good-sized white elephant on our hands.

In the meantime subsequent to the sale of Sunny Slope Father had engaged quite extensively in real estate transactions in Los Angeles County. He purchased many fine properties in the city, and in connection with Professor T. S. C. Lowe, builder of the famous incline up Mount Wilson, the Ward brothers, and Edward Webster, all residents of Pasadena, he opened up Raymond Avenue in that city and built thereon the old Raymond Opera House. In company with the same Webster and Mr. Woodbury, Father laid out the present glorious city Altadena, and with Messrs. Thompson and Ainsworth of Portland, Oregon, and Mr. Vail of Los Angeles he founded the seaport city Redondo Beach. This same company built the Redondo Beach Hotel.

Mr. Fargo was back and forth frequently from San Francisco to Ventura, and, although the stagnation of our investments was far from a gleeful matter, he made a huge joke of it and about evened himself in his sarcastic repartee with some of the retrenchers. Always jovial and good natured, he enjoyed the lack of restraint in the small town and soon knew all the best places to quench his thirst.

A large percentage of the population of Ventura were Mexicans, a number of whom kept restaurants, and, as Fargo was also a good trencherman, we patronized them quite regularly. We drove about the country considerably. There was living near New Jerusalem Señora Ortega, who was famous for the excellence of her viands, and we always managed to be near her place about the noon hour and enjoyed a wonderful repast in the open air under a large grape vine.

One day we were driving along on the road to Hueneme about ten miles from Ventura when our attention was drawn to thousands of wild geese feeding on a field of young barley on the Patterson ranch. The ranch buildings, located about a mile from the road, were of pretentious extent, and, noticing a "for sale" sign on the front gate, Fargo suggested, purely as a matter of curiosity, driving in.

The ranch consisted of 6,000 acres, with a three-mile frontage on the ocean; fully 5,000 acres were as level as a floor and fertile as a seedbed. The remainder was sand dunes along the coast. The property belonged to a Mr. Patterson of New York state. About half of it was seeded to barley, which was fed to hogs, of which thousands were raised. The remainder was devoted to raising draft horses. The property was in charge of Charley Daily, who, going along in his quiet manner, produced scores of draft animals that could take rank with the best raised in America.

We were informed the price was $40 per acre, and Fargo was so impressed with the property that he would have entered into negotiations on the spot for its purchase had I not prevailed upon him to first consult Father. He went to Los Angeles the following day for that purpose. Father would not listen to joining in the transaction, waving Fargo aside with the statement that in selling Sunny Slope he had been somewhat impelled by a desire to get my brother Harry and myself into some other walk of life. The project was abandoned, and another chapter thereby added to the comedy of our errors in our Ventura County investments. A little more than a decade later, when the Oxnards built their beet-sugar factory and established the town bearing their name near this property, they bought it for $300 per acre, and it soared to $1,500 per acre with the score of years following.

I visited San Francisco often and was always Mr. Fargo's dinner guest. If we were alone, we dined at his club, the new Pacific Union, if, however, we were attended by ladies—for whom he had a great weakness—we went to the Poodle Dog. He kept a fine span of horses and was a daily driver through the park to the Cliff House, winding up the afternoon with an hour or two at his friend Dickey's. Fargo, like my father, was a crony of all the big railroad and mining men of the early days, and through their acquaintance I knew all of those influential gentlemen very pleasantly in the later years of their lives. Mr. Charles Crocker of the railroad quartet was the most ardent disciple of the road. Senator Stanford drove little in the later years of his life. Huntington and Hopkins, who spent most of their time in the financial world of the East, were rarely seen on the road. John W. Mackay, as well as Senator George Hearst and J. B. Haggin, drove little, but James G. Fair and James Flood were out daily and always hobnobbed at Dickey's. There were many road drivers among the younger generation, my best friends of whom were A. B. Spreckels and Chris Smith.

# 12

## *Stallion Race - Horse Sales - Stamboul the Great*

### I

HERETOFORE, the race meetings in Los Angeles had taken place in October at the end of the circuit of eight fairs in the north, with a week's racing at each. As a consequence, during the arduous campaign many horses went wrong, many owners' hopes were shattered, and the entry list was greatly depleted by this late date. To forestall this occurrence and add fresh stimulus to their meeting, the Los Angeles Association offered very attractive purses and inaugurated the racing season this same year, 1888, in August.

Among others that came from the north was O. A. Hickok with Arab, the fastest trotter in California at the time, having a record of 2:16½. Arab was the joint property of Thomas H. Williams, Jr., Porter Ashe, Ira Ramsdell, and Hickok, and he had been raced very successfully the year previous on the eastern grand circuit by Hickok.

Williams, who was still in his twenties, was the son of General Williams, one of the leading attorneys of San Francisco, a man of great wealth, owning considerable rental property in that city and Union and Grand Islands, princely domains in the San Joaquin and Sacramento River districts. Williams, who was a profligate spender and had blossomed forth as a plunger on trotting races the preceding year at the State Fair in Sacramento, came along with Hickok and Arab. All of the entrants in Arab's race declined the issue with him, and, simply as a matter of compliment to the northerners in order to permit them to show their splendid horse, Father volunteered to start Stamboul against him.

Father had not the slightest idea or remotest hope of beating Arab; as a matter of fact, Stamboul had been out of the stud but two weeks. The public were of the same opinion, and in the auction pools Arab brought $100 and Stamboul $10. In this manner, after 5% was taken by the pool seller, a hundred dollars would win $4.50. Williams, who felt victory was a foregone conclusion, reasoned with me that he could not make money more easily than by putting up his check for $10,000 for about an hour and a half and drawing down $450 interest and proceeded to do so. We were very warm friends at the time, and he ceaselessly chided me for my lack of pride in my father's horse, saying as a matter of courtesy to him I should at least make one bet of $100 against a $1,000, in order, as he put it, that he might win some breakfast money. Finally in sheer self-defense, I made the bet with him. The race was called, Stamboul drew the pole, and he never looked more majestic. He weighed 1,120 lbs. in racing condition, and the combined weight of his four shoes was the insignificant total for a horse of his size of 24 ounces—7 ounces on each front foot, and 5 on each hind one. In swift action Stamboul carried his head dead in front, his neck absolutely rigid, and his almost mechanical action reminded one of the walking beam on a steamer.

The word for the first heat was given, with Stamboul at the rail, a neck in front. I sat in a box with Father, and, when the horses passed the quarter pole in the same relative positions, we both split on them, and, when our watches registered 32¾ seconds, a 2:11 gait, we could not believe our eyes. On they sped, the next quarter in 32 seconds, a 2:08 gait. We were then aghast, and, when we saw the glint of sunlight on Hickok's light-colored whip as he tapped Arab with it and still he could not pass Stamboul, we were dumbfounded.

Quite naturally after this great flight of speed the pace slackened, and Stamboul won the heat by a comfortable margin in 2:14¾. Stamboul took the lead from the start in the second heat and won it handily in 2:17½. Father could not understand the case and, considerably perturbed, went to Maben and inquired whether Hickok was doing his best to win, or was his party of owners engineering a betting coup. The final heat robbed Father of any such delusion, as Hickok made free use of his whip on his great little horse from start to finish but could not wrest the lead away, and Stamboul won the heat in 2:16½. I, instead of Williams, won the breakfast money.

The next meeting was at Oakland, and, as I was now master of my own affairs, when Stamboul was shipped north I also went along. At Oakland Stamboul met Guy Wilkes and Woodnut. It looked like a certainty, and I entered the arena as a plunger. Stamboul kept striking one hind shin as he passed his forefoot with it. The hot blood of his daddy Sultan asserted itself; he kept breaking and trotted scarcely half a mile during the five heats of the race without a break.

He managed to win two heats, but Guy Wilkes won the deciding one, and our party lost a cartload of money. The same three horses raced the following week at the State Fair; Guy Wilkes was not at his best, Stamboul was at his worst, and Woodnut, who sold for $20 in pools calling for upwards of $500, won the second, third, and fourth heats, Guy Wilkes winning the first. None of our party bet a dollar on Stamboul.

Fortunes were bet on a day's racing, the pool sellers were lightning fast, and those of us who bet big money had an open account, placed our orders to bet a certain amount, and, with first choice bringing $500 or even $1,000 at times, a large sum was placed in a few minutes. There were three or four races each day, rarely any of them under three heats, and, if the heats were split, the contest went to four or five or even seven. Pools were sold on each heat and the result of the race as well, and one could get action on his money ten or fifteen times in an afternoon. Moreover, there was a great amount of hedging, and one frequently hopped from the frying pan into the fire.

After Stamboul's miserable showing at Sacramento, he was taken to Santa Rosa, where he raced somewhat better but was beaten by Jane L., a mare from Oregon. My bosom friend John Goldsmith had himself substituted for Lindsay as driver of Jane L. When Stamboul had the race about clinched, by resorting to sharp practices, Goldsmith beat Stamboul the deciding heat. I lost my temper and slapped Goldsmith's face. Friends intervened, but he was thoroughly frightened and left town that night in a boxcar with some horses.

Father was in great distress over Stamboul's loss of form, as his heart was set on winning the $20,000 stallion race to be decided a few months later at the Bay District track in San Francisco. Maben had a light piece of steel plate inserted within Stamboul's hind shin boot, which prevented any pain when it was struck, and in the horse's next start, which was at Stockton, he trotted a steady race, but his ranting around, breaking and running in his races had deadened his speed. Maben returned to Rosemead from Stockton to attend to urgent matters, and Stamboul was sent to San Francisco and turned over to Hickok for the stallion race.

The day of the race arrived, and there were but three entries—Antevolo, Woodnut, and Stamboul. Antevolo was driven by his owner, Joseph Cairn Simpson, an aged gentleman, the editor of the *Breeder and Sportsman*, a fine publication devoted exclusively to harness horses. Mr. Simpson had as his fad, of which he was the originator, "tips," which were shoes that covered only the circular portion of the horse's feet. Though others tried them, Mr. Simpson was their sole constant exponent, and how he, an astute horseman, could be, I cannot see. I looked at Antevolo's feet and found his heels were at least four inches high, badly contracted, and his foot had grown to the shape of that of a mule; withal, he could trot and trot fast. He had been trained at Bay District, had shown some splendid miles, and had many admirers.

Woodnut was driven by his owner, Bi Holly, a sly old fox whose left hand knew not what his right hand did, who had many cohorts of the same ilk, and, harking back to the way he cleaned up Stamboul and Guy Wilkes at Sacramento—on which occasion, as a matter of fact, he simply profited by the misfortunes of his adversaries—their appetites were whetted for another killing.

Stamboul, by his erratic racing since his wonderful victory over Arab, had forfeited practically all his public prestige, and the race had an open look. After reaching San Francisco, Stamboul had shown us that he would at least be steady, and we felt fairly confident. Antevolo opened favorite at $500; Stamboul brought $400 and Woodnut $150. Father and I had placed an order for $5,000 in the pool box, and Stamboul soon went to favoritism.

When they were given the word, Antevolo took a slight lead; Hickok laid right alongside of him with Stamboul and made his move when entering the stretch, but Antevolo had enough foot left to beat him home. We at once counseled with Hickok, who, instead of being in any way perturbed, was very complacent. He admitted making a mistake in driving the heat, saying, "I'll go right at Mr. Antevolo from the start the next heat, and by the time we reach the half-mile pole, I'll have him and old man Simpson so dizzy that he (Antevolo) won't have that brush of speed left when we hit the stretch."

This was an unusual burst of enthusiasm for the taciturn Hickok. Antevolo was now favorite, and Father and I bet $2,500 more. True to his word, Hickok went "right at him," and Antevolo and Stamboul fairly sizzled around the first turn, and on they sped, head and head, to the half. Shortly after leaving there, Stamboul shook Antevolo off and came home a comfortable winner in 2:17¾. The third and fourth heats were repetitions of this one, each in 2:17½, and Stamboul repaid me my big Oakland loss with liberal interest.

Stamboul was restored to a pedestal, and Mr. Walker Hobart, a very wealthy mining man of San Francisco, offered Father $50,000 for him. Upon Mr. Hobart's agreeing to allow Father to breed five mares to Stamboul each spring as long as he remained in California, the offer was accepted.

## II

The instant Father decided to part with Stamboul, his further aspirations in the line of trotting-horse breeding ceased. Although he had not attained the confidently expected goal of establishing Stamboul as the fastest trotting stallion in the world, knowing that Mr. Hobart would give the horse every opportunity of accomplishing the glorious feat, Father felt content in the belief that he would ultimately share the glory, having been Stamboul's breeder. In embarking in the breeding game it had been Father's aim to create an individual strain of horses; this he had accomplished in a most spectacular manner. There was a big eastern demand for his stock, his cup of success was full, the time was propitious, so he concluded to disband Rosemead trotting stud.

In February 1889 I loaded forty-seven two- and three-year-olds for shipment to New York. Those of the older age were Sultan's last crop at Sunny Slope; the younger lot were about half each by Stamboul and Alcazar. They were loaded in three large baggage cars, hitched to the regular, fast passenger train, consigned to Peter C. Kellogg and Company, by Wells, Fargo and Company's express. The two-year-old Mascot, Stamboul's first foal out of renowned Minnehaha, was quite naturally considered the outstanding animal of the consignment. Father regarded Mascot's blood lines as the acme of his breeding ventures; he was as handsome a colt as one ever saw, was endowed with electrical speed, and Father had high hopes that the colt might excel his illustrious sire, Stamboul.

The sale was held in the old American Institute at Third Avenue and Sixty-Third Street. There was an eighth-of-a-mile ring in the building, and I showed all of the colts in harness. The auctioneer cried the sale from an embryo judges' stand, midway of one of the stretches, in which Father stood with him, giving any necessary information. The colts were hitched at the upper end of the ring, and, when I mounted the cart behind Mascot, the grooms asked my guess as to how much he would bring, to which I replied $12,500. The first time I drove by the auctioneer's stand, I heard $13,000 called, and from that amount the bids soared a $1,000 at a time until Mascot was knocked down for account of Marcus Daly, the Montana copper magnate, for $26,000, and the forty-seven head brought an aggregate of $114,400.[31] There is an interesting story that goes with the sale of Mascot. Bi Holly, of whom I have just spoken as the driver of Woodnut, was well acquainted with Marcus Daly and from time to time sold him horses. Mr. Daly had deputized Holly to go to New York and buy Mascot. Holly asked for instructions as to how much to pay, and Daly's reply was that price made no difference, to which Holly's rejoinder was that he would go on to the sale, but "he would be damned if he would pay over $10,000 for anybody's cat-hammed two-year-old"—and thus the matter rested.

Holly was very seriously afflicted with asthma, and, when he reached Chicago en route to the sale, he was taken from the train and kept there, violently ill. He immediately wired Daly, who thereupon communicated with Scott Queintin in New York, a new trainer whom he had recently hired at a big salary, to attend the sale and buy Mascot, and nothing could have been more propitious. Queintin looked more like a young Wall Street broker than a race-horse driver—carefully groomed, dressed in the height

[31] The Huntington Library has a copy of a telegram from L. J. Rose to Mrs. Rose dated March 7, 1889, as follows: "Biggest sale ever made forty seven brought hundred eighteen thousand."

of fashion, high silk hat, chamois skin gloves, stick and all. Dearly in love with himself and the limelight, Queintin would rather have paid $50,000 for the colt and had his picture in the morning paper than to have bought him for $10,000 with no ostentation.

Mr. J. H. Shultz, a very wealthy gentleman of Brooklyn, a liberal patron and warm personal friend of Father's, was the only other bidder, and, had Holly been present, Mr. Shultz would have secured the colt for his first bid above Holly's $10,000. We of course did not know this story until a few days later, when Holly, who had recuperated, drifted in to New York. Father and I were seated by the fire in his suite at the Hoffman House one evening when in walked Holly. He immediately unfolded his tale and kept repeating to Father, whom he called "Dad," "You owe me good and plenty, 'Dad,' for had I been here your Mascot would not have brought over $11,000." Father enjoyed the repartee thoroughly in his quiet manner. Finally, extracting a small roll of $1,000 bills from his pocket, he handed one to Holly. Holly, quite abashed, refused to accept it, explaining that he was only joking, thinking he might talk himself into a new suit of clothes. Father finally forced Holly to take the bill, telling him he fully realized the truth of his (Holly's) contention and was only too pleased to share his good luck with him to that small extent.

The price Mascot brought was the topic of the day in trotting-horse circles insomuch as it was the highest ever paid up to that time for an untried two-year-old of the harness tribe. Thus again had the current of Minnehaha's fame—somewhat analogous to the translation of her Indian name, "Laughing Water"—coursed constantly to greater triumphs. This, however, was the last of this wonderful little matron's earthly glories, as, after raising a year-younger brother of Mascot's, she died and was buried amidst the beautiful surroundings at Rosemead. Well may she rest on the laurels brought to her through the fame of her progeny. She was the dam of three by The Moor, one by Silver Threads, one by Kismet, six by Sultan, and two by Stamboul, everyone of whom except Mizpah—who like her ill-fated sire, Kismet, died before having an opportunity to assert her worth—lent nobly of their blood in later generations of the trotting family.

William Corbitt of San Mateo Stock Farm had sent along a carload to the sale, as also had Charley Durfee and Hancock Johnston, who had a carload in partnership. John Goldsmith, with whom I had buried the hatchet, was also along, and we were all stopping at the Hoffman House, which was also the rendezvous for all the Kentucky buyers. We had long nightly sessions at the round table in the palatial Hoffman House barroom, at which there was limitless discussion of the horse. William Crawford, known to every trotting horseman in the country at the time as the "Counsellor," a native of Pennsylvania but a Kentuckian by adoption, had during the preceding year, 1888, been in correspondence with Father regarding the purchase of Stamboul. Crawford had a syndicate of Kentuckians interested with him, and, while they were dickering, Mr. Hobart of San Francisco stepped in and bought the horse. The gentlemen were quite naturally somewhat disappointed, and Crawford, of very sarcastic mien, sought to vent his spleen by speaking disparagingly of Stamboul. Father finally accepted the gauntlet, one word led to another, and Father offered to bet $5,000 that Stamboul would trot a mile during the year 1889 in 2:12 or better. Crawford accepted the challenge, and William Corbitt was appointed stakeholder.

No money or collateral was forthcoming, and Corbitt, in his gruff manner, turned to Crawford, saying, "You are doing a lot of talking—why don't you put up?" Crawford replied, "I'll put up as fast as Rose will." "No you won't," said Corbitt, "Mr. Rose's word is good to me and is up already." Crawford drew his check on a Kentucky bank for $5,000, which Corbitt would not accept. It was finally agreed that, as Goldsmith and I were returning to California via Kentucky, I should take the check to the bank at Lexington and have it certified, which I did. Upon my return to California, I delivered it to Mr. Corbitt.

I told my father the minute we were alone that he would surely lose the bet, reasoning in the first place that the crafty "Counsellor" did not ever bet $5,000 on anything unless he had a peek in the box first. Please note, Stamboul had been turned over to Hickok, who was Crawford's closest friend, and together they had engineered many deals on the track.

The time rolled around for the trial, which was undertaken late in the fall of 1889 over the Bay District track in San Francisco. Stamboul was at his best, and, accompanied by a prompter driven by Charley Marvin, he stepped around the first turn in 33½ seconds. The next quarter was in 32½, 1:06 for the half. Hickok said to Marvin, when the horses were well on their way around the upper turn, "How fast to the half, Charley?" "1:06," was the reply. Hickok said, "Too fast, too fast," and took Stamboul back a trifle. He was still full of trot and had not faltered an instant—if damage had been done by the pace, it was then too late to rectify it—and Stamboul came on again when given his head and finished the mile resolutely with Hickok in no overly evident determined effort in 2:12¼.

Close contact with the horse-racing game had, even at that time, taught me so amply about the uncertainties of it that I was not of the ever "Doubting Thomases," and I may be doing Hickok an injustice. The significant fact, however, still remains that, although he had Stamboul eight months during which the horse trained perfectly, Hickok made but this one attempt to beat 2:12 with him.

Just one year later, February 1890, I again took a shipment of Father's horses to the sales ring in New York. There were 87 head in the consignment, as near a cleanup as was possible under the condition. Alcazar, the only remaining sire, was also included. About a half-dozen mares which had already foaled, Minnehaha's last colt, a two-year-old brother to Mascot, and two racing prospects were kept behind to be sold the following year. I had seven express cars in the load, and as on the former occasion the shipment was handled by Wells, Fargo and Company and its eastern connection with first-class passenger service guaranteed.

To escape the rigors of the winter cold along the routes farther north, I elected to go via Southern Pacific from San Gabriel to El Paso, thence over the Texas Pacific to St. Louis, and from there to New York. All went swimmingly until we reached El Paso early in the morning, where I awoke to the fact that my seven carloads of first-class matter were being shunted around the yards in forming a special freight train, made up of three freight carloads of California wine and an ordinary stock car filled with Texas broncos.

I pled in vain with every official I could reach, finally deciding, insomuch as the horses were less restless when in motion, that in lieu of losing time by standing in the yard awaiting developments I would allow the Texas Pacific to send me out with the freight crew. I fairly deluged the Western Union with messages to California, and, when about six hours later my freight pulled into the next division headquarters at Willow Springs, every Texas Pacific employee that had a hat stood with it in his hand, bowing and scraping to me as I alighted, offering his services. From that point onward I had the best of service.

I had the misfortune of losing two animals by death en route, but was, however, liberally recompensed in the meantime by the birth of a young aristocrat of rare lineage. Zoraya, a three-year-old black filly by Guy Wilkes out of a Nutwood mare, for which we paid Mr. William Corbitt $5,000 solely to be used as a brood mare because of her royal breeding, foaled a fine horse colt the night before reaching New York. The little fellow was about the greatest attraction in the outfit to visitors, and, when he and his young dam were sold, they brought $13,100 to the bid of Colonel R. G. Stoner of Paris, Kentucky. Reverie, a bay two-year-old filly by Alcazar out of Sallie Durbrow, who the year previous as a yearling had just missed becoming the champion of that age, was also in the consignment.

In trials against time, the animal making the attempt must equal or surpass the time contested against in order to be accredited with performance. Simply as a means of giving her a record, Reverie's first start as a yearling was for a record with no restrictions as to the time thereof, and she trotted a nice mile in 2:37. The yearling record at the time was 2:31¼; Reverie started against it later a number of times, trotting miles in 2:33 and 2:34, and one day stepped one in 2:31½, just a mere quarter of a second shy. Under the rules, however, she got no official credit for the performance, which was nonetheless highly regarded and flashed by telegraph all over the country.

Mr. Robert Bonner of New York, for many years publisher of the old-time fireside friend, the New York *Weekly Ledger*, a man of great wealth, had a penchant for owning the fastest trotter in America and for many years had been the leader in paying high prices for champions or near champions. Mr. Bonner had been in California a few months previous to this sale, had visited Rosemead, and inspected this filly, Reverie, which he was informed would be sold at auction in New York the following spring.

My large horse family were hardly settled in their quarters in the American Institute when Mr. Bonner put in an appearance. I had met him a decade earlier at Case's, on the New York speedway, when as a boy I was driving with E. S. Stokes, but naturally Mr. Bonner did not remember me. He was a fine, frank, and friendly gentleman, and we became well acquainted at once. I showed him my favorites among the band but soon learned the animal that had attracted him to the place, as we invariably got back to Reverie's stall.

The morning of his first visit, three days prior to the sale, I led the filly out for his inspection and offered to throw a harness on her that he might see her in action, which he declined. He was back bright and early the next forenoon and then requested to see her hitched; I stepped her briskly around the ring, and he was delighted with her way of moving. The succeeding day I again showed her to harness for him. The turns of the miniature track were perforce very sharp, and in my desire to show her speed I turned on so much steam I capsized the cart immediately in front of where Mr. Bonner was standing. I lit on my feet, however, instantly righted the cart, and it was all done so quickly the filly hardly knew what was happening.

The filly's docility under the circumstances, however, made a great impression on Mr. Bonner, and as he left he said, "I'll be at the sale tomorrow." Mr. Bonner came to the sale accompanied by Mr. Hamilton Busbey, editor of the *Turf, Field and Farm*, a contemporaneous publication in New York with the *Spirit of the Times*, both of which were exclusively harness-horse periodicals. Messrs. Bonner and Busbey sat immediately across the track from the auctioneer's box in which Father was sitting. As soon as I had flashed by with Reverie, Mr. Kellogg called for bids, and Mr. Bonner cried out sharply, "$10,000!"

Father immediately arose to his feet and earnestly said, "I hope no one raises Mr. Bonner's bid, for I would like to see this wonderful filly go into his barn." Mr. Kellogg promptly dropped his hammer, Mr. Bonner bowed his acknowledgment to Father, and Reverie went to Tarrytown to join

Maud S. and other equine celebrities—a little more glory to the memory of Minnehaha, through the paternal line of her son Alcazar.

A good-looking two-year-old bay stallion by Alcazar out of a Guy Wilkes's mare was knocked down to a gentleman from Boston for $2,950. In the course of a few minutes word reached Father that the buyer had discovered something wrong with one of the colt's hind legs and was dissatisfied with his purchase. There was no guarantee with the sale other than as to pedigrees and records, and as in all such sales it was a case of *caveat emptor* (the buyer beware). Disregarding all of this, Father had the colt immediately returned to the auctioneer's stand and stated the gentleman who had previously purchased him fancied he had discovered something wrong with one of the colt's hocks; however, if such was the case, it was unbeknown to him (Father). He counseled all to look carefully for themselves and be governed accordingly, as the colt was there to be sold if he brought but two dollars, adding casually that personally he had always admired the animal.

Father had the happy faculty of carrying conviction in all his utterances, and these few words bore good fruit. The colt was really a handsome fellow and as sound as a bell of brass. Bids were called for and rapidly mounted to $4,450, at which he was sold, an increase of $1,500 over the first sale. Alcazar brought $25,500. Voodoo, a grandson of Minnehaha through the maternal line of her daughter Eva, brought $24,400. The 86 head brought $238,800, an average of $2,770, the highest ever attained at a breeder's dispersal sale for a like number of animals before or since.

Mr. Bonner's first real champion was Dexter, whom he purchased in 1867. Dexter had gained great renown because of his speed and was advertised for an exhibition in Buffalo. Mr. Bonner journeyed there and witnessed the trial, in which Dexter all but set the world on fire by trotting a mile in 2:17¼. Mr. Bonner purchased him at once for $20,000 and immediately wired his New York friends: "I have today seen the two wonders of the world—this morning I saw Niagara Falls, and this afternoon saw Dexter trot a mile in 2:17¼—I could not buy Niagara Falls, but I have bought Dexter."

## III

There was a fair mile race track located on an alkali flat on the edge of Ventura, and races, such as they were, were held May Day, Fourth of July, and in the fall a meeting of four days after the bean harvest. Having been with trotting horses all my life, it was only natural I should be a fair reinsman; moreover, I had driven in a number of races at the Los Angeles Fair at different times.

Chrisman and Willoughby, who with some others purchased the stallion A. W. Richmond from Hancock Johnston of Los Angeles, had a pair of three-year-olds by him which were used by the local butcher for delivering meat in the rural districts. One of these, whom they called Richmond Jr., had shown quite an ability to trot, and with no more than a week's training at any one time I had driven him, winning three races handily and convincing myself the colt was quite a natural trotter. Richmond Jr.'s mate, Barney, although not so speedy as he, was far above the average and a gallant little fellow in harness.

As my fine pair of driving mares was well over the meridian in the age of horses, and, feeling certain the glamour of Father's sale would reflect itself to them, I took them along to New York this spring and sold them for brood mares for a little more than $2,500.

I had in mind at the time the purchase of this butcher-wagon team and upon my return bought them for $750. Richmond Jr. showed so much speed I decided to train him, and, when Father's horses in charge of Maben were sent north to the races in August, I shipped him along that I might busy myself with him every morning. He continued to improve, and I started him in a race at Stockton against horses I knew I had no chance of beating and gave particular attention to teaching him to get away from the score more rapidly. When around the first turn, he would fairly fly and gave such dazzling exhibitions of speed the judges called me into the stand, questioned my efforts to win, and rebuked me for going away so slowly. I explained the matter and offered to turn the horse over to anyone else they might choose. They were finally appeased, and I finished the race.

This race improved the horse greatly, and the following week I started him at San Jose against Una Wilkes, driven by John Goldsmith; Moro, belonging to my father, driven by Maben; C.C.S., driven by Andy McDowell; and a little brown horse by Abbotsford, driven by Alex Gordon.

Goldsmith and I bet $3,000 on my horse. Andy McDowell wanted to hippodrome the race by an agreement to an equal division of the purse in advance among the five contestants, then bet the total amount on my horse, shoo him in, and divide the winnings pro rata. I promptly declined the proposition, and, somewhat miffed, McDowell said, "Go ahead, then, I'll make you settle before it's over."

McDowell won the first heat in 2:22¾. I won the next in 2:23¼. Maben came along and won the third and fourth heats with Father's mare, Moro, in 2:23–2:24¼, in one of which McDowell was distanced. My prospects of winning looked far from good. Goldsmith was very much peeved, as he considered the money lost, and he suggested I get Maben to lay up a heat, which would give us a chance to hedge some of it. I told him that such a procedure was absolutely impossible, that I would under no conditions ask Maben, who, if I did, would no doubt give me a good cursing. Father was sitting in the grandstand, and finally, though realizing I was entering the lion's den in doing so, to placate Goldsmith I went to see Father and asked him to give me permission to have Maben lay up a heat, telling him Goldsmith and I stood to lose $3,000. Father gave me one look and said: "Don't you dare make any such proposition to Walter. I would not humbug all these people for twenty times $3,000, and what's more, I hope you lose it and go home to your little family and stay there, where you belong."

Goldsmith was as sore as he could be, rebuking me freely for not getting away faster. I was fully as much concerned as he, and we left the score at a scorching pace in the fifth heat. Goldsmith's voice could have been heard a mile away as he shouted his urge to my horse. Realizing it was a case of do or die, I tiptoed Richmond Jr. every inch of the way around the first turn; Maben and I were soon clear of the other two contestants, and I managed to beat him home in 2:22—the fastest heat of the race. According to racing rules, nonwinners of a heat in the first five are eliminated, which left Maben and me the sole contestants in the sixth and deciding heat, which I finally won.

During this same spring, 1890, Stamboul was turned over to John Goldsmith to train in an endeavor to beat the stallion record. Stamboul was a very "good doer," and, as it was difficult to take any of the surplus weight off him in the cool, bracing climate in the San Francisco Bay section, Mr. Hobart constructed a fine one-stall barn, with feed and sleeping room for his groom attached, at the fairgrounds at Stockton, where there was no lack of warmth. Goldsmith, who was still in the employ of William Corbitt at the San Mateo Stock Farm, went to Stockton every Wednesday and Saturday to work Stamboul and during the fall gave Stamboul a record of 2:09¾. Again had this mighty warrior reduced his record, and he was returned to winter quarters at Mr. Hobart's palatial stock farm in San Mateo County.

During the winter of 1890-1891, Father, with the love of horses still uppermost in his heart, decided to go into the running-horse game, purchasing a dozen two-year-olds from Senator Leland Stanford. They were turned over to Dave Bridges to train at Agricultural Park and late in the spring of 1891 shipped to New York to race. They were a useful lot of animals, and all won races; one of them, however, Fairy, was far above the average and won in the best of company on the metropolitan tracks.

Father also bought Fairy's sire, Argyle, from Senator Stanford to place at the head of a running-horse breeding farm. As success had come to him from a theory of his own in his trotting breeding venture, Father decided to reverse the usual order of things and, instead of depending on an imported sire, concluded to import matrons and use a native sire and asked me to go to Australia to buy ten mares for him. I was busy with my own affairs and greatly to my sorrow was forced to decline, whereupon he sent Captain

T. B. Merry, an expert on breeding, who wrote quite extensively under the nom de plume of "Hidalgo." Captain Merry bought Father ten mares and a two-year-old stallion at a cost of $22,000. The mares were of the choicest strains of Australian breeding, Muskets and Carbines principally. They were an odd-looking lot by comparison to the American thoroughbreds, were very much larger and far coarser in every way. Their bone was heavier than that of the most substantial trotting horse of this country.

A few years previous to this J. W. Robinson, proprietor of the Boston Dry Goods Store in Los Angeles, established a trotting-horse breeding farm near Rosemead, which he called Edgemont. Robinson imported a number of mares from Kentucky and, to be used as the head of his stud, purchased from Father for $10,000 Redondo, a fine three-year-old by Sultan; he also purchased Semi Tropic by Sultan for $4,500 as a racing prospect.

As previously stated, the second consignment of Father's horses which I sold in New York about put him out of the trotting-horse game, whereupon Mr. Robinson grasped the opportunity to secure Maben's services as a trainer. It was considerably like breaking up the family for Father to part with Maben, who for fifteen years had been a most devoted and competent helpmate, although both Maben and Father realized that it was for the best.

Maben's duties at Edgemont were not engrossing, and by an arrangement with Mr. Robinson Mr. Hobart hired Maben to go to Stockton during the summer of 1892 to take charge of Stamboul's training in a further effort of wresting Kremlin's stallion championship record of 2:07¾ from him. Maben remained in Stockton three months with Stamboul and early in the fall gave him a record of 2:07½. Early rains that season precluded another effort. Stamboul then went into winter quarters.

Perhaps some of my readers may have been wearied by the constant interjection of Maben and Stamboul into this narrative. If such is the case, I crave their forgiveness. Even so, a volume could be written of Stamboul's greatness, and his true worth would not be overestimated. Horsemen can thoroughly appreciate his wonderful speed achievements, and the layman should at least admire the constancy of his advancement to the coveted goal. Stamboul began his career as a two-year-old with a record of 2:37; then each of the succeeding seven years he bettered it in the following manner: 2:26½, 2:23, 2:17½, 2:14¾, 2:12¼, 2:09¾, and 2:07½. Is not this a glorious escutcheon? Does it not merit my enthusiasm? In his racing contests Stamboul never dodged the issue; he met all comers, fought valiantly for his laurels, never turned his tail to the feed box, and never took a lame step in his life. Nor was this all of his greatness.

Mr. Walker Hobart of San Francisco, who purchased Stamboul from Father for $50,000, died shortly after this performance, and the horse was not trained again in Mr. Hobart's interest. Following close upon Mr.

Hobart's death, Stamboul, along with Mr. Hobart's wonderful trotting stud, was consigned to the sales ring at New York, where he was purchased for $41,000 by Mr. E. H. Harriman. Stamboul was not trained again for speed but sought new laurels in the show ring. He had lived up to his early promise of equine perfection and at his first essay at Madison Square Garden Horse Show in the fall of 1893 was awarded the blue ribbon for the handsomest horse exhibited. He duplicated his performance the following year; after these triumphs he was not exhibited until three years later, when he again smothered all competition. Mambrino King, the property of Mr. Cicero J. Hamlin of Buffalo, New York, had for a number of years been classed as the handsomest horse in America, but Stamboul wrested the glorious distinction from him. Mr. Harriman was positively enraptured with the horse.

As all were aware, Mr. Harriman, with his tremendous railroad interests, was a very busy man, and he was also an extremely taciturn one. Notwithstanding this, when his gigantic Pacific Coast interest brought him west, he invariably telegraphed Maben—who had developed Stamboul—to meet him at the Van Nuys Hotel in Los Angeles. At the appointed hour to the second, Mr. Harriman would arrive, and, seated in the lobby of the hotel with Maben—casting every other care and interest to the winds for the time being—he would put in a solid hour doing naught but extolling Stamboul's many virtues. When Stamboul died, he was buried beneath a monument fit for a king at Mr. Harriman's beautiful country estate, Arden, in Goshen, Orange County, New York.

13

# *Tapo Ranch - A Long Ride - Desert Cattle Drive*

## I

THE INACTIVITY of our investments in Ventura finally got on my nerves, and in November preceding the horse sale of 1890 I decided to go into the cattle business and took a five-year lease on the well-watered, abundant feed-producing Tapo ranch of 14,000 acres, located 40 miles from Ventura. Concluding to give T. H. (Tom) Chrisman a working interest, we entered into negotiations for the purchase of 400 head of cattle belonging to Manuel Robles, ranging in the mountainous country near Cuyama, about forty miles from Ventura in another direction. Cattle were very cheap in those days, and the trade was made at $15 per head for all branded stock, all calves gratis.

A few days later I bought three hundred head from Rafael Reyes, a fine old fellow with whom my trade was full of pleasure. Reyes, a man of advanced years, weighed 280 lbs., had very protruding eyes, one of them completely covered with a white film, a bad scar on one cheek, a vicious-looking moustache, and, if ever a human being's appearance suggested Mephistopheles, Reyes was that individual.

He gave about the greatest demonstration of stamina in the native California horse that I have ever known. As stated, Reyes weighted 280 lbs., his saddle and blankets fully fifty more, and his large saddlebags, which he always carried filled with food for his insatiable appetite, weighed at least fifteen pounds additional. He rode a small gray horse that did not weigh an ounce over 850 lbs.; the country was mountainous and rough, but this valiant little animal never faltered, going up and down the steepest of places with this immense hulk on his back throughout the day.

These cattle were turned on the Tapo. Chrisman and I decided not to associate ourselves in the business, and I hired W. E. Dysart, who had been in charge of a band of cattle for a number of years on the Tapo for Lyons and Campbell, New Mexican cattlemen. Dysart continued in my employ throughout my cattle business, and I have never known a better cowman or as energetic and trustworthy employee.

The Tapo ranch was the last rural stand of the powerful De la Guerra family, who had previously owned the colossal adjoining Simi grant of 93,000 acres. Portions of the old adobe house still stood on Tapo, in which Dysart and I were very comfortably housed. My cow business was particularly lucrative on this place, and I shall always look back upon the tenancy of it and my association with Dysart as one of the very bright spots in my life.

The copious rainfall had produced a superabundance of grass, and Dysart advised buying more stock. I soon learned of a herd of four hundred ranging near Elizabeth Lake, belonging to the estate of "Miguel Grande" (big Michael) Leonis, a Basque, who recently had met death by falling from the seat of his farm wagon. During his life Leonis made his home near Calabasas with an Indian woman whom he called "Espíritu Santo" (the Holy Ghost), and I went there in quest of information as to the exact location and price of the cattle.

The ground had become absolutely waterlogged, even the beaten roads that appeared firm gave way under my horse, and he frequently mired down to his body, forcing me to dismount on various occasions in order that he might release himself. After about five hours of buffeting about in this manner, I reached the Leonis house, where I met Laurent Etchipari, also a Basque, who was handling the widow's affairs; he priced the cattle to my satisfaction, and I decided to start on the sixty-odd-mile trip to Elizabeth Lake to inspect them. After a weary afternoon ride I reached San Fernando, where I put up for the night. When I awoke the following morning, rain was falling in sheets. About noon the clouds broke away, and after eating lunch I started for Elizabeth Lake via Newhall and San Francisquito Canyon.

The next day at noon I reached Andrada's, a regular stopping place with ample eating and sleeping accommodations, with a particularly delightful adjunct at the time, a bar. Andrada, a good sort, saddled his horse and rode with me to look the cattle over. They were far above the average in quality, and I was correspondingly elated with my discovery of them.

I was on my way bright and early the following morning. The country traversed by San Francisquito Canyon was quite mountainous. The road wound its way up and down and around, frequently crossing the creek, which, though still somewhat swollen, hampered travel but slightly. In the early days when stage travel was in vogue, San Francisquito Canyon was the main highway of travel between Los Angeles and San Francisco, and the gaudily painted Concord coaches "chug-chugged" merrily to and fro daily. Andrada's station was at the northern mouth of the canyon; about three miles farther along the stage road passed Elizabeth Lake, a large sheet of fresh water situated on the outer rim of the Mojave Desert; then onward by way of Gorman's station, Fort Tejon, Bakersfield, and other San Joaquin

Valley points, and finally skirting the San Francisco Bay to the southward and up the west side thereof to San Francisco.

San Francisquito Canyon was also the getaway course for early-day malefactors in Los Angeles County. There were a few persons of shady reputation living in the canyon who, abetted by the rough topography of the country, acted as fences for horse thieves and shielded other evildoers of their ilk. In their apparently innocent home life along the road they were vigilant sentinels, and, by building a short line of barbed-wire fence across the mouth of a rugged-sided, sequestered canyon, they were well equipped for their nefarious transactions.

From the main line of travel at Elizabeth Lake, a road branched off to the east across the 175-mile stretch of Mojave Desert to Inyo County, over which travel was very light. Watering places, however, were available at distances easily within the scope of a day's drive, with loose horses and desert feed abounding. Two well-mounted expert horsemen from Inyo County would drift into Los Angeles and, piloted by a local accomplice, would ride about carelessly, reconnoitering the outlying country, and, when their quarry was well located, a rapid night foray would net them forty or fifty head of stolen horses. Sunrise the following day would find them comfortably ensconced, eating their breakfast, with their stolen band of animals browsing leisurely in good feed in a hidden canyon in the mountainous country near San Fernando. At nightfall they were again on their way, and long before daylight they had their booty safely stowed away in the hidden pasture of their friend in San Francisquito Canyon.

The following night found them twenty-five or thirty miles on the desert in the Willow Springs country and from there on, by allowing the animals to feed during the day and doing all driving by night, they avoided observation. By shunning the use of the road, no evidence of their passing was left in the shifting sands of the desert.

In the course of a week, when the populated portion of Inyo County was reached, the animals were rushed in during the night to the home plant of the thieves far up a fenced canyon, hidden securely from the eye of all, save an unsuspecting disciple of Isaak Walton who whipped the stream for rainbow trout.

Aside from its mining industry, Inyo County was devoted entirely to stock raising and afforded a ready market for traffic in animals. In the course of six weeks, when all evidences of the forced night marches had disappeared, the stolen animals, singly or in pairs, were brought forth from their mountain fastness and peddled to the unsuspecting. Whilst busy disposing of their plunder, the outlaws were active spotting animals for a later raid, and within three months they would be Los Angeles-bound with a stolen band under the same *modus operandi*. A flurry of excitement and activity was always created among the local peace officers. The resident accomplice, who had voluntarily sent along for sale one or two of his own animals, was most active and denunciatory, all the while doing his utmost to steer the officials in the wrong direction. The matter was soon consigned to the unaccountable and forgotten.

My ride down San Francisquito Canyon found me at the noon hour awaiting lunch, while my faithful *sabino* (light roan) merrily munched his hay, at my recently made friend Canos' place, and along toward evening I reached Camulos, where I stopped for the night. The Camulos ranch house was located fourteen miles from the town of Newhall. Camulos was one of the old Mexican grants, and within its mighty domain during the day of its pristine glory, when it was decreed to Don Ignacio del Valle, there were 22,000 acres.[32] Don Ignacio, who was one of the most prominent of his countrymen about Los Angeles during the golden era of the dons, at this time—1890—had been dead a number of years.

The acreage in Camulos had been reduced to 2,000; the curtailment in area, however, had in no manner robbed it of its glorious beauty or romantic splendor. A glowing tribute to its charms was the selection of Camulos by Helen Hunt Jackson as the scene of her fascinating tale *Ramona*. The property was ideally located along the banks of the Santa Clara River, its ample scope of arable land teeming with the production of the orange, olive, fig, pomegranate, and vine, nestled snugly between the range of hills on either side. An immense white cross truthfully emblematic of the household sanctity of Camulos stood on the highest point of one of the hills.

The family residing at Camulos consisted of the widowed Señora del Valle, her daughter Señorita Isabel, her sons, Ulpiano and Ignacio, Joventino, a son of Don Ignacio by an earlier marriage, and the wife and three charming daughters of Joventino. The senior son, Reginaldo, and Josefina, the oldest daughter, who married Juan Forster of San Juan Capistrano, lived in Los Angeles.

It was my rare privilege and great honor to be a frequent guest at Camulos, and it was the last—within my knowledge—of the grand haciendas to surrender the romantic glamour of the early-day customs of native Californians. Señora del Valle was one of the most charming of women, and strong evidence of her great girlhood beauty still persisted in her benign countenance in her advanced age. The señora was ardently devoted to her church and had a perfectly appointed chapel, sheltered by the branches of massive trees amid beautiful flowers near her door, where visiting padres held serv-

[32] Camulos was part of Rancho San Francisco, which contained 48,611.88 acres. The original grantee of the San Francisco was Antonio del Valle; Ignacio was a son.

ices on Sundays occasionally, and prayers were held daily by members of the family. At the first peal of the chapel's musical bells, all household duties ceased, and the family and scores of servants hastened thither. Señora del Valle was fairly sainted by her family and hordes of servants, and, as she moved about, Madonna-like in appearance, the serenity of her presence permeated the very atmosphere, and all was peace and love and hospitality. The Del Valle family was one of the few native ones that withstood the encroaching ravages of the gringos.

I left Camulos early the following morning for Tapo, where I spent the day riding the range with Dysart. Leaving Tapo the next morning, I galloped the forty miles to Ventura, then took the train to Los Angeles to close the deal for the cattle I had seen at Elizabeth Lake. I found that I was not alone in my appreciation of their quality. As they were the property of an estate, confirmation of their sale was a court procedure, and there I found a competitor who boosted the price on me to $20.10 per head, something over $2,000 on the herd. The cattle were well worth the money; I purchased them, and three days later with five *vaqueros* was back at Elizabeth Lake, counted and paid for them, and started the drive down San Francisquito Canyon. We held them one night near Newhall, and the following night found us comfortably housed at Tapo.

While we were closing the deal for these cattle, Etchipari, who delivered them, importuned me to purchase the herd of a little more than one hundred belonging to "Espíritu Santo," the Indian widow of "Miguel Grande," ranging on her place near Calabasas. The steer stock, from yearlings up, had been sold, and I was offered this bunch at $15 per head.

A. M. (Tony) Carrillo, whose father during the heyday of the dons owned the great Lompoc grant in Santa Barbara County, owned a bar and billiard room in Ventura, which I frequented regularly. Carrillo was a good fellow, always ready for a frolic, was a fair rider, and he was ever importuning me to take him along on one of my trips. As the number of cattle offered for sale by Etchipari was small, was also a very gentle herd, and, as the drive to Tapo would take but one day, I concluded this would be a good opportunity to initiate Carrillo.

Vejar's station, the halfway point—thirty-seven and a half miles—between Los Angeles and Ventura, was located near where the cattle were kept. Carrillo, my ever faithful friend Ramón Ortega, and I rode there leisurely one day, were well fed and properly put away for the night. In the morning I inspected the cattle and concluded to buy them, but, as Etchipari would not return from Los Angeles until late that night, no trade was made.

Etchipari was late in arriving, and it was noon the next day before we finished our deal. It was just a daylight drive to Tapo, and, as my time was quite limited, I concluded to save half of the following day by starting at once, having in mind to hold the cattle at Gormerly's station, about ten miles along the road at the point where I cut across the country to my place.

Gormerly's buildings stood immediately beside the road. He was a stockman himself, had good corrals and barns, and, although I was not acquainted with him, I naturally assumed in accordance with the unwritten law among stockmen which accorded to all traveling herdsmen the privilege of a night's accommodation—usually gratis—that I would at least be a welcome paying guest.

I was consequently astounded when Gormerly in a very gruff manner refused me the privilege of stopping, notwithstanding the fact I introduced myself fully and offered to pay him his own price solely for the use of his corral, volunteering to seek food and shelter for the night for our horses and selves at some other place. This was the only case in my long experience I ever heard of such cussedness, but he was absolutely obdurate. It was already dark, and, as the balance of my drive was through fields of others, in which there was loose stock that might mix with mine, there was no other alternative than to stop where I was in the country road.

Fortunately, the road, sixty feet in width, was well fenced on both sides, and the cattle could be easily held. The night was cold to a thin-blooded Californian; moreover, we had not had a bite to eat since daybreak. Our horses did not fare quite so badly, as there was a luxuriant growth of grass along the fences, where we allowed them to feed for a couple of hours. The night dragged wearily along; most of the cattle had bedded down; those which were still restless had but the one aim in view—to return to their former home. As a consequence one man stationed in the narrow well-fenced road in that direction could hold them.

Ramón, more inured to the cold than my amateur-*vaquero* friend and myself, did not mind the weather as much as we did. Carrillo and I foraged around, brought a liberal supply of wood, and built a fire in the road in the direction the restless cattle were bent upon taking and, stationing Ramón beside it, went stealthily to Gormerly's barn, which we found filled with old straw, and proceeded to burrow ourselves up to our necks. Our entrance must have startled the denizens of the place temporarily into quietude, for within a few moments, just as we were beginning to feel a little warmth, rats in swarms started a grand parade, literally loping around and over us, soon convincing us the place was not for weary *vaqueros*. We resumed our vigil in the cold, were on our way at the first peep of dawn, and by noon the cattle were happily feeding in a good field at Tapo.

During this same winter, 1890-1891, Father started a trade with Dan "White Hat" McCarthy in San Francisco for our hotel property in Ventura. McCarthy, who gained his sobriquet from the fact that he always wore a high, shaggy, light-colored beaver hat, was a keen-witted, illiterate, sharp horse trader, who made his headquarters in the rotunda of the old Palace Hotel. McCarthy was a spectacular character for many years in San Francisco. His clothes were so loud they almost screeched, and he never wore less than two heavy watch chains and a cumbersome diamond-horseshoe stickpin. He was a likable fellow, hobnobbed with all the prominent people around the hotel, everyone knew him—those that did not really care for him tolerated him because of his ready wit—but no one ever made a second horse trade with him.

Five years previous to this time McCarthy purchased a two-year-old colt by Joe Hooker for $115, which he named C. H. Todd. In 1887 he took the colt to Chicago and astounded the country by winning the American Derby, then went on to New York, and won two other stakes. Todd was a long price in the Derby, and McCarthy made a big cleanup. The colt in reality belonged to McCarthy's young son Joe, and "White Hat" put fifteen or twenty thousand dollars into outlying cheap corner lots in Chicago.

These lots had advanced considerably in value, and McCarthy offered to trade five of them for our hotel property in Ventura. Armed with a letter of introduction from the Farmers and Merchants Bank in Los Angeles to the First National in Chicago, in February 1891 I boarded the Santa Fe and upon arrival in Chicago was turned over to Mr. Peabody, who had charge of the First National's real estate.

It was a cold, raw, snowing day; we took a cab and drove a considerable distance out into a lumbering district, where I found many of the small buildings were constructed on piling and all of McCarthy's lots were considerably below street level, partly filled with water, which was covered with ice. The prospect was in no wise alluring, and Mr. Peabody placed $30,000 as the top-notch limit of the value of the lots. McCarthy had put them in at $100,000 in his proposition—I took the train back to Los Angeles the same day.

Our Ventura property including the price of the lot stood us just a shade under $75,000, and, not feeling willing to take so great a loss, we decided not to trade. McCarthy petered his lots away, and in less than a score of years later I ascertained they were worth $1,000,000, by which time to wind up some probate matters our hotel property sold for $10,000.

We concluded to make a final effort to salvage our investment. In doing so, however, we hopped from the frying pan into the fire. Two hotel men subsequently found to be first-class frauds—Hepburn and Terry—induced Father to furnish the place for them, and in his customary extravagant manner he gave them carte blanche. They bought the most expensive china, glassware, and table linen, costly bric-a-brac, expensive silverware and punch bowls, also chafing dishes at $125 per, Persian rugs, tapestries, and costly etchings to the tune of $25,000 for 27 suites in a country hotel.

They opened with a loud blast of trumpets with pomp and style fit for Fifth Avenue, New York, but in about a month they were asking guests for payment in advance to provide food for the next meal; thus they dragged along, never paying a cent of rent, until finally I detected them paying labor with chafing dishes and ejected them.

August 19th of this year, 1891, our first son, Fargo Fenton, was born to Mrs. Rose and me. The child was named partially for Mrs. Rose's uncle C. F. Fargo, who happened to be in Ventura at the time. The whole-souled old fellow was as happy over the distinction as a boy with a new red wagon and at his death bequeathed his namesake $5,000.

Two years previous to this I had joined G. W. Chrisman, J. G. Hill, H. K. Snow, Sr., and George Greenfield in the purchase of 260 acres of land located on the main road to Los Angeles near the town of New Jerusalem. At this time Snow and Greenfield wished to sell their portions, and Chrisman and Hill importuned me to join them in absorbing those two interests, whereby we would each own 33⅓% of the property. I had not in the two years I had been a co-owner ever gone to see the land and decided to investigate the proposition before going further.

Chrisman, who had constituted himself manager of the property when originally purchased, had improved it worthily. The place was rectangular in dimensions, a half mile in one direction and slightly less than a mile in the other. Intersecting sixty-foot roads had been laid out, which divided the property into four parts of practically the same size. Two hundred acres of the property were planted to English walnuts in rows, fifty feet apart, and a like distance separating them in rows; fifty acres were in a luxuriant stand of alfalfa, and five acres, on which there was a small residence and barn room for twenty-four animals and ample hay for them, were planted to various fruits.

The place was rented to some Chinamen, who raised beans between the walnut trees, on a crop rental basis of one-third to the landlord. The prospect was most alluring, and the place looked more like a city park than a bean ranch; as I could acquire the interest offered at actual cost, I lost no time in doing so.

In the early spring of this same year, 1891, my brother Guy returned to New York after a delightful three years spent in Paris, during which he painted constantly in the beautiful country contiguous to that city and had the rare honor for one so young—he was but twenty-one—of having one of his works hung in the Salon. He decided to remain in New York and took up illustration and from the first had all he could do from the important magazines. While pursuing his illustration work, Guy did not neglect his painting, and his canvases were given prominent positions in all the exhibitions of the "Society of American Artists." After a few months in New York the urge of California beckoned him homeward, and during the summer he came to Los Angeles for a visit with Mother and Father.

Notwithstanding the fact that a shotgun had all but snuffed out his young life, Guy had spent every one of his leisure hours frolicking in the open, with either a shotgun, a rifle, or a fishing pole in his hand. He had become very proficient in the use of all of them, and on one occasion while in Paris displayed such great skill in marksmanship in a shooting gallery that the excitable natives flocked about him and would not be convinced he was not one of Buffalo Bill's "Vile Vest" performers.

After a joyful six months spent in his beloved California, Guy returned to New York, where he again entered actively into his illustrating work. He did cover designs for *Scribner's*, *Harper's*, the *Century*, and the *Youth's Companion*. He also illustrated a de luxe volume of Bret Harte's works. In spite of his great success for so young an artist, Guy yielded to the call of beautiful Paris and went back to her in 1893.

## II

In January 1892 I went to Inyo County to look over a horse trade of something over 250 head, which had been presented to me. Heretofore, I had not operated in that section, and, realizing the importance of having a trusted lieutenant in the crew which it would take to move so large a band, I took with me my head stable groom, Alfredo García, an expert horseman, an alert lookout, and good companion.

We packed our saddles and riding outfits in large sacks I kept for the purpose, took the Southern Pacific to Mojave, where at 8 P.M. we changed to a stage line to Keeler—123 miles distant across the Mojave Desert—where connections were made with a narrow-gauge railroad that ran to Reno. The stage outfit was positively the poorest I have seen in my many years of western experience. The vehicle, known in stagecoach parlance as a "mudwagon," was of light construction, swung on the regulation thorough-brace leather springs connecting the axles, and, although the weather was really cold, the vehicle had no side curtains. The horses, very small and ill fed, were little more than shadows. Terrific sandstorms prevail in that locality, as anyone who has traveled by train to Mojave can attest. So many hats have been blown into limitless space from passengers' heads when alighting for meals at Mojave that it came to be said that a man stationed down the track three miles got rich collecting lost hats. Be this as it may, the night García and I pulled out of Mojave for Keeler we were thoroughly convinced that the hat story was truthful. We had not traveled ten miles before one of those gentle zephyrs, charged with the sharp-edged pieces of gravel of which the desert soil is composed, broke loose with such violence that it partly slued the vehicle around, and the pelting particles of granite caused the team to turn their tails to its fury. This occurred at least half a dozen times until we descended out of the path of the wind into Red Rock Canyon, 27 miles out at 2 A.M., where we changed teams.

Along about seven in the morning we arrived at Coyote Wells, where we had a good breakfast and changed horses again. Reaching Haiwee, the home camp of a flock of about five thousand Angora goats, we had an early and good supper. At Haiwee and even at Little Lake there were nice, open, well-watered meadows. We reached Olancha, a post office at the lower end of Owens Lake, along about 8 P.M. where we exchanged mails and horses and started on the tough remaining twenty-three miles of our drive to Keeler, where we arrived at four in the morning.

It had taken us thirty-two hours to make one hundred and twenty-three miles. We did not go to bed, preferring to sit around the fire till breakfast time and the departure of the train at seven for Independence.

I carried unlimited letters of credit from my bankers, Williams, Collins & Sons of Ventura, to Nathan Rhine, the leading merchant, who did all the banking business for the town of fifteen hundred or so of people. We soon knew everybody about the town, all of them the right sort of western type. There was a fair hotel, presided over by O. Mears. I had the good fortune to meet here Fred Holbert, with whom I did much business in succeeding years. He was a first-class cowman and was operating in that country principally for Gracien & Owens, wholesale butchers of Oakland, with his eyes at all times open for any stock deal, which, if attractive enough, he would handle for himself.

Holbert knew about every animal in that section and put me in touch with a number of good saddle animals. I bought a fine red sorrel, which I turned over to García to ride with a hackamore, and for myself purchased "Mike," a sturdy, brown, well-reined horse. Accompanied by Holbert, we rode out to see the band of horses which had been glowingly recommended, but, as was so often the case, they were not up to representations, and I abandoned the proposition.

Independence was right under the brow of Mount Whitney. Ice in the summer was obtained by a pack train of burros leaving early in the morning for the mountains and returning in the early afternoon with a load of frozen snow for the purpose. With Holbert acting as our guide García and I rode all over the country.

The next town north of Independence, something like twenty miles, was Big Pine, a thriving little place, and about an equal distance farther north was Bishop. Here I met a noteworthy character, Frank Shaw, who had extensive holdings out in Long Valley, where he ranged large herds of cattle and bred good mules. He had been an Indian fighter, had a number of notches in the butt of his gun, and was a rough-and-ready, all-around, hardy pioneer. Shaw had prospered and was one of the leading men of the community. He had lost an eye in one of his gun fights and wore a glass one. The Indians in those outlying districts are a degree or two lower in intelligence than the dumbest animals. Shaw used a number of them for doing different classes of labor in his very isolated neighborhood and told me the story himself; that when he had a number of them working together, as a means of preventing them from shirking in his absence, he would extract his glass eye and fasten it to a post, where it could watch them till he returned—and that the ruse worked admirably for a time. Let it be understood, this was Shaw's story.

In the opposite direction from Independence about fifteen miles, was the oldest settlement of the county, Lone Pine. Prospectors outfitted, and stockmen did their trading there. It was on the main line of travel—though little used—between Los Angeles and Reno. There was also a trail running out across the mountains into the San Joaquin Valley. Miners brought in their coarse gold, and there was always plenty of easy money in circulation, stimulating the influx of gamblers and tough characters fleeing from arrest for killings or horse thefts. Frequently one of the regulars of the gambling fraternity of Los Angeles, having a run of bad luck, would turn up missing some morning. In the course of sixty days he would show up, debonair and prosperous. Almost invariably the answer was, "I have been to Lone Pine."

Everyone was his own protector in Lone Pine, and, if the outlaw behaved himself, he found a haven free from search almost indefinitely. Mr. X.Y.Z., whom I had known as a law-abiding young man around El Monte before he embarked in horse rustling over the very trail I have before outlined, had established himself in a cozy little home on a fine ranch, which, besides its intrinsic value, had a strategical importance. He had married a schoolgirl acquaintance of mine from San Gabriel, had settled down, forsaken all his evil ways, and was living very happily in a prosperous condition, a respected citizen in the community. Of course, I knew his reputation and of his exploits in a general way, as all did. I spent the day with him on different occasions, and he took great pleasure in recounting his foraging expeditions in the pastures of horse owners, whom I knew well, looking back upon his lawlessness as a good joke. His mode of operating was to reach San Gabriel Mission in the early afternoon, and by midnight a notorious old Mexican, "Chico Mucho," whom I knew all his life, would have him a roundup of thirty or forty stolen horses, with which he would hasten to a near-by canyon, where he would hold them during daylight on grass and water. Under cover of darkness X.Y.Z. would make a point where there was water on the desert, then leisurely and unquestioned on out over the waste desert country to the good feed along the west side of the lake, where they would be held until nightfall. The animals were then driven to his home place, then into unfrequented meadows of luxuriant feed with fresh water. Where partially fenced by man, the rest nature's own doings with its precipitous canyon sides, cliffs, and chasms, the plunder was securely secreted from the eye of the unbidden.

After a very pleasant week's visit, García and I took leave of our friends and started homeward on our 250-mile ride. We rode the 55 miles to Mojave by midafternoon of the next day and remained there overnight, and the following morning I started García to Ventura by way of Willow Springs, Elizabeth Lake, and Camulos. Having heard of some steers that could be purchased at the right price at the Tejon ranch, I decided to investigate, and, when García and I parted, I rode up to Tehachapi and spent the night there. The following day I rode over the heavily snow-capped Tehachapi Mountains and pulled up for the night at Rancho Tejon.

The Tejon ranch at that time, January 1892, was a regal domain of 250,000 acres, still belonging to General Edward F. Beale, who purchased it for 50 cents per acre shortly after the discovery of gold in California. General Beale, we will remember, was in charge of the expedition with which Father traveled to California, shortly after his almost extinction by the Mojave Indians on the Colorado in 1858. I had counted upon seeing the general. He was away from home; however, my reception suffered nothing in cordiality thereby at the hands of his manager, Mr. Pogson, a cultured English gentleman, and his charming wife, who were lavish with their hospitality. I had never before visited the Tejon and was enthralled with the immense adobe built around a beautifully flowering patio and furnished in the splendor of a city mansion. General Beale, a man of great wealth, had as his standard the best, his immense herd of cattle was rated at the very top notch of excellence, and his cow horses were famous from one end of California to the other.

The Tejon was among the very last of California's great cattle ranches to continue the native Californian manner of breaking saddle horses. Chico López, a maestro of great renown in breaking a horse to rein with a Spanish bit, who had been *jefe* of the *vaqueros* at Tejon for upwards of a score of years, was still in charge, and I never have seen so many uniformly excellent horses. They were not only perfectly broken, but because of their fine blood lines were of more than average size and great beauty. At Mr. Pogson's generous invitation, I tarried a day, fairly feasting my eyes upon them.

When leaving, I rode down by way of old Fort Tejon and put up for the night at Gorman's station, a relic of stage days, where a number of the Gorman young men still resided. The next day I took a short cut over the mountain trail that ran by Steamboat Miller's and on down through Castaic Canyon, headed for Tapo.

## III

Holbert was a most energetic trader and in less than three weeks had summoned me back to Inyo County with the idea of having me buy a band of extra heavy steers to drive to Mojave and ship into Los Angeles for beef. No one had ever driven across the desert with fat cattle up to this time. Holbert reasoned, first of all, the weather was cool; that by taking a route with which he was acquainted, some distance off to the left of the stage road, we would encounter quantities of sand grass, a rooted grass growing in individual small bushy formation, of a very light straw color, very nutritious and even succulent at this stage of its growth. Furthermore, the initial lot of cattle in our calculations were very gentle and would be easy to handle; we could make night drives and rest in the heat of the day. These arguments, fortified by my confidence in Holbert plus the desire for conquest ever dominant in my life, induced me to tackle the proposition.

There were ninety head in the lot—all as gentle as dogs and most of them enormous, eight or nine years old. They had been fed alfalfa hay each winter and in early summer taken to Menache Meadows, up at the base of Mount Whitney, where they roamed in fine feed up to their bodies till late fall; then they were returned to their home places and fed alfalfa hay again. The consequence was one layer of fat upon another was added to their weight. Positively their loins and backs were tablelike; they were as tall as a good-sized horse and so gentle that in driving them one could ride quietly among them and stroke them with the hand.

Retail butchers do not care for extra large beeves, as they do not cut to good advantage, and for that reason this particular bunch of steers had become a drug on the market. As a consequence, I purchased them considerably below the market. As the expense of driving twice the number of animals would be practically the same and as a means of averaging up the band, which would give me some trading strength when I reached market, I purchased 110 prime fat small steers.

As usual, I was on the lookout for good-looking horses and found a nice dark bay with some white on him in Bishop. Hearing of another by the same sire out in the country a few miles, I went there and found a nice black, of the same size and conformation, and bought him. This was the nucleus around which my outfit crystallized. I rented a good pair of mules and a farm wagon, which the owner agreed to drive at so much per day for the outfit. I rented from one of Holbert's friends a set of light harness, with which we hooked my fancy pair as leaders ahead of the mule team. Holbert and four other horsemen and the cook made up the outfit. Well provisioned and with arrangements for carrying water for the cook, ample bedding, and a few sacks of grain, we moved slowly down the valley, renting feed in enclosed pastures the first few nights. We passed through Independence, on by Sheppard's to Cottonwood, where the formation is of almost solid volcanic rock, very flinty and wearing on the hoofs of animals. To avoid the long strip of narrow road through it, we turned the cattle to the left and down on the beach of Owens Lake.

This body of water, perhaps ten by thirty miles in area, into which for ages the good-sized Owens River has emptied, has no outlet. It is so thoroughly impregnated with salt, sodium carbonate, potassium sulphate, and other minerals that no vegetable growth ever starts and no animal life endures for any length of time. I have bathed in this water, emerging from which my body was covered with a reddish film; to remove this I got in the fresh water of Cottonwood Creek. The heavy saline precipitation had a wonderfully cleansing and agreeable effect, however, leaving the skin very soft. Wild duck living in this lake rapidly become emaciated, the flesh turning a coppery, reddish color, and a large death rate is in constant progress. Very heavy winds prevail here during which the waters are whipped into fair-sized foamy breakers. The day we were driving the cattle along the beach was one of the windiest I have ever known. The velocity and direction of the wind and the rapidly churning waters had driven hundreds of these half-dead duck onto the narrow beach, and, unable to rise to flight, they were trampled upon and killed by the score by the cattle, leaving behind a motley mess of bones and feathers.

We were able to pen the cattle for the last night at Olancha. From there on, however, the trip took on another aspect. We held them on good feed for a few hours at Little Lake, allowing them to have their fill of water before drifting them down on to the desert. In our number of days with them our observation caused us to decide to allow the cattle themselves to make their own pace, never hurrying them. Should a number show an inclination to stop and feed or even to lie down, we halted the moving ones and allowed the herd to rest. We paid no attention to hours, traveling just as conditions demanded—at times the entire night. Our supper might have been at 4 P.M. or 4 A.M.

We had a little adventure one night. The moon was shining bright. I was riding in the lead. It takes little to stampede cattle; oftenest the cause is imaginary. With no warning the entire herd broke into a run forward, some of them bellowing from fright. They were so big and fat I knew they could not run far. Although the country was safe for a horse to run over, there being no growth but small sagebrush, the tumultuous rumbling of their oncoming hoofs was not particularly comforting and would have been bad music had one's horse made a false step. After a run of about half a mile, we had them quiet again.

After leaving Little Lake, we had no water till Coyote Wells, about forty miles; then forty miles farther to Rose Springs, where we rested a few hours; then twelve miles on to Mojave. The weather having been cool and rather fresh and our travel very slow, the cattle did not suffer much from thirst. We had a sufficient supply of water in barrels to provide the horses with.

We shipped the cattle by railroad from Mojave to Los Angeles. Holbert and three of the men went with them. The other man rode my horse and led the team of horses to Ventura. Roberts with his team elected to camp at Mojave and await the return of Holbert and the other boys, so they could all go home together. I had gone on this trip clad in rather expensive clothing, all of which went into the discard upon reaching home. Not expecting to participate in driving any stock I might buy, I was ill prepared. This new undertaking, however, in which I had invested upwards of $10,000, prompted me to stand by. Due to the uncertainty of our hours, I had not removed my clothing or shoes for six days. I took the passenger train to Ventura, made myself presentable again, and doubled back to Los Angeles at once to close out the cattle.

My enormous steers were a source of great admiration as specimens of fat animals, but as a marketable commodity they were in no way attractive, and it was only by mixing them in with the small steers and cutting the price that I moved them. Charley Gasson, one of the earliest of Los Angeles' butchers, bought the first cut off from the herd, with the understanding he could include in the bunch a certain crumpled horned steer, that looked more like an elephantine dairy cow than anything else. This steer dressed 1,280 lbs. I charged Gasson to save me a porterhouse steak, which later I had cooked at the Hollenbeck Cafe, then one of the best eating places in Los Angeles; and Jim Mellus and Lon Hamilton, brother-in-law of U.S. Senator John P. Jones of Nevada, shared the splendid cut with me.

When I took account of stock for my undertaking, I found I had made $2,400 above every expense in the twenty-six days I had been engaged in it and had had the pleasure of writing a page in cattle history by driving the first fat cattle ever driven across the desert from Inyo County to Mojave. I found the team I purchased a splendid span and within six weeks sold them to State Senator D. T. Perkins of Hueneme, a business partner of U.S. Senator Bard, for precisely twice the amount I paid for them.

# 14

## *Guadalasca - Big Stakes - Rattlers and Fever Ticks*

### I

IN THE spring of 1893 I entered into partnership with the Hobson Brothers—Abe and Will—of Ventura in the cattle business, and we organized the Ventura Live Stock and Slaughtering Company, in which the Hobsons owned 50% and I 50%.

We took a five years' lease on the 2,300-acre Guadalasca Ranch, belonging to the estate of Lord William Richard Broome, who during his lifetime resided in Santa Barbara. The Guadalasca, located along the ocean about fifteen miles from Ventura, was being handled by the widow, Lady Frances Broome, from whom we purchased 750 head of fine cattle ranging on the ranch for $22.50 for the branded cattle, calves thrown in. Lady Broome reserved four hundred head of beef steers and a fenced field of fine feed until they were disposed of. We were as nice as we knew how to be with the lady but soon found her to be most unreasonable and suspicious. Having use for the field she had reserved, we made every effort to secure it, even offering to pay her a bonus of one-fourth of a cent per pound above what she could get for her steers from any butcher, which would have amounted to at least twelve hundred dollars. We could not budge her; it was evident there was a joker somewhere. Notwithstanding this fact, Lady Broome presented me with a very attractive well-reined gray saddle horse bearing the name of "Yankee Doodle." She had the horse delivered to my barn. I was more than surprised and wrote her a note of thanks couched in my best English, descending, however, into a bit of facetiousness in mentioning the feather which traditionally I would put in my cap as befitted Yankee Doodle. To my great sorrow I learned the lady was offended, saying I had chosen to "poke fun" at her.

Will Hobson and I went together and bought the cattle of the Hardison and Say Horse and Cattle Company ranging on their ranch near Santa Paula—about a thousand head of them. They were all black, or black and white Holstein stock, not particularly desirable as beef animals. True enough they grow large but are always rough and angular, light loined and quartered, and do not dress out as the Durham or Hereford. I went to Tehachapi and contracted to buy about two thousand head from different owners who had ranged them on the desert. I paid all the same price, $15 for the branded stuff, calves thrown in.

Lady Broome had disposed of her steers, so we moved the bunch from Santa Paula over. In about three weeks the strange cattle we had put on the ranch were dying by the scores daily. None, however, of the stock bought with the ranch were affected. We took Dr. J. J. Street, county veterinarian, out to diagnose the malady and advise us what to do. Usually those attacked were the hardier ones. They would lose weight incredibly fast, isolating themselves, standing motionless until approached, when they would shake their heads menacingly as though intending to attack and hook; they were so weak, however, they staggered when moving. In three days' time a fine fat animal weighing over a thousand pounds would shrink into a mere skeleton, the very sick ones never recovering. Dr. Street made all sorts of examinations without any definite conclusions, leaning somewhat to anthrax, with no great amount of definiteness, however. Deciding a change to green feed would be beneficial, we rented all alfalfa fields available up the river toward and beyond Santa Paula. In moving some of the cattle, we were soon in greater trouble. Many of them were so violently seized on the road that they could not be driven farther, standing or lying down where we left them, invariably dying. We took every precaution possible, always returning to succor or bury those left behind. It was not long before the board of supervisors was after us. Stating our case as having been guided by the county veterinarian in all our movements, protesting our desire and intention to do right by all, we were absolved from censure.

These were trying times, losing fifteen hundred dollars worth of cattle per day, multiplying expenses tremendously, on the go almost twenty-four hours a day; then to be assailed and even hampered in our movements by persons whose interests were in no wise jeopardized brought about some personal situations which came very near being tragical. The ravage kept up for about thirty days; our loss had been upwards of 1,250 head, besides a lot of expense and wear and tear upon ourselves.

The most significant fact to our groping minds was that throughout its frightful malignancy the epidemic had not fastened itself on a single animal raised on the Guadalasca, nor had any of the animals left on the Tapo shown any signs of sickness.

We knew not which way to turn. We were paying $9,000 per annum rental, and to have this calamitous condition interject itself was of serious consequence. There had been occasional vague rumors of death losses from disease on the Guadalasca, and, before renting it, Will Hobson and I rode the range carefully but found no telltale heaps of bones or other indications thereof. Moreover, we had positive assurance from Lady Broome in the presence of witnesses that no cattle had ever died from disease on the property.

There was nothing further to do that we could determine in the matter for the time being, so, leaving Hobson to run the business for the summer, I left for San Francisco, where Maben had taken Richmond Jr. along with the other horses he was training. Richmond Jr. started in but one race; in that instance my friend Andy McDowell evened up matters with me for not selling Richmond Jr. to him the year previous for $5,000 by beating him with Edenia, whom he purchased from Edgemont Stock Farm. The race was a fine contest, nonetheless, and Edenia had to step in 2:14¼ to turn the trick. At this same meeting there were racing two great little mares for their size, both bays, and to a casual observer they were so alike that either could be passed for the other. One of them, She, who belonged to Walter Hobart, the great polo player and expert gentleman rider, was being raced by my good friend Chris Smith of San Francisco—Jennie June, the other, belonged in the southern part of the state. These diminutive queens met, and after a spirited duel the palm of victory fell to the northern lady, She.

My very close friend A. B. Spreckels had blossomed forth as a trotting-horse breeder and later crowned his efforts by producing Hulda by Guy Wilkes, who took a record of 2:08 in Chicago. Spreckels was also a very close friend of Chris Smith's and quite naturally championed the cause of Smith's mare She. Dr. K. D. Wise of Los Angeles, a recent addition to the trotting game, espousing the merits of Jennie June in a blatant sort of way—which was his wont—offered to match Jennie June against She for $5,000 a side. He had no more than uttered the defy when Spreckels called him, telling him to put up. Wise wriggled about for a while but finally put up $500 for a race, play or pay, between the two mares to be decided two months later during the fair at Stockton, and I was appointed stakeholder.

I was detained by business at my ranch and did not attend the Stockton meeting. When the date for the race arrived, Wise refused to start his mare, played the welcher act, hiding behind the antigambling law of California, and enjoined me by wire from paying over the $1,000 stakes.

I immediately took the train to San Francisco to confer with Spreckels. We decided to give Dr. Wise all the trouble possible in forcing him to sue me. I turned the money over to Spreckels, who promised to defend the action and hold me free from loss. The suit, the first of its kind ever tried in California—Wise vs. Rose—was brought at Stockton and quite naturally was decided in Wise's favor. We had the satisfaction, however, of attaching the stigma to Wise of being a welcher, which clung to him throughout his racing career.

To please my friend Tommy Keating, I forsook the California circuit this season, 1893, and shipped Richmond Jr. to Salt Lake en route to Montana. I won two races with him at the Salt Lake meeting, then took him to Butte, Montana, where he again won two races; then we moved to Anaconda, where Richmond Jr. won his only start.

At the conclusion of a race one day at Anaconda, in which Keating had been driving against Pete Williams, these two drivers engaged in an argument, and Williams, who weighed at least eighty pounds more than Keating, made a motion as if to strike him. I was carrying a heavy stick and, stepping close to Williams, admonished him not to assault Keating. Williams gave me a nasty look, and the affair terminated.

That evening, as I sat at dinner with Mr. and Mrs. Charley Beard and Keating at the Anaconda Hotel, Miles Finlen, a prominent saloonkeeper and personal friend of Marcus Daly's, pulled a chair alongside of me at the table and placed a 45 colt in my lap, saying, "Pete Williams, half drunk, is out in the lobby, vowing to shoot you on sight." I thanked Finlen for his kindness, returned him his shooting iron, and told him as soon as I finished my dinner I would go to my room and get my own gun, with which I was better acquainted.

Williams, a burly bully, had a few years previously shot a Mexican in the back and killed him in San Jose, California, but had beaten the case through suborned evidence, and I realized that I must bring the matter to a finality one way or another lest he ambush me as he had the Mexican.

When I had finished dining, I went unobserved up the back stairway to the elevator and on up to my room, donned a light overcoat, placed my gun in the right-hand pocket, and descended into the lobby. I saw Williams before he saw me. The lobby was thronged with people waiting to buy pools on the following day's races, and I wormed my way through the crowd until about ten feet from Williams; then I called him, berating him in a scandalous manner, daring him to move his right hand an inch. I had taken the play away from him so suddenly there was no fight left in him. He was hustled out of the room by his friends, and a bad mix-up narrowly averted.

The affair created quite a stir. Williams was *persona non grata* with Marcus Daly, the copper king, because of his having defrauded Daly out of the stallion Silver Bow, and, when Mr. Daly saw me at the race track the following day, he complimented me highly and said: "If that so-and-so ever makes any more threats, get yourself a double-barrel shotgun, and blow his head off, and I'll stand back of you."

## II

This year, 1893, marked Father's third in the running-horse game in the East, and, although he had won fully his quota of races and some big bets, the matter was not altogether to his liking. He had had a different trainer each year—first Dave Bridges, then Billy Appleby, and lastly Hanger Jones—each of them an honest, capable horseman, but in turn for each the game was too big.

There is nothing mystic in the art of training a horse. Common sense, good care in the barn, and strict surveillance as to the feeding of animals goes a long way. The meat of the cocoanut, however, lies in the ability of a trainer to properly classify his horses and place them—as the saying goes—in their contests, and when Bridges, Appleby, and Jones came to match their wits with those of Hildreth, Healy, Rowe, Joyner, et al., they were lost.

Father had a nice string of fourteen head. Fairy, the champion of the band, though suffering from rheumatism to such an extent that she frequently had to be forced to stand when lying in her stall, beat Correction—one of the best of sprinters of that time—three-quarters of a mile, and Fairy was a certain 1:40 runner—about tops then—every time she faced the starter. Nomad, a two-year-old, battled himself into valorous distinction by the manner in which he responded to Snapper Garrison's merciless punishment and came unflinchingly on to win. Peri, Mignonette, Rico Lewis, Rinfax, Orizaba, and Oscar all gave good accounts of themselves, as also did Tycoon, Mikado, and Odette. The latter three were bred and raised by Ben Hill, who, in early days, owned the 5,000-acre El Cajon grant in San Diego County. Their sires and dams were of good strains, but along with many other good race horses that Ben Hill raised, Mikado, Tycoon, and Odette from birth roamed the hills surrounding famous El Cajon Valley, like so many range cattle. They were not even broken until two-year-olds, withal they matched strides successfully with first-class eastern-bred animals on the metropolitan tracks.

In the late summer Father decided to disband his stable and return to California. He sold Fairy for $10,000 to Mr. Richard Croker—then the boss of Tammany—who, after racing her successfully for a season, bred her to Iroquois, to whose cover she dropped the stake winner Indian Fairy. Choosing to retain Nomad for a sire, Father leased his running qualities during his three-year-old form for $10,000 to Dwyer Brothers, who were then in their heyday as the leading running-horse men of America. The remaining number were peddled at from $1,000 to $3,000 apiece.

Father loved to gamble, but, although a good poker player, he rarely played that game. He was rated high as a pitch player and spent his afternoons when in San Francisco playing with notables from far and near who visited the Palace Hotel for one hundred a game. Tom Williams, with the exuberance of youth and newly acquired wealth, was very apt to overmatch himself. He took my father on one afternoon. I believe he won one or two games in fifteen. Father also loved to play faro; his play was around $25,000 or $30,000, win or lose. He always told me—I know in absolute truth—that he won considerably more than he lost. With the sale of Fairy, the leasing of Nomad, and the sale of the others, he realized $42,000. Phil Daly was dealing faro at Long Branch that summer, where Father had played frequently against his game.

The night before Father's intended departure for Los Angeles, Mr. Daly, Ira Ramsdell, who was racing the good horses Homer and Rinfax in New York, my father, and another gentleman were seated in the Hoffman House cafe. Father suggested to Mr. Daly that he would like to play "a little high cards" as a farewell party. Mr. Daly informed him that he had a room near by, that he (Daly) would do the dealing, Father could keep "cases," Ramsdell could be lookout for Father, and the other gentleman for Mr. Daly. The party was soon in action.

At the end of three hours Father quietly announced that he thought he had had enough, having lost a cool $100,000. He said to Mr. Daly: "I have overplayed myself a little; I have but $42,000 with me. I need about $2,000 to get me out of town and home; here is forty thousand. I will give you a fifteen-day note for $60,000 and will forward the money to take it up the minute I get home."

Mr. Daly replied: "I would not think of taking your note, Mr. Rose. Don't give the matter another thought. Whenever it is convenient, you can send the money to me." Father came on home, arranged for the cash, and forwarded it to Daly at once.

Shortly following my return to Ventura after my summer's absence, Chrisman and Hill, my partners in the walnut ranch, having so many other irons in the fire, offered to sell me their two-thirds interest in the property for its exact cost as shown by the books—$157 per acre. Each succeeding year had marked a vast improvement in the appearance of the property; with the walnut trees now five years of age just beginning to yield, this increment, added to the crop rental from the beans grown, rendered the place practically self-supporting, and I accepted their proposition.

The experience of Hobson Brothers and myself with the cattle epidemic on the Guadalasca ranch had greatly dampened our ardor with reference to that property. We therefore decided to get from under the proposition and dissolve partnership. We divided the cattle on Guadalasca—the Hobsons took their portion of them to the Taylor ranch immediately adjacent to the town of Ventura; I took my share to Tapo and resumed sole proprietorship of that place. We leased 2,000 acres of virgin valley land on Guadalasca to Joe Lewis for $5,000 a year to be used in lima bean culture, and the 20,000 acres of hill land to some Basque sheepmen for $3,500 annually. I myself rented one field of 200 acres for raising oat hay and another piece of 1,000 acres of lowland lying along the ocean to be used as a horse pasture. In this manner we broke a little better than even on the transaction.

## III

On the thousand-acre tract of the Guadalasca ranch, which I have previously mentioned as having been rented by myself for a horse pasture, there were about one hundred acres of good arable land and a fine flowing well. Many bulrushes and other bulbous plants and weedy growths abounded, which afforded such advantageous conditions for hog raising that I decided to stock it with swine.

Another condition prevailing helped to decide me in stocking it with swine. The place was positively overrun with rattlesnakes, truly hundreds of them, rendering it quite dangerous ground for cattle and horses to graze upon. Knowing that the hogs would soon exterminate the rattlers, I felt I was accomplishing a dual purpose. An old mother hog seemed to enter into combat with the rattlers with gusto, kneeling on her knees, her most vulnerable part because of the thinness of the hide and the absence of adipose tissue. It would be but a few minutes before she would have the snake whipped into pieces. The theory of their immunity from harm from the fangs of the rattlesnakes is that the venom of the fangs is absorbed by the great amount of oil in the jowls and other fleshy parts of the hogs. It was not long before the snakes were all either killed or driven to the hills beyond the fences of this field.

One warm morning in early summer I saw while riding the Guadalasca range with Chico Nañes, one of the *vaqueros,* a most wonderful sight: five or six at least—I could not count them—large rattlesnakes had entwined themselves in a pyramid-like mass a foot and a half or two feet in height, supported by their tails, with their heads, which they kept darting about, striking viciously at space at the upper end of the formation. Keeping up a constant hissing and rattling it was about as vicious a spectacle as I have ever seen.

I have had a lot to say about the slowness of Ventura along real estate lines. It was not so, however, in revelry. The *fiesta* and *fandango* were numerous. I kept four Santa Barbara musicians—two guitars, a violin, and cornet—two or three months each summer to play at dances and for serenading. Barbecues and clambakes were regular affairs, and there was ample scope for the bibulously and sportively inclined.

I was tiring of all this hurrah. Our investments were hopeless, and with each trip I made to my ranch—which I had already christened "Roseland" with a fitting barbecue—the call back to the country grew stronger, and I resolved to move there. I constructed a good-sized house of bungalow type suitable for the country, with spacious verandas, five bedrooms, ample baths, a large dining room, glassed in on two sides, an extra large living room with a fireplace large enough for the children to walk into. We moved from Ventura to our new home in August 1894, and on the 11th of the following October our fourth child, the second son, Gilbert Blackman, named for my good friend Dr. James Blackman Gilbert, whom I had known in New York, was born.

The epidemic which killed a great number of the Hobsons' and my cattle on the Guadalasca ranch ultimately attained national importance. One day during this same fall, eighteen months subsequent to its occurrence, a Mr. Hill came to my house at Roseland direct from the Department of Agriculture at Washington, D.C., with proper credentials and instructions to make a thorough investigation and report.

I had some cattle in my pasture at Guadalasca, and, while driving there after lunch, Mr. Hill asked me if I had noticed any ticks. Myriads of them, I informed him. When we reached the ranch, I had the men rope a steer. There were hundreds of ticks in all stages of growth attached to the animal between its legs and on the tender parts of hide about the throat. Mr. Hill immediately found what he had expected—the Texas fever tick. On all California ranges in the spring of the year cattle and even horses are infested with what we have always called wood ticks, which fasten themselves upon the animal when foraging about in the brush or even high grass. The life of these parasites is but eight months, during which time they will not travel a foot horizontally; their movements are practically all vertically upwards on vegetation, and the animals passing by brush the ticks onto themselves. Multiplying very rapidly, even these wood ticks, though not malignant, severely sap the strength of an animal. As the larger ticks become filled with blood, some fall, and many of them are scratched off by the animal, nature in some way asserting itself in assisting the poor beasts to rid themselves of the pests before great harm has been done.

Taking it for granted that all of these ticks—of the presence of which we were thoroughly cognizant—were of the same well-known but not particularly injurious kind, they had not entered into our calculations at all as the cause of disease. I was positively stupefied when within a few minutes Mr. Hill showed me the two distinct varieties: the wood tick a light gray in color with no distinctive mark; the Texas fever tick a brownish gray, with a readily visible small white speck in the center of its head. Had we but known of a treatment later adopted—the use of crude petroleum applied locally—we could have saved ourselves large sums of money.

Reinforced with this information, the Hobsons and I delved into the matter extensively and finally ascertained that a man by the name of Harris, who had homesteaded a place in the hills between the Malibu Ranch and the Guadalasca, had a number of years prior brought onto his claim some steers from Texas and turned them loose on the open range. The cattle naturally drifted on to the Guadalasca and mingled with the herd along that border of the ranch which was not fenced. Felipe Reyes, who had been foreman on the Guadalasca for many years, informed me that, soon after he had noticed these stray Texas steers feeding with the ranch cattle, some of the latter took very sick and died. A strange factor to him, however, was that none of the Texas cattle got sick. The fever, though very malignant, did not always kill, and animals surviving its ravages feeding about with the rest of the cattle soon spread some of the ticks to them, and in this way the entire ranch became infected. An animal surviving an attack was immune from a further one, and its offspring likewise were immune from prenatal inoculation.

Lady Broome was cognizant of the fact that this sickness, though the nature of it was unknown to her, had passed through the entire herd, killing a goodly portion of them; and she well knew that each time new animals were brought in many of them, including young bulls, died with unerring regularity in the very field she was hesitant in surrendering, which from the start had been the infirmary, with consequent great losses.

After having thoroughly convinced ourselves that Lady Broome had not been candid with us in her statements of the absence of disease on her place, we brought suit against her for our losses of $45,000, the action resulting in the frequent jury fiasco. We were awarded $11,000 damages. The verdict should have been all asked for or none.

As stated before, the movements of ticks along the ground from place to place are negligible, and they are carried only by animals. This is true to such a degree that I have known fenced pastures side by side, one of which would be "ticky" and dangerous for healthy stock, whereas the other just across the fence would be free from them and perfectly healthy and safe.

The United States Department of Agriculture, in their determined and effectual crusade against the ravages and spread of the tick, quarantined localities in counties, certain counties in states, and even entire states, animals from which could only be shipped under government regulations. The only way of cleaning up a place is to starve the ticks to death by not using it for animals for a few years.

The winter of 1893-1894 was one of the driest ever known in California. Incredible as it may seem, fine sound horses weighing 1,300 and 1,400 lbs. could be bought for $1.25 each, and smaller ones could be had for the acceptance of them; in fact many animals were turned loose on the public roads to starve, and hundreds of splendid work and heavy draft horses were purchased to be used in making soap by the manufacturers of Los Angeles at $1.00 per head.

My cow-ranch foreman, Dysart, as usual was equal to the emergency. He had had some experience in selling western range cattle to the eastern feeders and at once advised shipping the thousand I had on Tapo to Kansas

City. We loaded them on the cars consigned to the George R. Barse Cattle Company, of Kansas City, Mo., and Dysart, accompanied by an understudy, Billy Elwell, was on his way.

The consignees halted the shipment at Newton, Kansas, where the cattle were turned in good pastures. Inside of a month Dysart with his protegé was homeward-bound, with a check for me considerably in excess of what I would have received for the animals had it been a good year and they had fattened in California.

As my lease on the Tapo ranch expired at this time, I quit the cattle business and parted with Dysart—the greatest asset I ever had—who had recently married and gone to live on a small place of his own in the Simi Valley. Before leaving, Dysart gathered up something over a hundred head of stray cattle belonging to me on Tapo and adjoining ranches. These I moved to a government claim I had taken up in the hills in Ventura County, just beneath the brow of Old Bony, a mountain landmark in that section.

# 15

## *Senator Rose - My Brother Guy - Roseland*

### I

MY FATHER was in no wise a politician; he was, however, always identified with the Democratic party. In the early eighties he was prevailed upon to run for the state senate, feeling that his influence would be worth while in passing some legislation favorable to Los Angeles County. He was elected and did his part. His sentimental love of nature asserted itself in a small way in a bill which he introduced and had passed at the same session. Mockingbirds were very plentiful in southern California, and about every Mexican family would rob a nest and raise the young birds for sale. Naturally many of the young things died. Regarding this as a wanton destruction of many of these happy, beautiful songsters, Father's bill made it a misdemeanor to rob their nests.

In the early nineties Father was asked to seek the nomination for Congress. For this he was opposed by our young friend George S. Patton, who had married Don Benito Wilson's daughter. Patton was practicing law—very capable and a gifted orator, a dyed-in-the-wool Democrat, born in Virginia, full of southern fire. He had taken part in many campaigns, lending his worthy efforts at all times, never having sought official preferment.

The convention met at Ventura and was deadlocked from the first ballot. Balloting continued for a number of days until eighty or ninety had been taken, whereupon the convention adjourned for two weeks to meet at Los Angeles. A lot of feeling had been developed. The fight was stubborn and while not altogether acrimonious was bitter enough. Some of the henchmen cut corners a little short to gain a point, and there was a fist fight or two.

One of Patton's delegates, Mr. Burke, whose son was Carlton Burke, one of California's most popular and famous polo players, had a run-in with Tom Savage, one of the Rose delegates, who was ward boss of a precinct in Los Angeles and considered himself a tough customer. The battle did not last long, however, friends interceding. Burke poked Savage in the jaw, which took a lot of the toughness out of him, as well as a few of his teeth.

Some friends of the Rose side took one of the opposing delegates, a man by the name of French, for a ride to the beach for supper during an adjournment—not the Chicago ride of today, just a drinking party. Nacho Belderraín engineered it, and there was quite a flurry over the delegate's absence when the convention reconvened. We were not seeking a victory achieved through sharp practices. Had there been anything of that kind in my father's make-up, we could have won by resorting to sharp though permissible methods which always have and always will obtain in politics. We could have won the nomination on one of the early ballots at Ventura; but Father would not listen to any mode of procedure which was not absolutely open and aboveboard.

The Patton forces had the organization, and there was no balloting until the absent Mr. French returned from his little outing. Balloting was resumed and continued from day to day until there had been one hundred and fifteen. Realizing that further continuance along these lines was futile, a compromise candidate was agreed upon and the nomination given to Charles Barlow, an ex-farmer who had been successful in the oil business in Bakersfield, and the campaign slogan, "Vote for Charley Barlow, the pumpkin roller," was adopted. Barlow was elected and served one term.

I have always charged my father's loss of the nomination to U.S. Senator Stephen M. White, one of California's most popular native sons and one of the brightest minds of his time. Mr. White was a native of Monterey County and grew up in the city of Los Angeles in the practice of law. He was a great lawyer and a most forceful and eloquent speaker and I believe the first of California's senators to be elected solely because of his merit. It was generally understood that the senator would remain passive in the congressional fight. He, however, was drawn into it and was one of Mr. Patton's delegates—not to be wondered at in politics, particularly in this case, as Senator White and Patton had gone through other campaigns speaking and pulling wires, were both politicians, with a code in common. Whereas Father was in no sense a politician and though not a "pumpkin roller," as the final nominee was dubbed, was looked upon as an outsider in the political realm.

Mr. Patton was naturally disappointed and retired to private life at his fine country estate on the old Wilson place. My father was even more so, feeling that his great help in building up the district entitled him to this much consideration. Patton in speaking before the convention made a splendid flowery address. My father, filled to the brim, paid Patton a complimentary tribute, disclaiming all forensic ability in the few words, "I am a worker, not a speaker."

My father was positively a crank on the subject of honesty and fair play, and I know of instances in his life where he caused himself to appear ridiculous in his rigid adherence to his code. He even went out of his latitude once when he was in the judges' stand at the race meeting at the county fair, in a race in which Silkwood—a great local favorite—was carded to start.

Auction pools were sold on the race downtown the night before, and people wagered to suit their fancy. Mr. Willets had always driven the horse in his races, and it was the general assumption that he was to drive him in this one. There had, however, been no specific statement or advertising to that effect, and a change of drivers or riders is always permissible, care being exercised that the substitution is a fair one as to comparative merit. This is one of the very many chances a bettor takes when playing horse races.

The morning of the race it was rumored that a Mr. Williams, a reputable driver but no better than Mr. Willets with this horse, was to drive him. For that matter a child could have driven Silkwood. My father did not inquire into the reason of the substitution of drivers; Mr. Willets might have been indisposed for all he knew. There was no complaint or objection from any source; everyone was contented except my father. He did not know whether the change was made for nefarious reasons or otherwise, nor did he inquire; he simply thought there might be a bugaboo someplace. So he took it upon himself when he went into the judges' stand that afternoon to declare "all bets off" made on the race the night before.

No one was particularly pleased, and many were greatly displeased. The pool sellers lost their commissions, the association its percentage, and an atmosphere of suspicion was cast about the race. The procedure was entirely wrong according to racing rules. If Father had any doubt as to the honesty of the transaction, as an official he should have waited for the race to come up and, if the least suspicious circumstance developed, promptly exercised his prerogative, substituted a driver to his own liking, and then could have punished the offenders and moreover would have caused them the loss of their money. The race was paced and won by Silkwood according to the consensus of opinion, as he was a pronounced favorite in the betting both the night before and the following day after the change of drivers was made. My father benefited no one, displeased many, and did not act according to rules himself—walked so straight he fell over backwards in this case.

Having become enamored of some copper claims he had acquired in Arizona, Father decided to disband his running breeding stud. The stallion Argyle was purchased by a breeder from Tennessee; the sale as a whole, however, was far from a success, and the very expensive half score of Australian matrons passed their declining days pulling plows in someone's vineyard.

Father also acquired, during his extensive real estate transactions in Los Angeles, seventeen acres in the hilly portion of the city for subdivision purposes. He called it the "Daisy Tract," in honor of one of my sisters. A short time after the property was placed on the market, shallow, small-producing oil wells were drilled all around the Daisy Tract almost to its edges.

A number of holes were sunk on the tract; every one of them, however, was dry. Father then made the crowning error of his spectacular career in spending something like $150,000 in erecting a smelter on his copper properties in Arizona, which ultimately resulted in a dead loss. Luck, the fickle goddess, seemed to have deserted Father. Nothing daunted him, however; he turned his attention more actively to the development of the orchards at Rosemead and derived great pleasure from spending two or three days of each week there, walking about among the wild flowers, communing with nature.

By this time, 1897, both cupid and the stork had been active in the Rose family. My sister Daisy married Mr. J. W. Montgomery, a successful businessman in Los Angeles, for whom she bore a daughter, Ruth. Maud married Mr. George D. Easton, a sterling young businessman of San Francisco; Mabel married Mr. Arthur Pike of San Francisco. My brother Harry married Miss Ada Currier of San Francisco. My brother Guy married Miss Ethel Boardman of Providence, R.I. Mrs. Wachtel had become the mother of four children, Valentine, Elizabeth, Leonard, and Markel. Mrs. Sanderson had become the mother of two children, Sadie, who passed away in early childhood, and Rowe. Several years later, W. S. Dixon of San Francisco became Mabel's second husband. Roy, the youngest of the eleven children, married Eleanor Ford of Los Angeles, and to them a few years later a son, L. J. Rose, III, was born.

## II

In February 1895 my brother Guy returned to New York from Paris and brought his wife to California for a visit. After six months happily spent in sketching his loved landmarks and in hunting and fishing, he with his wife returned to New York, where they took up their abode on Washington Square South. Guy did very little painting, teaching twice a week at Pratt Institute, and in summer conducting outdoor sketching classes in the country.

Unfortunately he was ill at intervals, and it was only now that the true nature of his ailment was discovered—lead poisoning caused by the absorption of white paint from the brushes. His eyes were affected and were operated upon. At times his hands became so inflamed that they had to be strapped flat to a board. Finally he was forbidden to use oil paints or even to have them in the house. This order was enforced for ten years, a lifetime to an artist born to handle the brush and express himself in color.

Through all his lean, troublesome years as instructor and illustrator, France was never quite out of his mind. In 1899 he returned to Paris again, and in 1904 he moved to Giverny. He had known and loved for years this charming village in the valley of the Seine, the home of a great French impressionist, Monet, who was found a near neighbor. Guy bought an old stone cottage, the home of many peasant generations, remodeled and added to it, and turned it into a delightful home and studio. Here he and his wife lived for eight happy years. The quiet congenial life of the country with the added pleasures of hunting, fishing, and motoring restored Guy's health in a measure, and he was finally permitted to paint again. He began to exhibit again in the Salon and joined his good friends Frieseke, Richard Miller, and Lawton Parker in sending work to New York.

In 1912 he returned to America again with his newer work, which included landscapes and figures out of doors. These with a few portraits painted that winter were exhibited in New York and later in Philadelphia and other cities. For two summers he taught and painted at Narragansett Pier. Then the home-coming lust seized him, and he returned to California "for good and all."

He had done little California painting since boyhood and had always had a longing to do some of the loved landscapes of his childhood. He bought himself a beautiful home in Pasadena and lived there happily, surrounded by birds and beautiful flowers, dogs, books, and everything dear to him. He suffered a mild paralytic stroke February 2, 1921, from which he never recovered and died in November 1925. He was cheerful at all times during his affliction and had to the last that sweet faculty, which he had so forcefully shown when hurt in boyhood, of treasuring every little joy that life could give him. He was a lovable character, a genuine man. At his death Guy left scores of canvases; and in a very short time thereafter people were clamoring for them. As do many other artists, he had to die to become fully appreciated.

## III

When I moved to my ranch Roseland with my family, there was just a bit of pioneering in it. The railroad station was three miles away and somewhat inaccessible during the rainy weather when the river was swollen. Gas and electricity were not available. Coal-oil lamps and candles were our means of lighting.

I welcomed it all with delight, however, not altogether for myself but for the children. True enough, in my individual life, going and coming frequently as I had, I was unconfined; but to be again in the country, to retire and awaken in its calm tranquillity with the singing of birds amid flowers and trees—at nature's very hearth again—carried me back to my glorious young childhood at Sunny Slope. I made up my mind at the outset to have my children as nearly as was possible spend their young lives as I had spent mine. A 260-acre ranch was not a great domain to those of us accustomed to the 50,000- and 100,000-acre haciendas of the dons; but it is a good-sized homesite, affording great freedom of action, and one is not apt to disturb the neighbors. The three children, Martha, Hinda, and Fargo, were more like little quail hovered together in their play, taking readily to their new surroundings, fancying themselves upon limitless plains, all of which, as far as they could see, was Papa's ranch to their young minds. Their baby brother Gilbert soon became one of them.

After the children had frolicked around for two years, learning the alphabet and numerals in the evenings, schooling became the paramount issue. There was a small school at New Jerusalem, attended by but inferior Mexican children. The little settlement was a tough place—a lot of drunkenness at all times—and naturally Mrs. Rose would not listen to the children going there. So the governness proposition presented itself. Very fortunately, Mrs. Rose's sister in San Francisco secured Miss Adelaide McConnell of Alameda, a fine young lady just out of the high school. And with the little governess there must be a suitable place for uninterrupted study. I built a fine one-room log schoolhouse in a rose garden at one edge of the lawn, with four desks, blackboard, and other paraphernalia, also a nice open fireplace, the roof thatched with heavy tule (bulrush). Later, with flowers and vines growing over it, it added considerable beauty to the garden.

There was always something transpiring: I was continually fussing around with a fractious team or saddle horse; my home-coming from Oregon with a hundred young mules—a countless number to the children—the men hitching a number of them, wild as deer, dashing down the road; bean harvest time, when an outfit of forty men and thirty horses would drive into the field, continuing working after dark by a huge bonfire of straw till the dew came on; the walnut harvest time, when Mexican women and their children—forty or fifty of them—came to gather the nuts. They picked them from the ground in buckets, filling sacks holding about sixty pounds, for which they were paid twenty-five cents each, at which they made good wages. Just before sundown a team drove through the orchard gathering and sewing up the filled sacks, hauling them near the barn. The following day three faithful old Chinamen passed them over an inclining shaker of one-inch-mesh galvanized wire, grading them. They were then dipped by hand in large baskets of this same wire in a chemical solution to bleach them, then spread on large trays to dry, preparatory to sacking for the trade in one-hundred-pound bags.

We were pioneers in this primitive way fully as much as we were in our wine making at Sunny Slope in 1864. All these families lived in a colony set apart for them, sleeping in tents, with brush shades for their cooking in the open. My little girls were brought by their governess for a glimpse of it occasionally. The boys had a free run, ate *tortillas* and *frijoles* with the children, and learned to speak Spanish from them. The Mexicans, never without musical instruments, playing their guitars or accordions in the bright moonlight or by the fitful flare of their campfires, gave the children a very correct idea of the Rancheria at Sunny Slope.

Roseland was now an earthly paradise—truly a land of milk and honey—the eucalyptus trees towering fifty feet, the cypress tapering beautifully from their broad expanse of limbs below to pinnacled tops; the two-hundred-acre forest of walnuts gradually reaching out toward each other in their broad umbrageous growth, bending low with the weight of their crop; the young orange trees dotted with their golden offerings; and other fruits and berries in great variety. There were also quantities of roses and chrysanthemums, asters and shasta daisies, violets, narcissus, daffodils, and jonquils—all basking in the golden sunlight under California's inimitable blue sky—Old Glory lying listlessly at the top of her mast. All was serenity and happiness.

Like a blast from the inferno, May 17, 1899, came the horrifying news of the death of my father. Old Glory is half-masted, and with this tragedy my story ceases, that my children may ever remember the time of its ending as the happiest of their lives, unbounded in freedom, untrammeled by worldly wisdom and its sorrows.

Always courageous and self-contained, my father had not confided in me in his financial distress. Had he done so, I could have helped him out. Truly enough, I was aware that his ventures had not been successful and that he was heavily involved; however, he still possessed valuable holdings, and had he weathered the passing storm incident to a temporary depression in real estate, he would have emerged triumphantly as he always had in his earlier tasks. His was more a case of disappointment than of adversity. Sentimentally ever harking back to the early days of the old dons, still a follower of their easy-going methods when friendships were genuine, he could not cope with the pound-of-flesh policy of the strictly business newcomer. I criticize not. He had his destiny. Even death could not rob him of the joys of having lived through the most glorious period of the most gloriously romantic country that the sun ever shone upon. Newcomers at the time of my father's passing gained not the slightest conception of its early charm. The California of Californians had waned even a score of years before. Commercialism had arrived and the easy-going, unwise (let us admit it if need be) old-timers with their casual methods were rapidly disappearing. Little by little at first, then with the tremendous influx of newcomers, by leaps and bounds the country has become a hotbed of business activity; every evidence of its earlier glory has vanished save the invisible, undeniable tinge of romance which persists in the very air we breathe.

Always generous, always willing to pay the price, having mastered the huge undertakings of his early career in his own extravagant way, Father could not school himself to latter-day exactions and refusals. Thwarted in his ideals, his pride mastered him. He was a great and good man—of deeds rather than words—mild mannered and gentle spoken, always with a smile, ever hopeful, ever valiant. His California had fled him now. His wheel of fortune was turning low. He chose to go, leaving behind a name—a household byword for forty years—honored and respected by everyone.[33]

[33]On May 17, 1899, the Los Angeles papers reported that L. J. Rose had taken his life. He left a note to his wife to the effect that he had grown weary of his burden of indebtedness.

THE END

# INDEX

L. J. ROSE OF SUNNY SLOPE
*has been set on the Linotype in*
ELDORADO
*a new type designed by W. A. Dwiggins who died in 1956. Eldorado's design was based on certain early nineteenth century American types, but has also a resemblance to the roman types of Aldus Manutius who printed in Venice at the end of the fifteenth century.*